# Development Cooperation between India and Neighbouring Countries: Possibilities and Challenges

# Development Cooperation between India and Neighbouring Countries: Possibilities and Challenges

*Editors*

**Subhrabaran Das**
*Professor & Head*
Department of Economics, Tripura University

**Salim Shah**
*Professor*
Department of Economics, Tripura University

**Priyadarshi Dash**
*Associate Professor*
Research and Information System for Developing Countries (RIS), New Delhi

**ALLIED PUBLISHERS PVT. LTD.**

Noida • Mumbai • Kolkata • Chennai • Bangalore

**ALLIED PUBLISHERS PRIVATE LIMITED**

D-5, Sector-2, **Noida**–201 301
Ph. Nos.: 0120-4320295/2542557/4352866 • E-mail: delhi.books@alliedpublishers.com

17 Chittaranjan Avenue, **Kolkata**–700072
Ph.: 033-22129618 • E-mail: cal.books@alliedpublishers.com

15 J.N. Heredia Marg, Ballard Estate, **Mumbai**–400001
Ph.: 022-42126969 • E-mail: mumbai.books@alliedpublishers.com

No. 25/10, Commander-in-Chief Road, Ethiraj Lane (Next to Post Office)
Egmore, **Chennai**–600008
Ph.: 044-28223938 • E-mail: chennai.books@alliedpublishers.com

P.B. No. 9932, No. 15, 3rd Floor (Next to Vijaya Bank), 5th Cross, Gandhinagar,
Karnataka, **Bangalore**–560009, Ph.: 080-41530285 / 22386239
E-mail: bngl.books@alliedpublishers.com

**Website: www.alliedpublishers.com**



ISBN: 978-93-89934-65-6



Published by Sunil Sachdev and printed by Ravi Sachdev at Allied Publishers Pvt. Ltd., D-5, Sector-2, Noida–201 301

# Foreword

RIS has since long been working on development of the North-Eastern region from the perspective of trade and investment integration. The North-Eastern states have become the epicentre of India's relationship with countries in South Asia and Southeast Asia, particularly with the BIMSTEC countries. RIS has a dedicated work programme on the whole gamut of trade integration with the Southeast Asian economies in the context of India's 'Act East Policy' and bringing the North Eastern Region in sharp focus in this regard. The 'Act East Policy' has provided scope for better engagement in trade, investment, supply chains and people-to-people connectivity. The incumbent government at the centre has been considering the eight states such as Assam, Arunachal Pradesh, Manipur, Meghalaya, Mizoram, Nagaland, Sikkim, Tripura as 'Asthalakshmi' in order to put special attention for promoting development in the region. Special emphasis has been given to strengthening trade and investment linkages with bordering countries, promote connectivity, nurturing resilient value chains, among others.

Over the past few years, RIS has supported and mentored the North East Training Research and Advocacy Foundation (NETRA) to emerge as an intellectual forum for young faculty members and researchers from the region to undertake evidence-based empirical work on key development issues facing the people of the region. The G20 Presidency of India gave us the opportunity to connect with various universities and research institutes in different parts of the country to explore their potential for bringing in research-based opportunities for strengthening university and institutional level country. It also provided a much-needed ecosystem for encouraging local articulation of ideas and perspectives on different multilateral issues. Further, RIS has documented the nature of activities undertaken under this programme by the host universities of the region in the form of a publication which could be considered as a template for engaging students from the region in future mega-events that India might lead in the coming years.

In recent past RIS, in collaboration with NITI Aayog, also prepared a report on localisation of SDGs and subsequently a few workshops were organized in different states of the North Eastern Region to disseminate the findings of the study and aggregate local views and opinions on those findings. The institute has also published the volume on "Rise of the North East: the Path to Prosperity, Inclusion and Sustainability".

In view of the importance of the region for local as well as national development, RIS and Tripura University organized the UGC-SAP Seminar on 'Development Cooperation between India & Neighbouring Countries: Possibilities and Challenges' on 22–24 March, 2022 at Agartala to deliberate upon key facets of socio-economic development and the possibility of cooperation with neighbouring countries. The deliberations covered several cross-cutting issues like the role of agriculture in livelihood and development, leveraging on trade and financial linkages between India and the neighbouring countries, demographic and social issues and environment & sustainability concerns. The papers presented in the conference covered a fair balance of empirical and conceptual works on various topics relating to the above-mentioned themes. Those papers highlighted the potential of the North Eastern States in different economic sectors and the nature of cooperation needed with neighbouring countries to tap such potential.

This volume presents a collection of papers from the conference which is timely as in view of the completion of 10 years of the 'Act East' policy in 2024. We are sure that the micro-level studies on agriculture, impact of climate change, potential of pharmaceutical sector, prospects of value chain, social sector issues like health and education and the importance of development cooperation, both at bilateral and regional levels, would provide useful inputs for planning and undertaking policy measures for ensuring inclusive and sustainable development of the North Eastern Region.

We also take this opportunity to thank all distinguished speakers and young scholars who participated in the deliberations in the seminar. Thanks are also due to colleagues from the Tripura University and the RIS faculty for their support for successful organisation of the programme and for bringing out this important volume.

**Sachin Chaturvedi**
*Director General*
*RIS, New Delhi*

# Preface

The South Asian region that has witnessed inter-state wars, civil wars, liberation movements, military dictatorships and cross-border terrorism in the post-colonial period is full of complexities and contestations. In many instances, India has taken responsible and leading roles in building peace in this region. Regional initiatives to establish the South Asian Association of Regional Cooperation in 1985, and subsequently formalizing BIMSTEC in 1997 and BBIN in 2015 are worth mentioning. The Look East Policy and its subsequent upgradation to Act East Policy manifest India's commitment to regional cooperation in the region. Development trajectories of the countries in the South Asian region have some specific challenges such as unaccounted migration, high informal trade etc. and also possibilities like better multilateral relationship, exchange of ideas and techniques, peace and development. Digitalisation, fintech, e-commerce, social media etc. are now emerging as effective cross-border communication tools and new forces of change and hope for the people in the sub-continent. In this backdrop, development cooperation is essential to build up bonding among the people and bilateral relationship among the neighbouring nations. In this regard, the role of both state actors and non-state actors like civil society and private entrepreneurs are very important towards achieving Sustainable Development Goals (SDGs) for the countries in this region.

India's "Neighbourhood First Policy" of 2008 shows her commitment to developing friendly and mutually beneficial relations with all its neighbours, where the Northeast can have a vibrant role owing to the region's strategic location, unique topography, natural resource endowments, potential human resources and communities. India is an active development partner for the regions with several projects, many of which are through Northeast, the region that is surrounded by five neighbouring countries viz. China, Myanmar, Bangladesh, Nepal, and Bhutan (and Tibet Autonomous Region also). The present volume, "***Development Cooperation between India and Neighbouring Countries: Possibilities and Challenges***" is an attempt to explore the possibilities of development cooperation between India and neighbouring countries, particularly surrounded by the region of Northeast India. The possibility of localized sustainable development in different sectors through development cooperation beyond the region is also an important coverage of the present volume. The book deals with a lot of emerging developmental issues of India and its neighbouring countries by covering four core areas of economic activities viz. *Agriculture and Allied Activities*; *Trade, Finance and Development*; *Demography and Social Sector*; and *Sustainable Development and Environment*. Where, Agriculture and Allied Activities deals with the issues of unemployment, agricultural adoption and impact of climate change; Trade, Finance and Development deals with pharmaceutical trade relationship, foreign investment, e-commerce and power sector reforms; Demography and Social Sector deals with health and educational performance, migration and resilience; Sustainable Development and Environment entails technological progress and productivity, road topology and landscape transformation, sustainable development goals, neighbourhood challenges and Act East policy. However, exploring the possibilities of development cooperation among the neighbouring countries surrounded by the region of Northeast India has been the prime focus of the present volume. The book is expected to be useful for the readers interested in neighbourhood developmental cooperation and geo-politics in regional economic development trajectories.

The present volume is an outcome of the international seminar on "*Development Cooperation between India & Neighbouring Countries*", organised by Department of Economics, Tripura University under its UGC-SAP-DRS II Project, jointly with the Research and Information System for Developing Countries (RIS), New Delhi. We would like to thank Professor Sachin Chaturvedi, Director General, RIS, New Delhi for his immense support in publishing this edited volume. The thoughtful debates and deliberations over the three days of the seminar actually pave the organisation of the present volume. So, a special appreciation is due to Professor Jahar Deb Barma, the then Coordinator of the UGC-SAP-DRS-II and Professor Indraneel Bhowmik, the then Head of the Department of Economics, Tripura University. Active support and cooperation from Research and

Information System for Developing Countries (RIS), New Delhi indeed adds quality to the seminar discussions and to shaping direction of the present volume. The authority of the Research and Information System for Developing Countries (RIS) deserves mentioning special gratitude. We would like to express our sincere gratefulness to the contributors of various chapters, without whose genuine and thought provoking efforts the present volume would not have been a possibility. We should clarify here that we are lumping together people who have helped and encouraged us in many different ways by reading and commenting on the manuscript, by their valuable observations and conversation. We also wish to thank the team of Allied Publishers, New Delhi for their wonderful job in bringing order to this manuscript for excellence publication.

**Subhrabaran Das**
**Salim Shah**
**Priyadarshi Dash**

# List of Contributors

| | | | |
|---|---|---|---|
| 1. | **Abdul Halim** | : | Former Professor, Bangladesh Agricultural University, Bangladesh |
| 2. | **Amlan Biswas** | : | MS student, Dept. of Agricultural Extension and Rural Development, Bangabandhu, Sheikh Mujibur Rahman Agricultural University (BSMRAU), Bangladesh |
| 3. | **Ariful Hoque** | : | Research Scholar, Department of Economics, Tripura University), Tripura West and Assistant Professor, Pandit Deendayal Upadhyaya Adarsha Mahavidyalaya (A Govt. Model Degree College), Eraligool, Karimganj, Assam, India |
| 4. | **Banalata Saikia** | : | Research Scholar, Department of Economics, Tripura University, Tripura, and Assistant Professor, Govt Model Women College, Chenga, Barpeta, Assam India |
| 5. | **Chandra Kanta Saha** | : | Research Scholar, Department of Economics, University of Burdwan, West Bengal, and Assistant Professor, Department of Economics, Sister Nibedita Government General Degree College for Girls, 20B Judges Court Road, Alipore, Kolkata-700027, West Bengal, India |
| 6. | **Debashish Mazumdar** | : | Professor of Economics, The Heritage College, Kolkata, West Bengal, India |
| 7. | **Dipikanta Chakraborty** | : | Assistant Professor of Political Sciences, National Law University, Tripura, India |
| 8. | **Dukhabandhu Sahoo** | : | Associate Professor, School of HSS & M, IIT, Bhubaneswar, India |
| 9. | **Elangbam Bijoykumar Singh** | : | Professor (Retd.), Department of Economics Department, Manipur University, Manipur, India |
| 10. | **Jayanti Behera** | : | Research Scholar, School of HSS & M, IIT, Bhubaneswar, India |

| | | | |
|---|---|---|---|
| 11. | **Kanchan Datta** | : | Associate Professor, Department of Economics, University of North Bengal, West Bengal, India |
| 12. | **Kazi Tamim Rahman** | : | Professor, Dept. of Agricultural Economics, Bangabandhu, Sheikh Mujibur Rahman Agricultural University (BSMRAU), Bangladesh |
| 13. | **Madhusudan Datta** | : | Professor of Economics (Retd.), University of Kalyani, West Bengal, India |
| 14. | **Mainak Bhattacharjee** | : | Assistant Professor, Department of Economics, Loreto College, Kolkata, West Bengal, India |
| 15. | **Md. Ashraful Islam** | : | MS student, Dept. of Agricultural Extension and Rural Development, Bangabandhu, Sheikh Mujibur Rahman Agricultural University (BSMRAU), Bangladesh |
| 16. | **Md. Safiul Islam Afrad** | : | Professor, Dept. of Agricultural Extension and Rural Development, Bangabandhu, Sheikh Mujibur Rahman Agricultural University (BSMRAU), Bangladesh |
| 17. | **Masud, Ahmed** | : | Research Scholar, Department of Economics, Tripura University, Suryamaninagar, Tripura and Assistant Professor, KNB Women's College, Badarpur College, Assam, India |
| 18. | **Paramita Saha** | : | Professor, Department of Economics, Tripura University (A Central University), Tripura West, India |
| 19. | **Pradip Debnath** | : | Research Scholar, Department of Geography and Disaster Management, Tripura University, Tripura, India |
| 20. | **Priyadarshi Dash** | : | Associate Professor, Research Information System for Developing Countries, New Delhi |
| 21. | **Pubali Das** | : | Research Scholar, Department of Economics, Tripura University, Tripura, India |
| 22. | **Salim Shah** | : | Professor, Department of Economics, Tripura University, Tripura, India |

23. **Sanjukta Niyogi** : Junior Research Fellow, Department of Economics, University of Burdwan, West Bengal, India

24. **Saptarshi Mitra** : Associate Professor, Department of Geography and Disaster Management, Tripura University, Tripura, India

25. **Shahriar Hasan** : Lecturer, Dept. of Agricultural Extension and Rural Development, Bangabandhu, Sheikh Mujibur Rahman Agricultural University (BSMRAU), Bangladesh

26. **Soumitra Saha** : Lecturer, Dept. of Agricultural Extension and Rural Development, Bangabandhu, Sheikh Mujibur Rahman Agricultural University (BSMRAU), Bangladesh

27. **Soumyananda Dinda** : Professor of Economics, Department of Economics, University of Burdwan, West Bengal, India

28. **Stabak Roy** : Assistant Professor, Department of Geography and Disaster Management, Techno India University, Tripura, India

29. **Subhrabaran Das** : Professor, Department of Economics, Tripura University (A Central University), Tripura West, India

30. **Suryakant Nayak** : Research Scholar, School of HSS&M, IIT, Bhubaneswar, India

# Contents

CHAPTER 1

# Emerging Development Issues: India & Neighbouring Countries

**Subhrabaran Das, Salim Shah and Priyadarshi Dash**

The South Asian region is full of different complexities and contestations. In the post-colonial period, the South Asian region has witnessed inter-state wars, civil wars, liberation movements, military dictatorships and has been suffering from the menace of cross border terrorism. In many instances, India has taken responsible and leading roles in building peace in this region. Regional initiatives to establish the South Asian Association of Regional Cooperation in 1985, and subsequently formalizing BIMSTEC in 1997 and BBIN in 2015 are worth noting. The Look East Policy and subsequent upgradation to Act East Policy manifests India's commitment to regional cooperation in the region; aiming at building all countries in the South Asian region and beyond.

Development trajectory of various geographical and economic regions of the world often provide rich insights about the implementation of diverse policies and programmes, their outcomes, scope for replication, and scope for international cooperation. The countries in the South Asian region have some specific challenges such as unaccounted migration, high informal trade etc. and also possibilities like better multilateral relationship, exchange of ideas and techniques, peace and development which may be glaring issues of future research for many such regions.

Now-a-days, technological innovations have become rapid and disruptive in the world as well as in the south and Southeast Asian regions. Digitalisation, fintech, e-commerce, social media etc. are now emerging as effective cross-border communication tools and new forces of change and hope for the people in the sub-continent. In this backdrop, development cooperation is essential to build up the bonding among the people and bilateral relationship among the neighbouring nations. This cooperation would strengthen the countries more through socio-cultural, political and economic exchanges among them. This approach would indeed be useful in economic upliftment of the neighbouring countries by facilitating peace and prosperity across the region. In this regard, the role of both state actors and non-state actors like civil society and private entrepreneurs are very important. With these cumulative efforts, all countries in this region can achieve their Sustainable Development Goals (SDGs).

The strategic location of the North-eastern region along with her unique topography, natural resource endowments, potential human resources and communities can pave the way of a strong multilateral relation with the neighbouring countries. India's "Neighbourhood First Policy" of 2008 shows her commitment to developing friendly and mutually beneficial relations with all its neighbours, where the Northeast can have a vibrant role. India is an active development partner for the regions with several projects in these countries and many of the projects are through Northeast. The region of Northeast India is surrounded by five neighbouring countries viz. China, Myanmar, Bangladesh, Nepal, and Bhutan (and Tibet Autonomous Region also). The region has already started its journey on the way of its development through different government initiatives and the progress is satisfactory in many instances. As per the latest estimates available on the SDG India Index, as maintained by the Niti Aayog, only Sikkim registered a value more than the Indian average in 2020. Thus, the faster development of the region is essential because of its strategic location and the potential for its sustainable development.

The present book is an attempt to explore the possibilities of development cooperation between India and the neighbouring countries, particularly surrounded by the region of Northeast India. The book also focuses on income-generating activities, people's benefits as well as economic mainstreaming that to be conducive in breaking the vicious cycle of poverty. The possibility of localized sustainable development in different sectors and regions of the North Eastern states through development cooperation beyond the region is also an important coverage of the present volume.

The book deals with a lot of emerging developmental issues of India and its neighbouring countries. It covers four core areas of economic activities viz. Agriculture and Allied Activities; Trade, Finance and Development; Demography and Social Sector; Sustainable Development and Environment in a cross-country perspective of the South Asian region. On a detail note, Agriculture and Allied Activities deals with the issues of unemployment, agricultural adoption and impact of climate change; Trade, Finance and Development deals with pharmaceutical trade relationship, foreign investment, e-commerce and power sector reforms; Demography and Social Sector deals with health and educational performance, migration and resilience; Sustainable Development and Environment consists of technological progress and productivity, road topology and landscape transformation, sustainable development goals, neighbourhood challenges and Act East policy.

Coming to chapter wise detailing, Chapter 2 i.e. "*Role of Agriculture and Some Other Macro Economic Variables for Unemployment Reduction: A Panel Data Analysis of Some G-20 Nations*" has tried to investigate the role of agriculture in value addition and some macroeconomic variables for unemployment reduction specially youth unemployment, using panel data regression model. Some selected G-20 nations are considered and the data are collected from World Development Indicators published by World Bank. The study finds that fixed effect model is better than random effect model, and gross fixed capital formation has been playing an important role for the reduction of youth unemployment for select G-20 nations.

Chapter 3 discusses on "*Adoption of Maize Production in Kaliganj Upazila under Lalmonirhat District of Bangladesh*" which tries to assess the adoption of maize production in terms of time and space by the growers in Kaliganj Upazila under Lalmonirhat district of Bangladesh. The study indicates that lack of storage facility at farmers' level followed by the limited availability of credit, lack of processing technique, poor technical information and lack of availability of hybrid seeds are the major problems in maize cultivation.

Chapter 4 focuses on "*Economic Impact of Climate Change on Agriculture: An Empirical Study of India and Bangladesh*". The study examines the long run relationships and short run dynamics between climate change as measured by per capita $CO_2$ emissions and temperature change and agricultural production measured by share of agriculture to GDP, using time series data of India and Bangladesh for the period from 1961 to 2018. The study finds that there is a long-run relationship between climate change and agricultural production over the period for both the countries. In short run, temperature change has a significant and negative impact on the share of agriculture in the GDP of both India and Bangladesh.

Chapter 5 highlights on "*India's Pharmaceutical Trade Relationship with South Asian Countries: Trends and Prospects*" which attempts to explore the prospects of India's pharmaceutical trade relationship with respect to South Asian (SAARC) countries in the light of some select trade indicators. An analysis of the trade intensity index (TII) brings out that India's pharmaceutical trade is more intense with Nepal and Sri Lanka, whereas it is lesser than expected with respect to Bangladesh and Pakistan, underlining that there is a significant gap to be filled and enormous potential to be realized. The revealed comparative advantage (RCA) shows that, except for India, none of the other South Asian countries enjoys a comparative advantage in pharmaceuticals. The analysis of trade complementarity index (TCI) reveals a fair degree of complementarity among the SAARC countries in trading pharmaceuticals, necessitating expanded trade to capitalize on this complementarity. The study also sheds light on the role of India's pharmaceutical industry in ensuring critical healthcare supplies in the South Asian Region during the outbreak of the COVID-19 pandemic.

Chapter 6 sheds light on "*An Enquiry into the Dynamics of India's Foreign Trade with SAARC and non-SARRC Nations during the Post-Globalization Period*". The study has examined the status of India's external sector in terms of export and import shares, export-import ratio, trade balance with neighbouring countries over the period from 1996 to 2020, along with eliciting the potential geopolitical factors underpinning the India's trade relations with her neighbors. The study brings out the pattern of India's trade dynamics with trading partners as to the inter-country convergence or divergence which essentially will shed light on the inter-country dynamic stability of India's trade relation.

Chapter 7 deals with "*Evaluating E-commerce as the Future of India's Trade with SAARC Countries*" and examines the impact of E-commerce on the international trade of India with the member countries in SAARC during 2001 to 2020. The gravity model shows that with the increase in the infrastructure for E-commerce in India and other countries, India's trade with the SAARC nations also increases. Infrastructure for E-commerce in India promotes the export to the SAARC countries. The study concludes that the dream objective of SAARC cherished through development of E-commerce infrastructure and reducing the tariff rates on E-commerce.

Chapter 8 particularly focuses on "*Impact of Indian Power Sector Reform on the Economy of North-Eastern Region*". The study examines the impact of power sector reform in India and also investigates emerging potential energy market across regions especially North Eastern region using power sector and related market data during 2000 to 2018. The study mainly focuses on current energy market scenario of the North-East Region and the parity between reforms in energy sector and Look East policy. North Eastern Region has potential to grow with renewable energy generation and consumption. The renewable energy market is generated not only within the country but also in South-Asian countries leading to an integrated South-Asian regional power market. There has been very high trading of renewable energy potentiality within country and cross countries in the South Asian region. Thus, an efficient clean energy trading may take place through RECs (Rural Electrification Corporations) across state as well as cross countries.

Chapter 9, "*Health and Educational Performance: A Comparative Analysis between India and China*", analyses and compares the availability of health care facilities and health status in terms of various health outcomes and also the variations in health status across demographic, economic, and occupation compositions. The study shows that both India and China have experienced improvements in the health system but that improvement is more substantial for China. The outcomes of their differential policy approach resulted in a remarkable reduction in undernutrition, mortality and morbidity in case of China, whereas the pace of such reductions was found to be much slower for India. The differences in their politico-administration resulted in differential trajectories for addressing these vulnerabilities.

Chapter 10 that focuses on "*Conceptualizing Cities in terms of Migrants' Vulnerability and Resilience during COVID-19*" has tried to explore how factors such as access to social protection schemes, loss of livelihood, levels of income, services relate to health and hygiene, the crisis of mobility and their interface with pandemic situations have an important bearing on the vulnerability of migrant workers. The study sheds light on City Resilience Index (CRI), supported by Rockefeller Foundation, which is a composite index obtained through different dimensions of resilience. It also throws light on understanding and measuring city resilience issues highlighting dimension of management and urban governance.

Chapter 11 highlights the "*Technological Progress and Productivity Measurement: Some Conceptual Issues*". Technological progress may sometimes simply mean getting rid of unwanted by-products that, in any case, are not counted as output. The by-products are treated as externalities polluting the environment but the implied costs are not internalized giving a partisan measure of output that fail to capture relevant technological progress under the growth accounting approach. Further, sectoral gross output measure needs a lot of information regarding intra-sectoral intermediate inputs and their prices. Fruits of technological progress are often passed on to the consumers in a competitive setup leading to decline in price of the product where technological progress originates. As a result, relative price and relative value added of the relatively non-progressive sectors rise giving a misleading measure of sectoral productivity change.

Chapter 12 covers the "*Impact of Spatial Arrangement of Road Topology on Landscape Transformation through Machine Learning Technique: Evidence from Sabroom, India and Ramgarh, Bangladesh*". This chapter analyses the possibilities and potentialities of road connectivity for developing regional trade and commerce of the neighbouring states especially between India and Bangladesh. An important notified link is the Sabroom-Ramgarh road link between India and Bangladesh through Maitri Setu over the Feni River. The development intervention has an initial impact on the infrastructural transformation and has led to changes in land use and land cover (LULC). The impact of spatial interaction on spatio-temporal changes of LULC within 15 km radius from Maitri Setu has been identified using multi-temporal satellite images and the maximum likelihood algorithm (MLA).

Chapter 13 particularly focuses on "*Reimagining Act East Policy*". The Indian development discourse today revolves around some prominent words like inclusive, resurgence, reimagining and mainstreaming which have immense policy implications, particularly for the marginalized Northeastern states of India. A main streamed northeast may acquire the paraphernalia of development at the cost of its identity. Resurgence extols the virtues of a past and its reappearance will help in solving the current problems and building integrity. With India's Act East Policy (the earlier, Look East Policy), successive governments have sought to revive and strengthen age-old ties with the far east, across the sea and overland across Myanmar. Just as global economic power has been shifting from the west to the east, the geography of Asia is changing. These phenomenal changes expected to provide significant developmental benefits to the Northeastern states of India, given the changing progressive outlook of the governments towards the new regime of development discourse.

The last chapter (Chapter 14) covers "*Understanding India's Neighbourhood Challenges through the Lens of Geo-psychology*". The region of South-Asia has always been experiencing the protuberance of conflict among the states. The high noon of the peace process in the South Asia lies in understanding the geo-psychology of the nations of the region. India, being the regional power has been committed to the peace and prosperity of the region. Through its earnest 'neighbourhood first' policy, India is constantly working on a cordial neighbourhood circle. The study attempts to use the theory of geo-psychology in the analytical study of India's neighbourhood policy.

On the whole, the present volume has gone for a wide coverage of developmental issues in the perspective of neighbourhood development cooperation for the South Asian Region, where India has been playing an instrumental role for long time being. The book in reality is an attempt to intertwine with the neighbouring countries sectoral performance and trade dynamics for the region's development trajectories. Exploring the possibilities of development cooperation among the neighbouring countries surrounded by the region of Northeast India has been the prime focus of the present volume. It also focuses on income-generating activities, people's benefits as well as economic mainstreaming that to be conducive in breaking the vicious cycle of poverty towards fulfilling the SDGs. Thus, the present volume is expected to be helpful for the readers who are interested in neighbourhood developmental cooperation and geo-politics in regional economic development trajectories.

# SECTION – I

# Agriculture & Allied Activities

CHAPTER 2

# Role of Agriculture and Some Other Macro Economic Variables for Unemployment Reduction: A Panel Data Analysis of Some G-20 Nations

**Kanchan Datta**

## 2.1 Introduction

Unemployment is one of the most important problems in many nations especially in Asian continent. The experience of openness shows that economic growth of the nations are rising but at the cost of employment that is why today inclusive growth is a matter of research among many policy makers. It implies the fruits of economic growth are not reaching to the poorer section of the society or in other words, inequality in the distribution of wealth is increasing in many developing nations. According to Kuznets (1964), when a country develops the sectoral contribution with respect to output and employment move towards industrial and service sector. From the real world situation we can also see that most of the least developed or poor nations heavily depend on agriculture both in terms of production and employment. Under these circumstances it becomes pertinent to investigate or explore the possibility of reduction in unemployment specially youth unemployment by encouraging the agriculture sector.

In the literature study mainly from Lewis (1954), Fei & Ranis (1961), Schultz (1964), Echevarria (1997), Kogel & Prskawtz (2001), Gardner (2005), it is found that most of the research works related to agriculture are mainly focussed on investigating the relationship between agricultural growth and economic growth or impact of agricultural growth on macro-economic variables. These works are based on two fundamental theoretical backgrounds. One is agriculture led growth hypothesis and the other one is economic growth led agricultural growth.

According to the first hypothesis with the growth of agriculture sector, income of the farmers increases and their demand also increase hence it stimulates the production and income of the non-farm sector which ultimately helps the overall economic growth. According to the second hypothesis for the growth of farm sector it is essential to develop the non-farm sector in other words development of non-farm (industry and service sector) ultimately benefits the farm sector. According to their logic with an increase of agricultural output declines prices of food items, it creates an opportunity to the industrialists to pay lower wages which in turn increases the profitability and competitiveness of the industrial sector since price of the industrial output also declines due to decline in wage rate. They are also opined that it would ultimately increase saving and investment and hence employment also increases. Moreover, with the decrease of food expenditure, real income increases which may have an expansionary effect on non-farm sector in terms of output and employment.

From the another angle Steger (2000) in his research paper has opined that relatively higher total factor productivity growth in the farm sector can lead to higher factor productivity growth for the entire economy, there by leading to a higher GDP growth and a higher rate of saving. Higher savings naturally tends to raise investment and employment which results a reduction of unemployment. However, Hwa (1988) already has thrown some lights on how an increase in the agricultural output might lead to an increase in total factor productivity and lower unemployment. Here agricultural production has taken as a measure of the linkages between the rural sector and the industrial sector. With the increases of agricultural production, in one hand the supply of raw materials for industrial sector increases on the other hand, demand for industrial output that are used as an input in the agricultural sector also increases. From another angle, higher productivity in the agricultural sector can increase the incomes of the person engaged in farm sector, which raises the demand for domestically produced industrial output. Hence it may raise the possibility of job creation in the upstream and downstream of industrial or non-farm sector which results reduction of poverty also (Dethier and Effenberger, 2012).

However agricultural growth would neutralises the reduction of unemployment or rather increases the unemployment problem through the adoption of mechanisation or sophisticated technology which reduces demand for labour to a great extent. In this context, Irzeet. al (2001) opined that if agricultural growth is due to the technological progress that are labour savings then value addition from farm sector may not reflect the additional employment. So it can be said that the net employment effect of an increase in agricultural output is not clear.

Moreover, another group of researchers like Matsuyama (1992) opined that, in the era of globalization of free trade, if a country has comparative advantage in farm sector, to raise export it can draw resources from non-farm sector to farm sector which would exert negative effects on the long run economic growth and employment.

Rosenzweig (2003), defines another possibility is that, with the increase of agricultural productivity as well as income, raises the wage rate of the workers of the non-farm sector. Now, in the agriculture sector generally there is inelastic demand for labour, on the other hand in the non-farm sector elasticity of demand especially for the unskilled labour is elastic. Hence with a slight increase in of wage rate may lead to retrenchment or higher level of unemployment. So the positive association between agricultural growth and unemployment is also empirical possibility. Hence there is plethora of examples in the literature to incorporate agriculture value addition as a variable to reduce unemployment.

A report by the ILO (International Labour Organization, 2012) mentions that in early 2012 the labour market reality is cruel: one in three persons from the working population is either unemployed or is poor. In other words, the data show that from the total labour force of 3.3 billion, 200 million are unemployed and 900 million are living with their families below the poverty line of $2 per day (Stanila, 2013). The most affected segment of the population is the young, 75 million of them being unemployed. Globally, youth are three times more likely to become unemployed (compared to the adults) and this can lead to long-term deterioration of the labour market (ILO, 2011).

In contemporary economic policy the globalization or openness plays an important role on employment. Although workers in developing countries see globalization as a threat (since the traditional jobs disappear or are relocated), employment growth in developing countries that is generated through globalization is thought to lead to poverty reduction (Jenkins, 2006). There are a variety of ways in which globalization affects labour, foreign direct investment (FDI), increased trade openness and international technology transfer being the most mentioned. Trade is an important factor in economic development. In a report of the European Commission (2010) three major benefits of trade openness are listed: (1) economic growth, (2) consumer benefits, (3) employment. In these circumstances it is easy to conclude that trade openness of an economy is an important lever for developing countries to get out of unemployment and poverty. In this study, the degree of openness as the ratio of trade to GDP is measured.

On the other hand regarding the importance of capital formation for reducing unemployment there are ample studies in the literature. Some of these works are like, Rowthorn (1999) shows that the capital labour ratio affects unemployment in the long-run when the elasticity of substitution between capital and labour is less than unity—he finds that this elasticity is, typically, between 0.6 and 0.8. Modigliani (2000) shows that there is a strong negative correlation between the investment and unemployment rates—this was dubbed the "Modigliani puzzle" by Blanchard (2000, pp. 140). Bean and Dréze (1991) focus on the sluggish wage response to the productivity growth slowdown in Europe in the aftermath of the oil price shocks and show that wage stickiness reduced employment and, hence, the capital stock profit rate. In turn, this prompted a decline in investment and capital accumulation that further increased unemployment. Arestis *et al.* (2003) claim that capital formation is an important variable in determining unemployment and wages. The model shows that the Non-accelerating Inflation Rate of Unemployment (NAIRU) is a declining function of capital stock and they find significant effects of capital accumulation on unemployment in the UK and Germany. In this study gross fixed capital formation as a percent of GDP is considered another important variable which may reduce unemployment.

## 2.2 Objectives of the Study

In this paper an attempt has been taken to investigate the role of some macro-economic variables mainly agriculture (measured by agricultural value addition), GDP per capita Growth, Gross Fixed Capital Formation, government's final consumption, Openness/Trade and Inflation for reducing the unemployment especially youth unemployment in some selected G-20 nations.

## 2.3 Methodology of the Study

The study is based on the secondary data. The data sources are World Development Indicators and the time periods cover from year 2000 to 2019 and the nations are Argentina, Australia, Brazil, Canada, China, France, Germany, India, Indonesia, Italy, Japan, Russia, South Africa, and Saudi Arabia. The variables used in this study includes Unemployment, youth total (percentage of total labour force ages 15–24) (modelled ILO estimate), Agricultural value added (percent of GDP), GDP per capita growth (annual percentage), General government final consumption expenditure (percent of GDP), Gross fixed capital formation (percent of GDP), Trade (percent of GDP), Inflation, consumer prices (annual percent).

For the analysis of data Panel Data regression models are used in this study. Panel data are also known as longitudinal or cross-sectional time series data. Through this data set the behaviours of entities across time can be observed. A panel regression specification can be written as follows.

$$y_{it} = \alpha_i + \beta_k x_{k,it} + \mu_{it} \qquad \text{... (1)}$$

Where, *i* denote the cross section units (in this study Nations, 1 to 15) and *t* denotes the time period for the year 2000 to 2019.

$y_{it}$ is the dependent variable, $x'_{it}$ represents $i^{th}$ independent and control variables.

$\beta_k$ is the coefficient for respective independent and control variables. $\mu_{it}$ is the error term.

The individual effects may be either assumed to be correlated with the right hand side variables (fixed effects model: FEM) or be incorporated into the error term (random effects model: REM) and assumed uncorrelated with the explanatory variables (Baum, 2001).

Fixed effect model analyses the impact of variables that vary over time. Generally it is assumed that something within each cross sectional unit may impact or bias the independent variables and we need to control for this. Moreover, the time –invariant characteristics are unique to the individual and should not be correlated with other individual characteristics.

When working with panel data models the first step is to test whether the data series can be estimated through a panel data model or through a pooled OLS. Therefore, Baltagi (2008) considers that the question is "To pool or not to pool the data?" A simple probability test has the null hypothesis the OLS model and the alternative hypothesis the FE model.

The next step would be to decide whether a FE model or a RE model is more appropriate for the data series. The decision between the two models can be made based on different tests, economic reasons and/or information criteria. Baltagi (2008) suggests all of these methods; hence one can estimate both models and choose between them according to the information criteria and/or based on economic arguments. In our study we have used Hausman's specification test for selecting which model is better Fixed or Random effect model.

For the random-effects model, the $\alpha_i$ from model (1) is incorporated into the error term and assumed uncorrelated with the explanatory variables. Considering this assumption we have the model (2) as a random effect model specification:

$$y_{it} = x'_{it} * \beta + \varepsilon_{it} \qquad \dots (2)$$

Because the $\alpha_i$ is incorporated in $\varepsilon_{it}$ in each time period, we might say that we have to deal with autocorrelation of the error. Therefore the general least square method is used for the estimation of a RE model. An advantage of the RE model is that it allows using explanatory variables that are constant over time; a great disadvantage is that if the FE model would be more appropriate those estimates would be inconsistent.

After controlling for the effects, the default standard errors assume that the error $\mu_{it}$ is independent and identically distributed (Cameron, Trivedi, 2009). Also, the model is estimated assuming the homoscedasticity of the residuals. When heteroscedasticity is present the standard errors of the estimates will be biased and one should compute robust standard errors correcting for the possible presence of heteroscedasticity. The most commonly deviation from homoscedastic errors in the context of panel data is likely to be error variances specific to the cross-sectional unit. When the error process is homoscedastic within cross-sectional units, but its variance differs across units we have the so called group-wise heteroscedasticity. Another problem is the serial correlation of the idiosyncratic error term, but Wooldridge proposed a very simple test for checking the autocorrelation of the residuals. In order to overcome these problems, we should estimate the regression model using robust standard errors. Some authors have provided a number of tests in order to identify the problems encountered (Drukker, 2003, Baum, 2001, Green, 2000). All these techniques are applied in this study.

## 2.4 Findings

Tables 2.1 & 2.2 show descriptive statistics and correlation matrix of the variables of this study respectively. Highest standard deviation is observed in gross capital formation, whereas, the minimum variance is observed in log youth unemployment level. The correlation matrix shows trade and capital formation are highly correlated similarly government's consumption expenditure and capital formation are also highly and negatively correlated.

**Table 2.1:** Descriptive Statistics

| *Variable* | *Obs.* | *Mean* | *Std. Dev.* | *Min* | *Max* |
|---|---|---|---|---|---|
| lyouthunem | 340 | 2.679 | .647 | 1.275 | 4.108 |
| lagrivad | 335 | 1.166 | .869 | –2.132 | 3.074 |
| ltrade | 335 | 3.503 | 1.223 | –5.613 | 4.565 |
| linf | 280 | 1.175 | 1.065 | –3.283 | 3.067 |
| lgfcapi | 338 | 5.895 | 7.712 | 2.482 | 28.326 |
| lgfcon | 338 | 2.472 | .996 | –.57 | 3.401 |
| lgdppcg | 335 | 1.166 | .869 | –2.132 | 3.074 |

*Source:* World Development Indicators published by World Bank. (https://databank.worldbank.org/source/world-development-indicators)

**Table 2.2:** Matrix of Correlations

| *Variable* | *Lyout-hunem* | *lagrivad* | *ltrade* | *linf* | *lgfcapi* | *lgfcon* | *lgdppcg* |
|---|---|---|---|---|---|---|---|
| lyouthunem | 1.000 | | | | | | |
| lagrivad | 0.190 | 1.000 | | | | | |
| ltrade | 0.521 | 0.090 | 1.000 | | | | |
| linf | –0.153 | 0.280 | –0.451 | 1.000 | | | |
| lgfcapi | –0.558 | –0.196 | –0.928 | 0.452 | 1.000 | | |
| lgfcon | 0.599 | 0.080 | 0.907 | –0.509 | –0.970 | 1.000 | |
| lgdppcg | 0.190 | 1.000 | 0.090 | 0.280 | –0.196 | 0.080 | 1.000 |

*Source:* Author's Calculation from World Development Indicators published by World Bank (https://databank.worldbank.org/source/world-development-indicators)

Table 2.3 below shows the results of pooled regression model. Since pooled regression does not care about panel data that is it considers all intercepts are identical and there is no heterogeneity, hence we generally do not consider pooled regression results as effective for panel data analysis.

**Table 2.3:** Results of Pooled Regression

| *lunytot* | *Coeff.* | *Std. Err.* | *t–value* | *p-value* | *95% Conf* | *Interval* |
|---|---|---|---|---|---|---|
| lagrivad | .6846175 | .063726 | 10.74 | 0.000 | .5589033 | .8103317 |
| lgdppcg | –.0368807 | .0283723 | –1.30 | 0.195 | –.0928516 | .0190901 |
| lgfcex | 1.533278 | .1696285 | 9.04 | 0.000 | 1.198647 | 1.86791 |
| lgfcfor | –1.325022 | .1564706 | –8.47 | 0.000 | –1.633696 | –1.016347 |
| linf | .0101187 | .0361182 | 0.28 | 0.780 | –.0611328 | .0813702 |
| ltrade | .5191327 | .1051242 | 4.94 | 0.000 | .3117509 | .7265145 |
| Constant | –.2685584 | .8787334 | –0.31 | 0.760 | –2.002063 | 1.464946 |

*Source:* Author's Calculation from World Development Indicators published by World Bank. (https://databank.worldbank.org/source/world-development-indicators)

**Table 2.4:** Results of Fixed Effect Model

| *lunytot* | *Coeff.* | *Std. Err.* | *t-value* | *p-value* | *95% Conf* | *Interval* |
|---|---|---|---|---|---|---|
| lagrivad | –.211* | .081 | –2.61 | .01 | –.372 | –.051 |
| lgdppcg | .001 | .012 | 0.10 | .923 | –.022 | .024 |
| lgfcex | .084 | .217 | 0.39 | .7 | –.344 | .512 |
| lgfcfor | –.686* | .15 | –4.59 | 0 | –.982 | –.391 |
| linf | –.024 | .018 | –1.28 | .201 | –.06 | .013 |
| ltrade | .101 | .087 | 1.16 | .247 | –.07 | .272 |
| Mean dependent var | | 2.749 | | SD dependent var | | 0.563 |
| R-squared | | 0.148 | | Number of obs | | 194 |
| F-test | | 5.076 | | Prob> F | | 0.000 |
| Akaike crit. (AIC) | | –195.042 | | Bayesian crit. (BIC) | | –172.166 |

*Source:* Author's Calculation form World Development Indicators published by World Bank. (https://databank.worldbank.org/source/world-development-indicators)
*Note:* *denotes p<0.01.

**Table 2.5:** Results of Random Effect Model

| *lunytot* | *Coeff.* | *Std. Err.* | *t-value* | *p-value* | *95% Conf.* | *Interval* |
|---|---|---|---|---|---|---|
| lagrivad | –.092 | .073 | –1.27 | .205 | –.235 | .05 |
| lgdppcg | .001 | .012 | 0.05 | .958 | –.023 | .025 |
| lgfcex | .14 | .211 | 0.66 | .508 | –.274 | .554 |
| lgfcfor | –.605* | .142 | –4.27 | 0 | –.883 | –.327 |
| linf | –.022 | .019 | –1.14 | .255 | –.059 | .015 |
| ltrade | .104 | .088 | 1.17 | .24 | –.069 | .277 |
| Constant | 3.954* | .894 | 4.43 | 0 | 2.203 | 5.705 |
| Mean dependent variable | | 2.749 | | SD dependent variable | | 0.563 |
| Overall r-squared | | 0.036 | | Number of observation | | 194 |
| Chi-square | | 25.767 | | Prob.> chi2 | | 0.000 |
| R-squared within | | 0.138 | | R-squared between | | 0.036 |

*Source:* Author's Calculation form World Development Indicators published by World Bank. (https://databank.worldbank.org/source/world-development-indicators)
*Note:* *denotes p<0.01.

**Table 2.6:** Hausman (1978) Specification Test

| | *Coefficient* |
|---|---|
| Chi-square test value | 22.14 |
| P-value | .001 |

*Source:* Author's Calculation form World Development Indicators published by World Bank. (https://databank.worldbank.org/source/world-development-indicators)
*Note:* *denotes p<0.01.

Table 2.4 and 2.5 shows the results of estimation of Fixed effect model and Random effect model. Table 2.6 show the result of Hausman's specification test. Hausman's test results shows that fixed model effect is better compared to random effect model. Hence, it is important to test the presence of Random effect model compared to pooled regression model

**Table 2.7:** Breusch and Pagan Lagrangian Multiplier Test for Random Effects

| Lunytot[c_id,t] = Xb + u[c_id] + e[c_id,t] |
|---|
| Estimated results: |
| \| Varsd = sqrt(Var) |
| lunytot \| .3165271 .5626074 |
| e \| .0220964 .1486487 |
| u \| .158541 .3981721 |
| Test: Var(u) = 0,chibar2(01) = 508.97,Prob> chibar2 = 0.0000 |

*Source:* Author's Calculation form World Development Indicators published by World Bank. (https://databank.worldbank.org/source/world-development-indicators)

The LM test results show the presence of Random effect model and reject the pooled regression model. Usman test results show that Fixed effect model is better than Random effect model in this study. For diagnostic checking we have to check the presence of hetero-scedasticity through Wald test. The results are shown below in Table 2.8.

**Table 2.8:** Modified Wald Test for Group Wise Heteroscedasticity in Fixed Effect Regression Model

| $H_0$: sigma(i)^2 = sigma^2 for all i |
|---|
| chi2 (13) = 810.21, Prob>chi2 = 0.0000 |

*Source:* Author's Calculation form World Development Indicators published by World Bank (https://databank.worldbank.org/source/world-development-indicators)

This test results show that we have to reject the null hypothesis and accept that there exist heteroscedasticity. Hence we need to estimate again the fixed effect model with robust standard error. The results are shown in the Table 2.9.

**Table 2.9:** Results of Fixed Effect Model with Robust Standard Error

| *lunytot* | *Coefficient* | *Std.Err.* | *t-value* | *p-value* | *95% Conf* | *Interval* |
|---|---|---|---|---|---|---|
| lagrivad | –.2114901 | .1294468 | –1.63 | 0.128 | –.4935305 | .0705502 |
| lgdppcg | .0011469 | .0114855 | 0.10 | 0.922 | –.0238778 | .0261716 |
| lgfcex | .0835634 | .4468906 | 0.19 | 0.855 | –.8901276 | 1.057254 |
| lgfcfor | –.6862969 | .2428482 | –2.83 | 0.015 | –1.215418 | –.1571762 |
| linf | –.0236247 | .0279904 | –0.84 | 0.415 | –.0846105 | .037361 |
| ltrade | .1007442 | .1969141 | 0.51 | 0.618 | –.3282948 | .5297831 |
| Constant | 4.545289 | 2.091448 | 2.17 | 0.050 | –.0115854 | 9.102163 |
| sigma_u | | .66836226 | | | | |
| sigma_e | | .14864874 | | | | |
| rho | | .9528664 (fraction of variance due to $u_i$) | | | | |

*Source:* Author's Calculation form World Development Indicators published by World Bank. (https://databank.worldbank.org/source/world-development-indicators)

From the above results it is clear that agriculture value addition though negatively related to youth unemployment but it is not statistically significant. Similarly for inflation also, though high inflation reduces youth unemployment but the estimated coefficient is not statistically significant. The estimated value is negative but not statistically significant. The estimated coefficient of General government's final consumption expenditure and per capita GDP growth and trade that is openness is positive though statistically not significant. But only the estimated coefficient of one variable that is gross fixed capital formation is negatively and statistically significant. It implies only capital formation can reduce youth unemployment.

## 2.5 Summary and Conclusion

Over the past 25 years unemployment has been raised dramatically in almost all nations of the world. Not only unemployment there has been a widespread increase in earnings inequality. The wages of unskilled and uneducated workers have fallen in relative as well as absolute terms (Rowthorn, 1999). Many variables are directly or indirectly related to employment. For example agriculture, capital formation, government's consumption expenditure, trade, inflation etc.

This study finds that gross fixed capital formation playing an important role for the reduction of youth unemployment for the G-20 nations. Globalization or openness which is measured by Trade as a percent of GDP is positively related to youth unemployment, though the estimated coefficient is not statistically significant. Dynamic panel regression has not applied in this study, future researchers can able to test this relationship by applying dynamic panel regression model.

## References

[1] Arestis, P. and Biefang-Frisancho, Mariscal (2000). Capital Stock, Unemployment and Wages in the UK and Germany, *Scottish Journal of Political Economy,* Vol. 47(5): pp. 487–503.

[2] Baltagi, B. (2008). Econometric analysis of panel data. John Wiley & Sons.

[3] Baum, C.F. (2001). Residual diagnostics for cross-section time series regression models", *The Stata Journal,* Vol. 1(1), pp. 101–104.

[4] Bean, Ch. and Dréze, J. (1991). Europe's Unemployment Problem, The MIT Press, Cambridge, MA.

[5] Blanchard, O. (2000). "The Economics of Unemployment: Shocks, Institutions and Interactions," Lionel Robins Lectures, https://old.nes.ru/public-presentations/Papers/zvi0.pdf

[6] Cameron. C. and. Trived K., Microeconometrics Using Stata, Second Edition, Stata Press.

[7] Dethier, J.J. and Effenberger, A. (2012): Agriculture and development: A brief review of the literature. Economic Systems, Vol. 36(2), pp. 175–205.

[8] Drukker, D.M. (2003). Testing for serial correlation in linear panel-data models", *The Stata Journal*, Vol. 3(2), pp. 168–177.

[9] Echevarria, C. (1997). Changes in the sectoral composition associated with economic growth, *International Economic Review*, Vol. 38(2), pp. 431–452.

[10] European Commission (2010). "Trade as a driver of prosperity", https://www.cep.eu/fileadmin/user_upload/cep.eu/Analysen_KOM/KOM_2010_612_Handelspolitik/SEC_2010_1269.pdf

[11] Fei, J.C. and Ranis, G. (1961). A theory of economic development. American Economic Review, Vol. 51(4): pp. 533–565.

[12] Green, W. (2000). Econometric Analysis, Prentice-Hal

[13] Gardner, B.L. (2005). Causes of rural economic development, *Agricultural Economics,* Vol. 32, pp. 21–41.

[14] Gordon, R.J. (1997). "Is there a trade-off between unemployment and productivity growth," in D.J. Snower and G. de la Dehesa (eds), Unemployment Policy: Government Options for the Labour Market, CU Press, Cambridge.

[15] Hwa, C. (1988). The contribution of agriculture to economic growth: Some empirical evidence, World Development, Vol. 16(11), pp. 1329–1339

[16] International Labour Office (ILO) (2012). *Global Employment Trends. Preventing a deeper jobs crisis* (Geneva), https://www.ilo.org/wcmsp5/groups/public/---dgreports/---dcomm/---publ/documents/publication/wcms_171571.pdf

[17] International Labour Office (ILO). 2011. *Global Employment Trends for Youth: 2011 update* (Geneva), https://www.ilo.org/wcmsp5/groups/public/---ed_emp/---emp_elm/---trends/documents/publication/wcms_165455.pdf

[18] Irzeet, X., Lin L., Thirtle, C. and Wiggins, S. (2001). Agricultural productivity growth and poverty alleviation, *Development Policy Review*, Vol. 19, pp. 449–466.

[19] Jenkins, R. (2006). "Globalization, FDI and employment in Viet Nam", *Transnational corporations*, Vol. 15, No. 1, pp. 115–142.

[20] Kogel, T. and Prskawetz, A. (2001). Agricultural productivity growth and escape from Malthusian trap. *Journal of Economic Growth,* Vol. 6, pp. 337–357.

[21] Kuznets, S. (1964). Economic growth and the contribution of agriculture. In: Eicher C., Witt L. (eds): Agriculture in Economic Development. McGraw Hill, New York.

[22] Larisa, S., Mădălina, A. and Amalia, C. (2013). Employment in the EU countries: A panel data analysis, *Theoretical and Applied Economics*, Volume XX(1), pp. 87–102.

[23] Lewis, W.A. (1954). Economic development with unlimited supplies of labour. *The Manchester School*, Vol. 22, pp. 139–191.

[24] Marika, K., Hector, S. and Pablo, F. (2008). Capital Accumulation and Unemployment: New Insights on the Nordic Experience, *Cambridge Journal of Economics*, Vol. 32(6), pp. 977–1001.

[25] Matsuyama, K. (1992). Agricultural productivity, comparative advantage and economic growth. *Journal of Economic Theory*, Vol. 58, pp. 317–334.

[26] Modigliani, F. (2000). "Europe's economic problems," Prepared for testimony before the Monetary Committee of the European Parliament, 3rd Monetary and Finance Lecture, Freiburg, 6 April.

[27] Murad, A.B. and Serhan, C. (2017). The relationship between the relative GDP share of agriculture and the unemployment rate in selected Central and Eastern European countries, Agric. Econ. – Czech, Vol. 63(7), pp. 308–317.

[28] Rosenzweig (2003). Adaptation and mitigation strategies in agriculture: an analysis of potential synergies, Mitig Adapt Strat Glob Change, Vol. 12, pp. 855–873.

[29] Rowthorn, R. (1999). "Unemployment, wage bargaining and capital-labour substitution," *Cambridge Journal of Economics*, 23, pp. 413–425.

[30] Schultz, T.W. (1964). Transforming Traditional Agriculture. Yale University Press, New Haven, Conn.

[31] Stanila L. (2014). "Determinants of Earnings Inequality—Case Study for Romania", *International Journal of Business and Social Science*, Vol. 5, No. 9(1), August, pp. 238–244.

[32] Steger, T. (2000). Economic growth with subsistence consumption, *Review of Development Economics*, Vol. 62(2), pp. 343–361.

[33] Tiffin, R. and Irz, X (2006). Is agriculture the engine of growth? Agricultural Economics, Vol. 35, pp. 79–89.

# Appendix

| *Variables* | *Symbol Used* | *Definition** |
|---|---|---|
| Unemployment, youth total (% of total labor force ages 15–24) (modelled ILO estimate) | lyouthunem | Youth unemployment refers to the share of the labor force ages 15–24 without work but available for and seeking employment. |
| Agriculture, value added (% of GDP) | lagrivad | Agriculture corresponds to International Standard Industrial Classification (ISIC) divisions 1–5 and includes forestry, hunting, and fishing, as well as cultivation of crops and livestock production. Value added is the net output of a sector after adding up all outputs and subtracting intermediate inputs. It is calculated without making deductions for depreciation of fabricated assets or depletion and degradation of natural resources. |
| GDP per capita growth (annual %) | lgdppcg | Annual percentage growth rate of GDP per capita based on constant local currency. Aggregates are based on constant 2010 U.S. dollars. GDP per capita is gross domestic product divided by midyear population. GDP at purchaser's prices is the sum of gross value added by all resident producers in the economy plus any product taxes and minus any subsidies not included in the value of the products. It is calculated without making deductions for depreciation of fabricated assets or for depletion and degradation of natural resources. |

| *Variables* | *Symbol Used* | *Definition** |
|---|---|---|
| General government final consumption expenditure (% of GDP) | lgfcon | General government final consumption expenditure includes all government current expenditures for purchases of goods and services (including compensation of employees). It also includes most expenditures on national defence and security, but excludes government military expenditures that are part of government capital formation. |
| Gross fixed capital formation (% of GDP) | lgfcapi | Gross fixed capital formation includes land improvements (fences, ditches, drains, and so on); plant, machinery, and equipment purchases; and the construction of roads, railways, and the like, including schools, offices, hospitals, private residential dwellings, and commercial and industrial buildings. |
| Trade (% of GDP) | ltrade | Trade is the sum of exports and imports of goods and services measured as a share of gross domestic product. It is treated as openness in this study. |
| Inflation, consumer prices (annual %) | linf | Inflation as measured by the consumer price index reflects the annual percenttage change in the cost to the average consumer of acquiring a basket of goods and services that may be fixed or changed at specified intervals, such as yearly. The Laspeyres formula is generally used. |

*Source:* World Development indicators published by World Bank. (https://databank.worldbank.org/source/world-development-indicators)

CHAPTER 3

# Adoption of Maize Production in Kaliganj Upazila under Lalmonirhat District of Bangladesh

**Md. Safiul Islam Afrad, Md. Ashraful Islam, Abdul Halim, Kazi Tamim Rahman, Shahriar Hasan, Soumitra Saha and Amlan Biswas**

## 3.1 Introduction

Maize is well known as one of the oldest crops for its versatile nature with highest grain yield and multiple uses in the world. Despite the fact that maize expansion was ineffective in Bangladesh throughout the 1960s due to the government's push to promote a rice-based Green Revolution technology, maize production and yield have surged in recent years. Maize has a vast genetic variety that allows it to grow well in every environment, and it is cultivated in Bangladesh both in the winter and summer. With time, the cultivated area of maize in Bangladesh has increased to about 0.50 million ha with annual production of 40.2 million metric tons' grain in 2019–20 from merely 10.2 million metric tons from 0.17 million ha in 2010–11 and over 90 percent of maize is used as poultry feedstuff and the remaining in fish sector and as human food products (Rahman and Rahman, 2014; BBS, 2020).

There is a lot of potentiality to improve and expand the maize production in Bangladesh. Because of its many applications, maize is in high demand all around the world, including Bangladesh. It would probably be possible to minimize food shortages to a large amount if Bangladeshis' rigid food habits are to be varied from rice to maize. Because, in comparison to rice and wheat, it is a high-yielding and low-cost crop (Moniruzzaman *et al.*, 2009). Besides, the continuous growth of poultry industry in the country creating demands for maize. But farmers cultivating maize are not completely aware of the benefits of maize cultivation. Due to this reason, many of them are not interested to invest for maize cultivation as they do not have proper information on maize farming and marketing techniques (Hasan, 2008). Maize farming has been the subject of a small number of socio-economic studies in Bangladesh, which have found that it is a more valuable crop than rice and mustard (Hussain, 1995). Maize cultivation is not only lucrative, but maize growers' technical and economic efficacy is substantially greater than rice and wheat farmers' (Rahman *et al.*, 2016). So, it is absolute time for the farmer to come forward in maize cultivation.

The success of any technology depends on its dissemination among the potential users which is ultimately measured by the level of adoption of that technology. Very insufficient number of studies has been conducted on the adoption of maize production technologies in northern districts of Bangladesh. So, in terms of dissemination and adoption the present condition of maize production technologies needs to be explored. Given this background, the present study specifically addressed this critical research gap and systematically examines the socio-economic characteristics of the maize growers, extent of adoption of maize production by the growers, relationship between the socio-economic characteristics of the farmers and their adoption of maize production, and impediments in adopting those technologies.

## 3.2 Methodology

### 3.2.1 *Research Design*

The descriptive and diagnostic research design has been employed in the present study, and carried out at the Kaliganj upazila under Lalmonirhat district of Bangladesh. Three villages viz. Aminganj, Binbiniarchar and Mohisamuri has been randomly selected based on the intensive cultivation of maize. Farmers associated with agricultural activities in the study areas are the target population of the study. Disproportionate random sampling technique has been applied to select 85 respondents.

### 3.2.2 *Measurement of Variables*

Adoption of maize production technology is the dependent variable of this study. Wahab (1979) has constructed a multidimensional adoption scale to measure the rate of an adoption of a practice. The scale covers both duration as well as area dimensions under the use of the particular practice under measurement. The formula constructed by Wahab (1979) to compute the Adoption Quotient (AQ) for an individual has been adapted to express the AQ in percent (multiplying the AQ by 100). The AQ can range from 0 to 100, where 0 (zero) indicates no adoption of the practice and 100 indicates full adoption. The modified formula for calculating the AQ is presented below:

$$AQ = \frac{T2}{T3} \times \frac{T1}{T3} \times \frac{A1}{A2} \times 100$$

Where,

AQ = Adoption Quotient

$T_1$ = Year since the practice under study was introduced

$T_2$ = Year since the user became aware of the practice

$T_3$ = Year since the practice was adopted by the user

$A_1$ = Actual area (ha) under the practice during the surveyed year

$A_2$ = Potential area (ha) under the practice under study during the surveyed year

The independent variables of the present study are age, educational level, family size, farm size, farming experience, extension contact, annual family income, organizational participation, cosmopoliteness, training experience, knowledge in maize cultivation, area under maize cultivation.

Age of a respondent is measured based on the actual years, education in years of schooling, family size in total number of family members, farming experience based on the duration of a respondent engaged in agricultural works, farm size based on total farm land area (ha) owned by the respondents, extension contact by counting the number of information gathering sources, annual income based on his total annual earnings from different sources expressed in BDT, organizational membership based on the nature and duration of participation in different organization, cosmopoliteness based on their exposure to media, training experience based on the duration of a respondent engaged in training programs, knowledge based on their achieved score from different questions regarding maize cultivation, maize area based on maize cultivated area (ha) owned by the respondents.

### 3.2.3 *Problems Faced by Farmers during Maize Production*

To identify the problems that respondents faced, they were interviewed individually. They were requested to express their extent of problem. Based on their extent of problem facing, problem confrontation index (PCI) is calculated by using the following formula:

$$\text{Problem Confrontation Index (PCI)} = NAA \times 0 + L \times 1 + M \times 2 + H \times 3$$

Where, H = High, M = Moderate, L = Low and NAA = Not at all

Statistical Package for Social Science (SPSS) is used to analyze data and statistical tests like percentage, frequency count, mean, standard deviations were carried out. The Pearson coefficient of correlation is computed in order to explore the relationships between the selected characteristics of the farmers and their adoption of maize production.

## 3.3 Results and Discussion

### 3.3.1 *Farmers' Socio-demography*

The age category reveals that two thirds of the respondents (69.4 percent) were in young and middle-aged categories. Majority of the (61.2 percent) respondents had primary tohigher secondary level education which is appreciable. Most percentage of the respondents (58.8 percent) has medium family size where majority of the respondents (48.2 percent) had medium farming experience. Most percentage of the respondents (84.7 percent) possessed small farm size with low extension contacts (65.9 percent). (58.8 percent) respondents belong to low-income category because most of their income is dependent upon the farming sources. Data presented in Table 3.1 indicates that the highest proportion of the respondents (77.65 percent) have no organizational participation. Overwhelming percentage of the respondents (83.52 percent) has low cosmo-politeness. Table 3.1 also reveals that a very big portion (74.2 percent) of them received no training. Highest proportion of the respondents (82.47 percent) had high knowledge on maize cultivation where most percentage of the respondents (88.2 percent) has small to medium maize cultivation area.

**Table 3.1:** Salient Features of the Selected Characteristics of the Respondent Farmers

| *Characteristics (Unit of measurement)* | *Categories* | *Respondents (n=85)* | | *Mean* | *SD* |
|---|---|---|---|---|---|
| | | *No.* | *%* | | |
| Age (years) | Young (22 to 35) | 26 | 30.6 | 44.99 | 11.92 |
| | Middle (36 to 50) | 33 | 38.8 | | |
| | Old (above 50) | 26 | 30.6 | | |
| Educational level (Schooling year) | Illiterate (0) | 33 | 38.8 | 4.84 | 4.93 |
| | Primary (1 to 5 class) | 22 | 25.9 | | |
| | Secondary (6 to 10 class) | 20 | 23.5 | | |
| | Higher Secondary (>10) | 10 | 11.8 | | |
| Family size (No. of members) | Small (up to 5) | 24 | 28.2 | 5.61 | 1.92 |
| | Medium (5–7) | 50 | 58.8 | | |
| | Large (above 7) | 11 | 12.9 | | |
| Farming experience (Years) | Low (1 to 10 years) | 14 | 16.5 | 26.42 | 13.22 |
| | Medium (11 to 20 years) | 30 | 35.3 | | |
| | High (above 20 years) | 41 | 48.2 | | |
| Farm size (Hectare) | Small (up to 1.0 ha) | 72 | 84.7 | 0.73 | 0.66 |
| | Medium (1.01 to 3.0 ha) | 11 | 12.9 | | |
| | Large (above 3.0 ha) | 2 | 2.4 | | |
| Extension contacts | Low (1 to 5) | 56 | 65.9 | 6.04 | 2.24 |
| | Medium (6 to 10) | 25 | 29.4 | | |
| | Large (above 10) | 4 | 4.7 | | |

| *Characteristics (Unit of measurement)* | *Categories* | *Respondents (n=85)* | | *Mean* | *SD* |
|---|---|---|---|---|---|
| | | *No.* | *%* | | |
| Annual family income (BDT) | Low (up to BDT 110000) | 50 | 58.8 | 141494.0 | – |
| | Medium (BDT 110001 to 240000) | 22 | 29.9 | | |
| | High (> BDT 240000) | 13 | 15.3 | | |
| Organizational participation (Day) | No participation | 66 | 77.65 | – | – |
| | Had participation | 19 | 22.35 | | |
| Cosmopoliteness | Low (up to 10) | 71 | 83.52 | 7.36 | 3.80 |
| | Medium (11 to 13) | 11 | 12.94 | | |
| | High (above 13) | 3 | 3.53 | | |
| Training experience | Upazila Agriculture Office | 15 | 17.7 | – | – |
| | Private Company | 7 | 8.1 | | |
| | Didn't receive training | 63 | 74.2 | | |
| Knowledge on maize cultivation technologies | Low knowledge (up to 15) | 8 | 9.4 | 22.82 | 3.35 |
| | Medium knowledge (16 to 20) | 7 | 8.2 | | |
| | High knowledge (above 20) | 70 | 82.4 | | |
| Area under Maize Cultivation | Small maize cultivation area (0.10 to 0.30ha) | 38 | 44.7 | 0.37 | 0.26 |
| | Medium maize cultivation area (0.31 to 0.60 ha) | 37 | 43.5 | | |
| | Large maize cultivation area (above 0.60 ha) | 10 | 11.8 | | |

*Source:* Field Survey, 2021.

## 3.4 Adoption of Maize Production

### 3.4.1 *Extent of Adoption of Maize Cultivation*

Based on the respondents' extent of adoption of maize cultivation the respondents are classified into three categories presented in Table 3.2.

**Table 3.2:** Distribution of the Respondents According to their Extent of Adoption of Maize

| *Adoption Categories* | *Respondents* | | *Mean* | *SD* |
|---|---|---|---|---|
| | *Number* | *Percent* | | |
| Low adoption (up to 33) | 6 | 7.1 | 76.75 | 27.214 |
| Medium adoption (33.01 to 67) | 26 | 30.6 | | |
| High adoption (above 67) | 53 | 62.4 | | |
| **Total** | **85** | **100.0** | | |

*Source:* Field Survey, 2021.

Information contained in Table 3.2 reveal that majority 62.4 percent of the respondents have high level of adoption of maize cultivation compared to 30.6 percent having medium adoption while 7.1 percent had low level of adoption. Findings clearly indicated that almost all (92.9 percent) of the respondents had medium to high adoption of maize production. Sharda *et al.* (2018) reported that 85.0 percent respondents had moderate to high adoption of Kharif maize production technology. Almost similar findings are also reflected in the studies of Afrad *et al.* (2020) and Ghosh (2016) in adoption of BARI piaz1 and BARI ada2 cultivation in Bogura district and BRRI dhan28 cultivation in the coastal area of Bangladesh, respectively.

### 3.4.2 *Comparative Adoption of Different Maize Varieties*

Farmers in the study location are cultivating different maize varieties. Among the varieties, four major cultivated varieties are Palwan, Bahuboli 555, Dalia 4455 and Kabri 50. A comparative adoption of the four varieties is computed based on total average area covered as presented in Table 3.

**Table 3.3:** Distribution of the Respondents Based on their Adoption of Different Maize Varieties

| *Varieties* | *Adoption Quotient (AQ)* | *Mean Cultivated Area (ha)* | *Rank* |
|---|---|---|---|
| Palwan | 78.1 | 0.318 | 1st |
| Dalia 4455 | 73.3 | 0.535 | 2nd |
| Bahuboli 555 | 72.4 | 0.453 | 3rd |
| Kabri 50 | 70.3 | 0.385 | 4th |

*Source:* Field Survey, 2021.

Findings contained in Table 3.3 show that among the four cultivated maize varieties in the study location, Palwan ranked first (with adoption quotient of 78.1 percent) followed by Dalia 4455 ranked second (with AQ of 73.3 percent), Bahuboli 555 ranked third (with AQ of 72.4 percent) and Kabri 50 ranked fourth position (with AQ of 70.3%). Almost similar findings are also observed in the study of Podder (1999).

## 3.5 Relationship between Selected Characteristics of the Farmers and their Adoption

Relationship between the selected characteristics of the respondents and their adoption of maize production has been presented in Table 3.4.

The estimated value of (r) is $-0.232^{*}$ for level of education (Table 3.4), of which adoption is negatively significant at 5 percent level of significance. It indicates that the higher the educational level of the respondent, the lower the adoption of maize cultivation technology. Education is the process of developing capabilities of the individuals so that they can adequately respond to their situation. This might be due to the reason that the educated farmers consider the diversified aspects of maize cultivation including its production, processing, preservation and marketing. They might find similar drawbacks among these aspects; therefore, they don't whimsically get involved in maize cultivation.

**Table 3.4:** Relationship between Selected Characteristics of the Farmers and their Adoption of Maize Production

| *Selected Characteristics* | *Correlation Coefficient (r)* |
|---|---|
| Age | –0.211 |
| Family member | 0.029 |
| Level of education | –0.232* |
| Annual family income | –0.194 |
| Farming experience | –0.206 |
| Farm size | –0.337** |
| Cosmopoliteness | 0.049 |
| Knowledge | 0.112 |
| Area under maize cultivation | 0.029 |
| Organizational participation | 0.088 |

*Source:* Field Survey, 2021.

*Note:* ** Correlation is significant at 1% level, *Correlation is significant at 5% level.

The relationship between farm size and adoption of the respondents was found to be negatively significant at one percent (Table 3.4) as the value of (r) is –0.337. It means that if there is any increase in the farm size of the respondent, there would decrease in their adoption of maize cultivation technology. Innovation always involves some sort of risks; a new variety may fail in new areas. Generally, the farmers having large farm size can take the risk of practicing new variety. In this case, it different trend has been observed which might be due to the fact that the large farm holders hardly involve in the farming activities, heavily dependent on sharecropper and or hired labor. Again, the large farmers are usually educated persons may find some disadvantages of maize cultivation technology. Another reason may be that farmers don't get quality seeds of modern varieties and depend on the seeds to be supplied from own produced seeds or old varieties. But Rahman (2001), Hussen (2001) and Sarkar (1997) in their studies reported significant positive relationships between farm size and adoption of modern technologies. Dissimilar findings also observed by Hedayet (2011) and Islam (2008) in their studies on adoption BRRI dhan47 and mungbean, respectively.

## 3.6 Problems Faced in Cultivation of Maize

The farmers faced different problems in cultivating maize of them 15 were identified. For clear understanding of the fact, a problem confrontation index (PCI) has been used which is shown in Table 5. Results presented in Table 3.5 indicate that lack of storage facility at farmers' level (with PCI score 212) is the top most problem followed by the limited availability of credit which ranked 2nd, lack of processing technique to consume as food ranked 3rd while poor technical information ranked as 4th and lack of availability of hybrid seed ranked as 5th problem with corresponding PCI scores of 190, 172, 69 and 51 respectively.

**Table 3.5:** Rank Order of the Problems faced by the Maize Growers

| *SI#* | *Problem Items* | *PCI* | *Rank* |
|---|---|---|---|
| 1. | Lack of suitable land for maize cultivation | 18 | 14th |
| 2. | Limited seed availability at farmers' level | 36 | 7th |
| 3. | Non-availability of hybrid seed | 51 | 5th |
| 4. | Higher input cost (seed, fertilizer, pesticide) | 38 | 6th |
| 5. | Non-availability of credit | 190 | 2nd |
| 6. | Lack of irrigation facilities | 35 | 8th |
| 7. | Poor knowledge on maize production | 34 | 9th |
| 8. | Lack of technical information | 69 | 4th |
| 9. | Labor shortage | 31 | 11th |
| 10. | Harvesting complexity | 14 | 15th |
| 11. | Lack of crushing machine | 32 | 10th |
| 12. | Cannot consume as food | 172 | 3rd |
| 13. | Lack of storage facility at farmers' level | 212 | 1st |
| 14. | Lack of marketing of maize | 27 | 12th |
| 15. | Others (if any) | 21 | 13th |

*Source:* Field Survey, 2021.

Lack of storage facility is common problem for rural farmers of Bangladesh which hinders large scale commercial crop production. In the study area the farmers did not have storage capacity for storing their maize. Getting credit is another vital problem of maize production, because its production requires huge inputs including seeds, fertilizers, labors which are credit dependent. Most of the times, farmers cannot get the credit facilities. The maize processing for food is quite unknown to the farmers which are machinery dependent. These machineries are not available in Bangladesh, especially to the Char land dwellers. Similar findings were also reflected in the study of Hedayet (2011). Moniruzzaman *et al.* (2009) where they observed lack of capital and high price of fertilizers as the major problems faced by the maize growers. According to Yahaya *et al.* (2020), maize growers face a number of challenges, including shortage of capital (73.0 percent), high farm input costs (69.0 percent), inadequate credit facilities (67.0 percent), insufficient storage facilities (53.0 percent), insufficient processing facilities (50.0 percent), pest and disease infestation (46.0 percent), poor road network (40.0 percent), and poor extension services (33.0 percent).

## 3.7 Conclusions

Majority of the respondents are young and middle aged (69.4 percent), having primary to higher secondary level of education (61.2 percent), medium family size (58.8 percent), medium farming experience (48.2 percent), small farm size (84.7 percent) with low extension contacts (65.9 percent), low-income category (58.8 percent), no organizational participation (77.65 percent), low cosmopoliteness (83.52 percent) and no training participation (74.2 percent). 82.47 percent respondents have high knowledge on maize cultivation where (88.2 percent) respondents have small to medium maize cultivation area. (92.9 percent) respondents had medium to high adoption of maize production. In the study area, 'Palwan' is ranked first among the four cultivated maize varieties. Level of education and farm size was found negatively significant at five percent and one percent level of significance respectively. Lack of storage facility at farmers' level followed by the limited availability of credit, lack of processing technique to consume as food, poor technical information and lack of availability of hybrid seed were the top most problem in maize cultivation.

## References


[1] Afrad, M.S.I., Akter, M.R., Haque, M.E. and Zakaria, M. (2020). Adoption of spices cultivation technology by the growers in Shibganj upazila under Bogura district of Bangladesh. The Agriculturists, Vol. 18(1), pp. 81–93.

[2] BBS (2020). Yearbook of Agricultural Statistics in Bangladesh, Bangladesh Bureau of Statistics. Ministry of Planning, Government of the people's Republic of Bangladesh, Dhaka.

[3] Ghosh, M.K. (2016). Adoption of BRRI dhan 28 in the coastal areas of Bangladesh. International *Journal of Agricultural Extension and Rural Development Studies*, Vol. 3(3), pp. 25–35.

[4] Hasan, M.F. (2008). Economic efficiency and constraints of maize production in the northern region of Bangladesh, *Journal of Innovation Development Strategy*, Vol. 2(1), pp. 18–32.

[5] Hedayet, A.K.M. (2011). Adoption of BRRI dhan47 in the Coastal Saline Areas of Bangladesh. MS Thesis, Department of Agricultural Extension Education, Bangladesh Agricultural University, Mymensingh.

[6] Hussain, M.S., Islam, M.N. and Anwar, M.M. (1995). Comparative study on hybrid and composite variety of maize in selected areas of Bangladesh. Annual Report. Agricultural Economics Division, BARI: Gazipur, Bangladesh, pp. 44–52.

[7] Hussen, M.A.M. (2001). Farmers' knowledge and adoption of modern sugarcane cultivation practices. MSc. Thesis, Department of Agricultural Extension Education, Bangladesh Agricultural University, Mymensingh.

[8] Islam, A. 2008. Farmers' Knowledge System and Dissemination of Mungbean Cultivation in the South-western Region of Bangladesh. MS Thesis, Department of Agricultural Extension and Rural Development, Bangabandhu Sheikh Mujibur Rahman Agricultural University. Gazipur.

[9] Monlruzzaman, M.S. Rahman, Karim, M.K. and Alam, Q.M. (2009). Agro-economic analysis of maize production in Bangladesh: a farm level study. *Bangladesh Journal Agricultural Research,* Vol. 34(1), pp. 15–24.

[10] Podder, S.K. (1999). Adoption of Mehersagar banana by the farmers of Ciazaria union under Sakhipur thana of Tangail district. MS Thesis, Department of Agricultural Extension Education, Bangladesh Agricultural University, Mymensingh.

[11] Rahman, M.S. (2001). Knowledge, attitude and adoption of the farmers regarding Aalok 6201 hybrid rice in Sadar upazila of Mymensingh district. MS Thesis, Department of Agricultural Extension Education, Bangladesh Agricultural University, Mymensingh.

[12] Rahman, S. and Rahman, M. (2014). Exploring the potential and performance of maize production in Bangladesh, *International Journal of Agricultural Management*, 3, pp. 99–107.

[13] Rahman, S., Kazal, M.M.H., Begum, I.A. and Alam, M.J. (2016). Competitiveness, profitability, input demand and output supply of maize production in Bangladesh. *Agriculture*, Vol. 6(2), pp. 1–14.

[14] Sharda, W., Kapse, P. and Ahire, R.D. (2018). Knowledge and adoption of kharif maize production technology among the farmers. *International Journal of Current Microbiology. Applied Science.* Special Issue-6: pp. 1478–1484.

[15] Sarker, D.C. (1997). Correlates of selected characteristics of potato growers with their adoption of improved potato cultivation practices of five villages of Cumilla District. MSc. Thesis, Department of Agricultural Extension Education, Bangladesh Agricultural University, Mymensingh.

[16] Wahab, M.F. (1979). An analysis of factors influencing adoption and non-adoption of high yielding varieties of rice in Bangladesh. Unpublished MS Thesis, Asian Institute of Technology, Thailand.

[17] Yahaya, U.F., Emeghara, U.U., Onwuegbunam, N.E., Akanni-John, R., Olagunju, O.E., Suleiman, R., Aasa, O.S., Agbomakha, F.I., L. Ganiyu, L., and Olukotun, O. (2020). Costs and returns analysis of maize production in Lere local government area of Kaduna State, Nigeria. *South Asian Journal of Social Studies and Economics*, Vol. 8(1), pp. 45–54.

CHAPTER 4

# Economic Impact of Climate Change on Agriculture: An Empirical Study of India and Bangladesh

**Mashud Ahmed and Paramita Saha**

## 4.1 Introduction

The climate change and climate variability are closely associated with agriculture and its allied activities. Agriculture sector is the most vulnerable to climate change across the world (Mendelsohn and Dinar, 2009; Nastis *et al.*, 2012). Climate change reduces agricultural production in two ways: directly by causing damage to standing crops and indirectly by influencing cropping decisions (Trinh *et al.*, 2021). The impact of climate change on agriculture has received a lot of attention since it is related to food security and poverty for the majority of the world's population (Dinar *et al.*, 1998). It will directly contribute to future food insecurity by raising food costs and diminishing food production.

Climate change can cause various socio-economic problems including poverty, unsustainable development, health and safety (Swart *et al.*, 2003). Climate variables interact directly with input variables such as land, water, fertilisers, and pesticides in agricultural production. Therefore, empirical studies on climate change and agricultural productivity have indicated its negative impact on developing countries (Cline, 2007; Xie *et al.*, 2019). In India, the agriculture sector employs the majority of the people, directly and indirectly. Agriculture, hydropower, forest management, and biodiversity all get negatively affected by climate change (Senapati *et al.*, 2013). In literature, it is observed that projected climate change over the period 2010–2039 will reduce crop production by 4.5 to 9 percent. In the long run (2070–2099), the impact is substantial, with yields falling by 25 percent or more in the absence of long-term adaptation (Guiteras, 2009). In Bangladesh, where lives and livelihoods largely depend on agriculture, the effect of climate change on agriculture appears to be a great threat for national food security (Sikder and Xiaoying, 2014). Marginal impact estimates suggest that increase in temperature and rainfall leads to increase in net income from crop farming in Bangladesh (Hossain *et al.*, 2019).

Government of India has pledged to cut India's total projected carbon emissions by one billion tonnes by 2030, to reduce the carbon intensity of the nation's economy by less than 45 percent by the end of the decade, and achieving net-zero carbon emissions by 2070 at the COP26 Summit in Glasgow in November 2021. The Prime Minister of Bangladesh Sheikh Hasina, on the other hand, has urged wealthy countries to follow up their pledges to reduce greenhouse gas emissions and to provide the promised $100 billion in annual financial aid to less developed countries to help them adapt to climate change and mitigate further temperature rises.

In this background, the present study seeks to answer the research question whether climate change is related to share of agriculture in Gross Domestic Product (GDP) or not. Therefore, the main objective of this study is to examine long-run and short-run relationships of the change in the share of agriculture in GDP with climate variables, particularly temperature change and per capita $CO_2$ emissions, in India and Bangladesh.

## 4.2 Data Sources and Methodology

The data of annual $CO_2$ emissions (metric tons per capita), share of agriculture in annual GDP (growth in percentage) have been collected from the world bank's data portal (https://data.worldbank.org) whereas the data on annual mean surface temperature change ($^0$C) are taken from the Food and Agricultural Organisation (https://www.fao.org/faostat) for the period spanning from 1961 to 2018. Due to non-availability of the secondary data of other climate variables like changes in rainfall, an increase in the frequency of extreme weather events, sea level rise etc., this study is confined only with the above-mentioned variables.

The observed time series plots of the share of agriculture in GDP, $CO_2$ emissions per capita and annual mean surface temperature change (natural log) for India are presented in Figure 4.1.

Where lnAGDP, $lnCO_2$ and lnTempch represent natural log value of the share of agriculture in GDP, Carbon dioxide emissions and Temperature change, respectively.

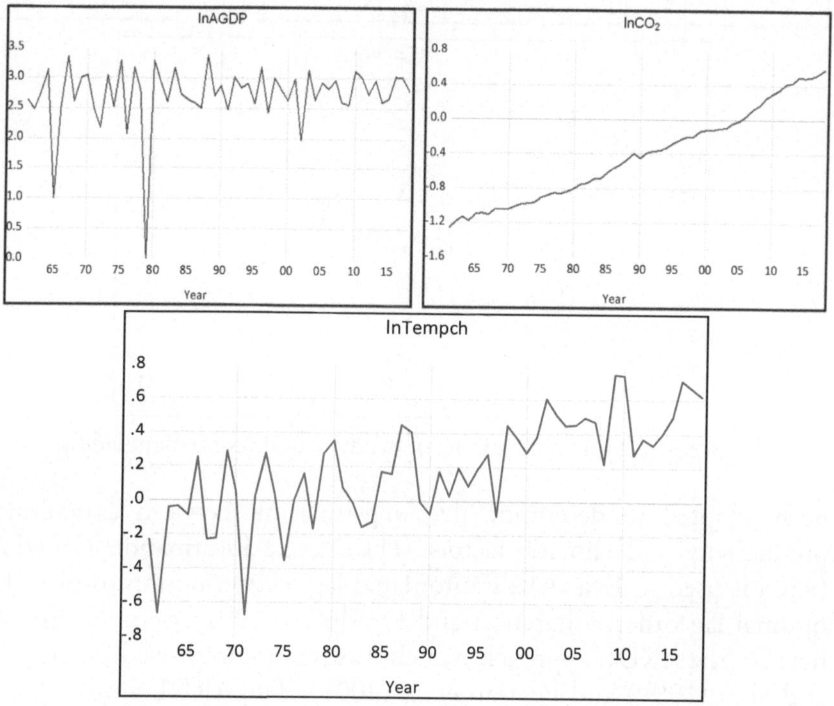


**Figure 4.1:** Time Series Plots of Study Variables for India

Now, the observed time series plots of the share of agriculture in GDP, $CO_2$ emissions and annual mean surface temperature change (natural log values) for Bangladesh are presented in Figure 4.2.

Where lnAGDP, $lnCO_2$ and lnTempch represent natural log value of the share of agriculture in GDP, Carbon dioxide emissions and Temperature change, respectively.

There are different methods to study the impact of climate change and variability on agricultural production. In the present study, the Autoregressive Distributed Lag (ARDL) bounds testing technique has

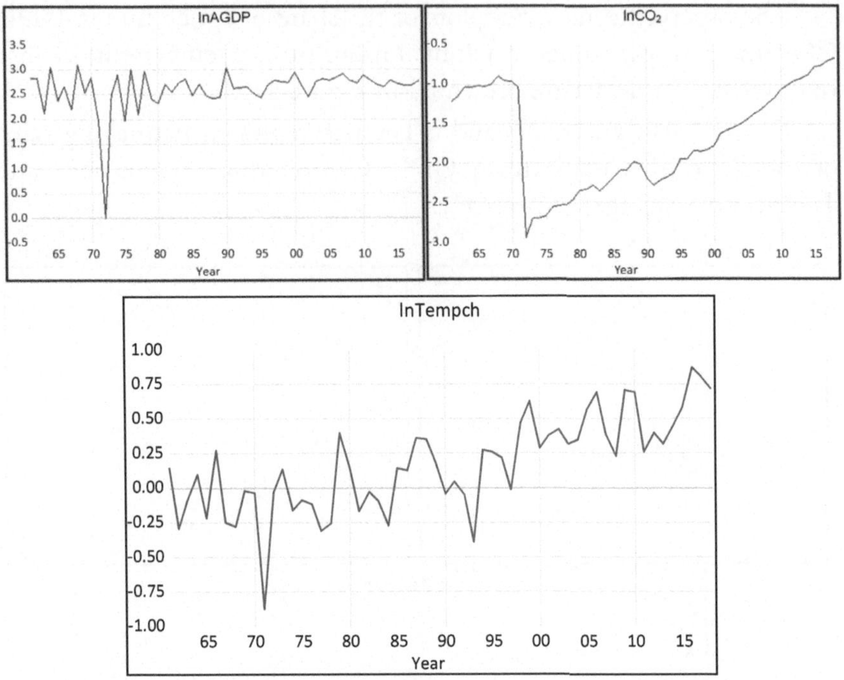


**Figure 4.2:** Time Series Plots of Study Variables for Bangladesh

been adopted to determine the long-run link between agricultural productivity and climatic factors. The Akaike information Criterion (AIC) is used in Eviews12's automated lag section option to pick the optimal lag order. Charemza and Deadman (1992) were the first to develop the ARDL approach, which was further improved by Pesaran and Shin (1999) and Pesaran *et al.* (2001). The ARDL approach has some advantages over other methods. For example, The ARDL approach can be used even in cases when different variables have different orders of integration. In other words, if the variables are stationary at either I(0) or I(1), ARDL approach can be applied. Secondly, the ARDL test ensures more consistent estimates in the case of small samples compared to the other techniques.

The model to investigate the association of climate variables including temperature change and carbon dioxide emission with the share of agriculture in GDP for both India and Bangladesh throughout the period 1961–2018, can be specified as:

$$AGDP_t = f(Tempch, CO_2) \qquad \ldots (1)$$

In equation (1), $AGDP_t$ indicates the share of agriculturein GDP for a specific country over time, Tempch represents the change in the annual mean surface temperature and $CO_2$ denotes per capita carbon dioxide emissions. Equation (1) can also be written as:

$$AGDP_t = \beta_0 + \beta_1 Tempch + \beta_2 CO_2 + \mu_t \quad \ldots (2)$$

This study used all variables in their natural logarithmic form to minimize the multicollinearity and volatility of the annual time series data. A log-linear model is specified as follows by applying natural logarithm to equation (2).

$$LnAGDP_t = \beta_0 + \beta_1 LnTempch + \beta_2 LnCO_2 + \mu_t \quad \ldots (3)$$

ARDL approach is based on two steps. First step, it is needed to determine the existence of a long run cointegrating relationship among the variables by using the Wald-coefficient test or F-statistics and by comparing them with critical values set out by Pesaran *et al.* (2001). Pesaran *et al.* (2001) reported two types of critical values: lower bounds and upper bounds. The critical values for the I (0) variables are referred to as lower-bound critical values while the critical values for the I (1) variables are meant to as upper-bound critical values. If the calculated F-Statistic is higher than the upper bounds, it means the null of hypothesis of no co-integration is rejected, indicating the evidence of a long-run cointegration relationship between the variables, regardless of the order of integration of the variables. If calculated F-statistic is below the lower bound, we cannot reject the null hypothesis of no cointegration, indicating the absence of a long-run equilibrium relationship. If calculated F-statistic is between lower and upper bounds, a conclusive inference could not be made without knowing the order of integration of the underlying regressors. The mathematical representation of the ARDL bounds-testing model for this study can be expressed as follows:

$$\Delta\, LnAGDPt = \beta_0 + \beta_1 \sum_{i=1}^{n} \Delta\, LnAGDPt_{t-i} + \beta_2 \sum_{i=1}^{n} \Delta\, LnTempch_{t-i} + \beta_3 \sum_{i=}^{n} \Delta\, LnCO_{2\,t-i} + +\gamma_1 LnAGDP_{t-1} + \gamma_2\, LnTepch_{t-1} + \gamma_3 LnCO_{2\,t-1} + \varepsilon_t \ldots (4)$$

Where Δ represents change, $\beta_0$ is the intercept, n denotes the lag order and $\varepsilon_t$ is the error term. The existence of cointegration relationship between variables from Equation (4) is examined by testing the significance of the lagged levels of variables using the F-statistic or Wald-coefficient test.

In order to study the short-run relationship between the variables, the error correction model (ECM) based on the ARDL approach is established as follows.

$$\Delta \text{LnAGDPt} = \gamma_0 + \gamma_1 \sum_{i=1}^{n} \Delta \text{LnAGDPt}_{t-i} + \gamma_2 \sum_{i=1}^{n} \Delta \text{LnTempch}_{t-i} + \gamma_3 \sum_{i=1}^{n} \Delta \text{LnCO}_{2\,t-i} + \gamma_4 ECM_{t-1} + \varepsilon_t \quad \text{... (5)}$$

Where ECM (–1) term is a lagged value of the residual of model in which the long-term relationship is obtained. ECM (–1) is the speed of adjustment parameter which is expected to be negative.

## 4.3 Results and Discussions

### 4.3.1 *Unit Root Tests*

Before proceeding to ARDL test, it is required to investigate the order of integration for each series considered under the study. In order to find out the order of integration, the Augmented Dickey-Fuller (ADF) test is applied. The unit root test on the natural logarithms of the variables in level and first difference forms are shown in Table 4.1. Order of integration is shown a mixture of I(0) and I(1). In other

**Table 4.1:** Unit Root Test Results

| *Variables* | *ADF Unit Root Test* | | *Order of Integration* |
|---|---|---|---|
| | *Level* | *First Difference* | |
| **India** | | | |
| LnAGDP | –9.863573*(–3.490662) | – | I (0) |
| $LnCO_2$ | –1.591749(–3.490662) | –9.694125* (–3.492149) | I (1) |
| LnTempch | –7.475508*(–3.492149) | – | I (0) |
| **Bangladesh** | | | |
| LnAGDP | –7.491959*(–3.490662) | – | I (0) |
| $LnCO_2$ | –1.675092*(–3.490662) | –7.969308* (–3.492149) | I (1) |
| LnTempch | –5.685645*(–3.492149) | – | I (0) |

*Note:* t-statistic of intercept and trend model with 5% significance level, parentheses denote critical values. *Indicates statistically significant at 5% level of significance.

words, the results indicate that natural logarithm of the share of agriculture in GDP(LNAGDP) and temperature change (LNTEMPCH) for both India and Bangladesh are stationary at level while the natural logarithm of $CO_2$ ($LNCO_2$) is stationary at first difference for both the countries. Therefore, the condition for the order of integration to apply ARDL model is satisfied.

### 4.3.2 *Cointegration Testing Results*

The results of ARDL bound test are presented in Table 4.2. The calculated values of F statistic are found to be above the critical values at 5 percent level of significance. This implies that there is a long-run relationship among the variables during the study period.

**Table 4.2:** Cointegration Test Results of ARDL (1, 0, 1) and ARDL (3, 4, 4) for India and Bangladesh

| *Test Statistic* | *Estimated Values* | *k* |
|---|---|---|
| F-Statistics | 24.02841* AGDP of India<br>11.17842 * AGDP of Bangladesh | 2 |
| Critical Value Bounds (Peseran *et al.*, 2001) | | |
| *Significance* | *Lower Bound (I0)* | *Upper Bound (I1)* |
| 10% | 2.63 | 3.35 |
| 5% | 3.1 | 3.87 |
| 1% | 4.13 | 5 |

*Note:* * signifies rejection of the null hypothesis at 5% significance level.

### 4.3.3 *Long-Run ARDL Estimates*

Long term coefficients, calculated according to the estimation results of ARDL (1, 0, 3) and ARDL (3, 4, 4) models for India and Bangladesh are presented in Table 4.3. The results show that per capita $CO_2$ emission and temperature change have positive but statistically insignificant association with the share of agriculture in GDP of India, in the long run. However, $CO_2$ has negative but insignificant impact on the share of agriculture in GDP of Bangladesh, while temperature change has shown a statistically significant and positive association with the share of agriculture in GDP of Bangladesh, in the long run. The coefficient of temperature change for Bangladesh implies that a1 per cent increase in temperature will be causing growth of 0.31 percent in contribution of agriculture to GDP of Bangladesh, in the long run. The results are also supported by the time series plots of the study variables as presented in Figures 4.1 and 4.2 for India and Bangladesh, respectively.

**Table 4.3:** Long-Run ARDL Estimates

| **India** | | | |
|---|---|---|---|
| *Dependent Variable: D(LnAGDP), ARDL (1, 0, 3)* | | | |
| *Regressor* | *Coefficient* | *t-values* | *Probability* |
| $LNCO_2$ | 0.101384 | 0.440994 | 0.6612 |
| LnTempch | 0.198494 | 0.363848 | 0.7176 |
| C | 2.744065 | 14.09615* | 0.0000 |
| **Bangladesh** | | | |
| *Dependent Variable: D(LnAGDP), ARDL (3, 4, 4)* | | | |
| *Regressor* | *Coefficient* | *t-values* | *Probability* |
| $LnCO_2$ | –0.007592 | –0.207120 | 0.8370 |
| LnTempch | 0.319830 | 3.583387* | 0.0009 |
| C | 4.162481 | 6.045027* | 0.0000 |

*Source:* Authors' own calculation using EViews12.

*Note:* * Indicates significant at 5% level of significance.

### 4.3.4 *Short-run ARDL Estimates:*

The results of the short run ARDL estimates along with the coefficients of error terms are presented in the Table 4.4. The important outcome of the short run dynamics is the calculation of the coefficient of ECM (–1). Error correction coefficient indicates the speed of adjustment back to the long-run equilibrium after a short run shock. The ECM coefficients are negative and statistically significant for both the countries. For example, the coefficient of $ECM_{t-1}$ for the share of agriculture in GDP of India is –1.253095. This implies, nearly 125 percent of the disequilibria of the previous year's shock adjusting back to the long run equilibrium in the current year. In the similar way, the coefficient of $ECM_t-1$ for the share of agriculture in GDP of Bangladesh is –1.641099, implying the disequilibria in the short run is adjusting back to the long run equilibrium in the current year with a rate of 164 percent.

**Table 4.4:** Short-run ARDL Estimate

| India | | | |
|---|---|---|---|
| *Dependent variable (LnAGDP), ARDL (1, 0, 3)* | | | |
| *Variable* | *Coefficient* | *t-values* | *Probability* |
| D(LnTempch) | –0.940106* | –3.401473 | 0.0014 |
| D (LnTempch (–1)) | 0.006901 | 0.027163 | 0.9784 |
| D (LnTempch (–2)) | –0.802004* | –3.123978 | 0.0030 |
| ECM (–1) | –1.253095* | –10.10548 | 0.0000 |
| **Bangladesh** | | | |
| *Dependent variable: D(LnAGDP), ARDL (3, 4, 4)* | | | |
| *Variable* | *Coefficient* | *t-values* | *Probability* |
| D (LnAGDP (–1)) | 0.410331* | 2.155088 | 0.0372 |
| D (LnAGDP (–2)) | 0.334046* | 2.893972 | 0.0061 |
| D ($LnCO_2$) | 1.330953* | 11.05392 | 0.0000 |
| D ($LnCO_2$(–1)) | 0.2269772 | 1.305786 | 0.1991 |
| D ($LnCO_2$(–2)) | 0.088597 | 0.453282 | 0.6528 |
| D ($LnCO_2$(–3)) | 0.566551* | 3.203279 | 0.0027 |
| D (LnTempch) | –0.071907 | –0.654086 | 0.5168 |
| D (LnTempch (–1)) | –0.753033* | –4.925982 | 0.0000 |
| D (LnTempch (–2)) | –0.353038* | –2.288117 | 0.0275 |
| D (LnTempch (–3)) | –0.418429* | –3.237696 | 0.0024 |
| ECM (–1) | –1.641099* | –6.933051 | 0.0000 |

*Source:* Authors' own calculation using EViews12.

*Note:* * Indicates significant at 5% level of significance.

In short run, temperature change has a statistically significant negative impact on the share of agricultural GDP but $CO_2$ has no significant impact in India. In case of Bangladesh, $CO_2$ has significant and positive association with the share of agriculture in GDP while temperature has a statistically significant and negative relationship with the share of agriculture in GDP, in short run.

### 4.3.5 *Diagnostic Tests*

Table 4.5 contains diagnostic test results of the ARDL models for agricultural GDP of India and Bangladesh. The values of R-Square and adjusted R-square of the models for both the countries are highly satisfactory. For example, the adjusted $R^2$ value of 0.7416 for the model of India suggests that temperature change and $CO_2$ emission jointly explain a significant part (74.16 percent) of the variation in the share of agriculture in GDP during the period 1961–2018. The Breusch-Godfrey serial correlation LM test and the Breusch-Pagan-Godfrey heteroscedasticity test suggest that there is no serial correlation and no heteroscedasticity of the residuals at 5 percent level of significance. In other words, the functional forms of the models are good fitted, free from serial correlation and heteroscedasticity.

**Table 4.5:** Diagnostic Checking of the ARDL Model

| *Dependent Variables* | *R Square* | *Adjusted R Square* | *Serial Correlation* | *Hetero-scedasticity* |
|---|---|---|---|---|
| D(LnAGDP) (India) | 0.7560 | 0.7416 | 0.7878 (0.4649) | 1.6638 (0.1505) |
| D(LnAGDP) (Bangladesh) | 0.9112 | 0.8906 | 3.0020 (0.0616) | 1.1303 (0.3638) |

*Note:* Null hypothesis for serial correlation is $H_0$: No serial Correlation, for Heteroscedasticity $H_0$: Homoscedasticity and the values in the (…) are probability values.

## 4.4 Conclusion

In recent years, the topic climate change has got much popularity in agricultural research, as it is predicted that climate change would have a severe impact on agricultural productivity and the share of agriculture in GDP across the countries. The present study reveals the long-run and short-run associations of the share of agriculture in GDP and climate variables, particularly temperature change and $CO_2$ emission, in India and Bangladesh. The study finds the existence of long-run relationship among climate change and agricultural productivity over the study period from 1961 to 2018, for both the countries. The results indicate that per capita $CO_2$ emission and temperature change have positive and insignificant association with the share of agriculture in GDP of India, in the long run. However, a positive and statistically significant relationship is observed between temperature change and the share of agriculture in GDP of Bangladesh, in the long run. In short run, temperature change has a significant and negative impact on the share of agriculture in GDP of India but $CO_2$ has no significant impact. The $CO_2$ emission has a positive and statistically significant impact on the share of agriculture in the GDP while temperature has a statistically significant and negative relationship with the share of agriculture in GDP of Bangladesh, in short run. Agriculture sector is the major source of GDP for both the countries. Therefore, it is important for the respective governments to make suitable mitigation policies and to encourage the farmers to take appropriate adaptation strategies to combat the adverse effects of climate change on agriculture.

## References

[1] Mendelsohn, R.O. and Dinar, A. (2009) Climate change and agriculture: an economic analysis of global impacts, adaptation and distributional effects. Edward Elgar Publishing. Cheltenham, UK.

[2] Nastis, S.A., Michailidis, A. and Chatzitheodoridis, F. (2012) Climate change and agricultural productivity. African journal of agricultural research, 7(35), pp. 4885–4893.

[3] Dinar, A., Mendelsohn, R., Evenson, R., Parikh, J., Sanghi, A., Kumar, K..... and Lonergan, S. (1998) Measuring the impact of climate change on Indian agriculture. The World Bank, Technical Paper no. 402.https://ideas.repec.org/p/fth/wobate/402.html

[4] Trinh, T.A., Feeny, S., and Posso, A. (2021) The Impact of Natural Disasters and Climate Change on Agriculture: Findings from Vietnam. Economic Effects of Natural Disasters, pp. 261–280. Academic Press. https://doi.org/10.1016/B978-0-12-817465-4.00017-0.

[5] Swart, R., Robinson J. and Cohen, S. 2003, "Climate Change and Sustainable Development: Expanding the Options" Climate Policy, 3(01), pp. 19–40.

[6] Cline, W.R. (2007). Global Warming and agriculture: Impact estimates by Country. Centre for Global Development and Peterson institute for International Economics, Washington, DC.

[7] Xie, B., Brewer, M.B., Hayes, B.K., McDonald, R.I. and Newell, B.R. (2019). Predicting climate change risk perception and willingness to act. *Journal of Environmental Psychology*, 65, pp. 1–11. https://doi.org/10.1016/j.jenvp.2019.101331.

[8] Guiteras, R. (2009). The impact of climate change on Indian agriculture. *Manuscript, Department of Economics, University of Maryland, College Park, Maryland.*

[9] Senapati, M.R., Behera, B. and Mishra, S.R. (2013). Impact of climate change on Indian agriculture and its mitigating priorities. *American Journal of Environmental Protection, 1*(4), pp. 109–111.

[10] Sikder, R. and Xiaoying, J. (2014). Climate change impact and agriculture of Bangladesh. *Journal of Environment and Earth Science*, 4(1), pp. 35–40.

[11] Hossain, M.S., Arshad, M., Qian, L., Zhao, M., Mehmood, Y. and Kächele, H. (2019). Economic impact of climate change on crop farming in Bangladesh: An application of Ricardian method. *Ecological Economics*, 164, pp 106354. https://doi.org/10.1016/j.ecolecon.2019.106354`

[12] Charemza, W.W. and Deadman, D.F. (1992), New Directions in Econometric Practice: General to Specific Modelling. Cointegration and Vector Autoregressions, Edward Elgar Publication, England.

[13] Pesaran, M.H. and Shin, Y. (1998), "An autoregressive distributed-lag modelling approach to cointegration analysis", *Econometric Society Monographs*, 31, pp. 371–413.

[14] Pesaran, M.H., Shin, Y. and Smith, R.J. (2001), "Bounds testing approaches to the analysis of level relationships", *Journal of Applied Econometrics*, 16(3), pp. 289–326.

# SECTION – II

# Trade, Finance and Development

CHAPTER 5

# India's Pharmaceutical Trade Relationship with South Asian Countries: Trends and Prospects

**Ariful Hoque and Subhrabaran Das**

## 5.1 Introduction

Development cooperation among the neighbouring countries is an important and essential aspect not only beneficial for the economic development but also helpful to maintain the diplomatic as well as friendly relation with them. This relationship would be more strengthened through grants-in-aid and bilateral trade among the neighbouring countries. Numerous studies have already been conducted on the benefits of increased bilateral trade between India and its neighbouring countries (e.g. Hassan, 2000; Qamar, 2005; Sikdar, 2006; Batra and Khan, 2005; Hussain, 2011; Taneja *et al.*, 2013a; Ahmed and Batool, 2014; Pant and Pande, 2014;Tyagi, 2014).Evidence also suggests that economic integration and regional trade affect a country's economic growth and well-being favourably (Heng and Gayathri, 2004; Dennis, 2006; Ma, 2022; Mashood *et al.*, 2022). Empirical literature also shows that a small country gains more when it liberalizes its trade relationship with a large country (Alesina *et al.*, 2005; Ahmed and Batool, 2017). The SAARC (South Asian Association for Regional Cooperation) has been founded in 1985 based on the initiatives of Bangladesh. It is an association of eight countries that includes Bangladesh, Bhutan, India, the Maldives, Nepal, Pakistan, Sri Lanka and Afghanistan (Afghanistan became a member in 2007). It aims to promote peace, healthy neighbourly relations and purposeful cooperation among the member countries of the region. Following the establishment of SAARC, member countries have signed an agreement known as SAPTA (SAARC

Preferential Trading Agreement) in 1993, which has later been transformed into SAFTA (South Asian Free Trade Area) in 2006 with a view to facilitate regional trade and economic cooperation. Being the largest country of the region, India accounts for roughly 90 percent of the regional trade with Sri Lanka, Nepal and Bangladesh (Taneja *et al.*, 2013b). India is, therefore, the most significant player in South Asian trade integration. Both bilaterally and through SAFTA, India has taken a number of initiatives to strengthen its trade ties with neighbouring countries. Further, since all the neighbouring countries share many commonalities with India in terms of history, language, religion and culture, the country has adopted a more liberal trade policy with these countries. India's continued efforts would, therefore, strengthen the process of regional economic and trade integration even more than before.

Given the growing importance of pharmaceutical sector in the international trade, it is one such area where South Asian countries can integrate and strengthen their regional trade cooperation. The global pharmaceutical market is estimated to be worth US$ 1423.5 billion in 2021, and it is expected to grow at an annual rate of 8.5 percent from 2021 and touch US$ 1738.2 billion by 2023[1]. This sector assumes significance because it is directly associated with human health and well-being. Its significance also emanates from the goal of protecting lives and improving healthcare services. The pharmaceutical sector is considered as the cornerstone of any country's public healthcare system (Pant and Pande, 2017). The pharmaceutical industry of India has emerged as one of the most technologically advanced and dynamic segments of Indian manufacturing. It has attained a significant scale in developing cost-effective modern drugs on its own to emerge as "the pharmacy of the world". In addition to fulfill the domestic needs, the industry is also concentrating on R&D activities, clinical trials, contract research and manufacturing services (CRAMS), and exporting to more than 200 countries, including highly regulated American and European

[1] Business Research Company. (2020). Global Pharmaceuticals Market Opportunities and Strategies Report, retrieved from https://www.thebusiness researchcompany.com/press-release/global-pharmaceuticals-market opportunities (accessed on 22/08/2022).

markets (Das and Hoque, 2023). Around 95 percent of the country's pharmaceutical requirements are met by the Indian pharmaceutical industry (Das and Das, 2015). Over the years, the industry has made significant contributions to the country's economic growth. It employs more than 2.7 million people in different areas of drug manufacturing and research and development, either directly or indirectly[2]. The industry has recorded a compound annual growth rate of 6.6 percent during 2015–2019 and touched US$ 20 billion in 2019[3]. It has experienced a downturn at the onset of the COVID-19 pandemic, but reverted quickly and has been growing rapidly since early 2021. It is expected to grow at an annual rate of 12.3 percent during the period 2020–2030, and will touch the value of US$ 120 billion by 2030[4]. Not only has the industry been successful in catering domestic pharmaceutical requirements, but it has also become the largest exporter of generic pharmaceuticals products globally. The Indian pharmaceutical industry manufactures around 60000 distinct generic brands throughout 60 therapeutic areas, accounting for 20 percent of global generic drug supply[5]. Pharmaceutical exports from India have grown by 18.2 percent over the previous year in FY2021, the highest growth in exports during the last eight years[6]. The value of India's pharmaceutical exports has risen from 4476.7 million in 2007 to 21011.6 million in 2021. During the same period, India's share of global pharmaceutical exports has also increased from 1.22 percent to

---

[2] Department of Pharmaceuticals (2020).*Annual Report, 2020–21*. Ministry of Chemicals and Fertilizers, Government of India. https://pharmaceuticals.gov.in/annual-report (accessed on 21/07/2022).

[3] FICCI (2022). Impact of the Pharma Industry on the Indian Economy in the Post-COVID Era, *A Report by KPMG in India and FICCI, April, 2022*, https://ficci.in/studies.asp (accessed on 02/07/2022).

[4] IBEF (2022).*Indian Pharmaceuticals Industry Report, March, 2022*, India Brand Equity Foundation. https://www.ibef.org/industry/pharmaceutical-india.aspx (accessed on 23/08/2022).

[5] Department of Pharmaceuticals. (2021). *Annual Report, 2021–22*. Ministry of Chemicals and Fertilizers, Government of India. https://pharmaceuticals.gov.in/annual-report (accessed on 23/08/2022).

[6] FICCI (2022). Impact of the Pharma Industry on the Indian Economy in the Post-COVID Era, *A Report by KPMG in India and FICCI, April, 2022*, https://ficci.in/studies.asp (accessed on 02/07/2022).

2.92[7]. India's pharmaceutical industry exports pharmaceuticals to over 200 countries across the world, with the United States being the largest export market (Hoque and Das, 2021). The top five export destinations for India's pharmaceutical products in 2020–21 are the United States (31.57 percent), South Africa (3.41 percent), the United Kingdom (2.93 percent), Russia (2.41 percent) and Germany (2.36 percent)[8]. During 2020–21, drug formulations and biologicals account for 77.02 percent of India's pharmaceutical exports, followed by bulk drugs and drug intermediaries (18 percent), surgicals (2.77 percent), and Ayush and Herbals (2.21 percent)[9].

In this study, an attempt has been made to analyze the trends and prospects of pharmaceutical trade between India and other South Asian countries and the possibilities for future expansion. Specifically, this study seeks to address the following objectives

- To investigate the prospects of India's pharmaceutical trade relationship with respect to South Asian countries.
- To examine the role of India's pharmaceutical industry in ensuring essential medical supplies in the South Asian Region during the outbreak of the COVID-19 pandemic.
- The rest of the paper is organized in the following manner: Section 5.2 outlines the main data sources and the methodology to be followed in this study. Section 5.3 presents the empirical results of the study, and Section 5.4 provides conclusion and policy suggestions.

## 5.2 Data Sources and Methodology

The present study is based on secondary sources of information. In order to address the objective of the study, relevant secondary data have been extracted from the Commodity Trade (Comtrade) database of the United Nation. The data have been extracted for the two basic

[7] Comtrade (2022). https://comtrade.un.org/ (accessed on 23/08/2022).

[8] Pharmexcil (2020). *Annual Report 2020–21*, Pharmaceuticals Export Promotion Council of India, Ministry of Commerce and Industry, Govt. of India. https://pharmexcil.com/annual-report (accessed on 23/08/2022).

[9] IBEF (2021). *Indian Pharmaceuticals Industry Report*, India Brand Equity Foundation, November, 2021. https://www.ibef.org/industry/pharmaceutical-india.aspx (accessed on 23/08/2022).

groups of pharmaceutical products, namely drug formulations (SITC Code 542, Revision 3), and bulk drugs and intermediaries (SITC Code 541). This study also uses data from different secondary sources like annual reports, news papers and so on, wherever necessary. The study period is 15 years from 2007 to 2021. In order to evaluate the prospects of India's pharmaceutical trade relation with South Asian countries, this study employs a few selected trade indexes, namely the Trade Intensity Index (TII), the Revealed Comparative Advantage (RCA) Index and the Trade Complementarity Index (TCI). These indexes are briefly discussed below.

### 5.2.1 *The Index of Trade Intensity (TII)*

To analyze the intensity of India's pharmaceutical trade with SAARC countries, Export Intensity Index (EII) and Import Intensity Index (III) have been calculated. The TII is used to measure the intimacy of a country's trading relationship with another (Goyal and Vajid, 2018). It is used to 'determine whether the value of trade between two countries is smaller or greater than would be expected on the basis of their importance in world trade' (World Integrated Trade Solution, 2010). TII is of two types, viz. Export Intensity Index (XII) and Import Intensity Index (MII). Following Kojima (1964) and Srivastava and Green (1986), these indexes are stated as follows:

$$XII_{ijk}{}^{(t)} = \frac{x_{ijk}{}^{(t)}/X_{ik}{}^{(t)}}{M_{jk}{}^{(t)}/(M_{wk}{}^{(t)} - M_{ik}{}^{(t)})} \text{ ; and} \quad \dots (1)$$

$$MII_{ijk}{}^{(t)} = \frac{m_{ijk}{}^{(t)}/M_{ik}{}^{(t)}}{X_{jk}{}^{(t)}/(X_{wk}{}^{(t)} - X_{ik}{}^{(t)})} \quad \dots (2)$$

In equations (1) and (2), $XII_{ijk}{}^{(t)}$ represents the export intensity index of country i's trade in product k (pharmaceuticals) with partner j at time t and $MII_{ijk}{}^{(t)}$ is the import intensity index of i's trade in product k with country j. $x_{ij}{}^{(t)}$ stands for country i's export of product k to partner j and $X_{ik}{}^{(t)}$ is i's total exports of product k. $M_{jk}{}^{(t)}$ indicates partner country j's total imports of product k, $M_{wk}{}^{(t)}$ is total imports of k$^{th}$ product by the world and $M_{ik}{}^{(t)}$ is the total imports of product k by the country i. Similarly, $m_{ijk}{}^{(t)}$, $X_{jk}{}^{(t)}$ and $X_{wk}{}^{(t)}$

respectively denote country i's imports of product k from j, country j's total exports of product k and world's total exports of product k. An index value greater (smaller) than unity implies a larger (smaller) than expected trade flow between two partners.

### 5.2.2 *The Index of RCA*

The index of RCA, developed by Balassa (1965), is the most frequently used measure of comparative advantage of a country. A number of studies have applied this index to ascertain the comparative trade performance of a country in relation to a particular commodity/sector (e.g. Pitigala, 2005; Ahmad *et al.*, 2017; Banik and Kim, 2020; Ahmed *et al.*, 2020). The index of RCA for country i for k$^{th}$ product (pharmaceuticals) in the t-year can be expressed as,

$$RCA_{ij}{}^{(t)} = [(\frac{x_{ik}{}^{(t)}}{X_i{}^{(t)}})/(\frac{x_{wk}{}^{(t)}}{X_w{}^{(t)}})] \qquad \dots (3)$$

In equation (3), $x_{ik}{}^{(t)}$ denotes the value of export of k$^{th}$ product by the i$^{th}$ country in the t-year and $X_i{}^{(t)}$ represents the value of total export of all products by the i$^{th}$ country in the t-year. Similarly, $x_{wk}{}^{(t)}$ refers to the export value of k$^{th}$ product by all countries in the time t and $X_w{}^{(t)}$ indicates the value of export of all products by all countries in the t-year. The range of value of the index of RCA is $0 \leq RCA \leq \infty$. A country is said to have comparative advantage in the export of product k if the value of RCA is higher than unity. In contrary, a country is said to have comparative disadvantage in product k if the value of RCA is lesser than unity. The index of RCA, thus, determines a country's strong/weak export sectors.

### 5.2.3 *The Index of Trade Complementarity (TCI)*

The index of trade complementarity has been developed by Michaely (1996) which assesses the degree to which two countries are 'natural trading partners' i.e. how much what one country exports coincides with what other country imports. The TCI is used to measure the adequacy of export supply by country i with country j's import demand (Sikdar, 2006; Vahalik, 2014). In the present study, the TCI is calculated as the arithmetic mean of the coefficient of specialization (CS) and the coefficient of consistency (CC) using the methodology followed by Xu (2017), Li (2018) and Chen *et al.* (2020), and is given by the following equations

$$CS = 1 - \frac{1}{2}\sum_k \left| x_{ik}{}^{(t)} - m_{jk}{}^{(t)} \right| \quad \text{... (4)}$$

$$CC = \frac{\sum_k x_{ik}{}^{(t)} m_{jk}{}^{(t)}}{\sqrt{\sum_k (x_{ik}{}^{(t)})^2 \sum_k (m_{jk}{}^{(t)})^2}} \quad \text{... (5)}$$

$$TCI_{ij}{}^{(t)} = \frac{1}{2}(CS + CC) \quad \text{... (6)}$$

Where $TCI_{ij}{}^{(t)}$ refers to the trade complementary index between country i and j at time t. $x_{ik}{}^{(t)}$ is the share of exports of k[th] product (bulk drugs/formulations) by country i in its total pharma exports in the t-year, and $m_{jk}{}^{(t)}$ represents the share of imports of k[th] product by country j in its total pharma imports in the t-year. The value of TCI lies between $0 \leq TCI \leq 1$. When the index value is closer to one, there will be stronger trade complementarity and more opportunities for trade cooperation between two countries (Li, 2018). When the value of TCI is smaller and closer to zero, there will be lower degrees of complementarity between the two trading partners.

## 5.3 Results and Discussion

### 5.3.1 *India's Pharmaceutical Trade with SAARC Countries*

India's pharmaceutical trade with SAARC countries has remained very low over the years. The South Asian countries account for a very small share in India's pharmaceutical exports and imports. As per WITS data, India's total pharmaceutical trade with SAARC countries stands at US$1059.4 million out of a total of US$26576.3 million in 2021, which accounts for 3.99 percent of its global pharmaceutical trade. India has a favourable trade balance with all of the SAARC countries, possibly because their pharmaceutical industries are still in their infancy. Table 5.1 presents the trends in India's pharmaceutical exports to SAARC countries during 2007–2021. India's pharmaceutical exports to SAARC countries have increased over four-fold from US$246.39 million in 2007 to US$1043.42 million in 2021, registering an average annual growth of 11.6 percent over the last 15 years. The share of India's exports to SAARC countries in its total pharmaceutical exports has remained below 6 percent throughout the years and it has exhibited a somewhat declining trend. It has declined from 5.5 percent in 2007 to 4.97 percent in 2021. On examining the patterns of bilateral trade, it is observed that, over the years, Sri Lanka has been the largest export destination for India's pharmaceutical products, with an average share of 1.39 percent. From a level of US$80.69 million in 2007, India's pharmaceutical export to Sri Lanka has increased almost three-fold to US$227.52 million in 2021. Pharmaceuticals Export Promotion Council [Pharmexcil] (2018) has reported that Sri Lanka imports approximately 90 percent of its medicinal requirements from different sources, with India alone accounting for 49 percent of its total imports, followed by Pakistan (8 percent), and the USA (3 percent). India's second largest export partner in South Asia is Nepal, which accounts for 1.18 percent of total pharmaceutical exports, followed by Bangladesh (0.75 percent). Barring a few years, pharmaceutical exports from India to both Nepal and Bangladesh have shown an increasing trend over the years. On the import side, India is the single largest and second largest import partner of Nepal and Bangladesh, accounting for approximately 80 percent and 12 percent of their total pharmaceutical imports, respectively[10]. Pharmaceutical exports from India to other South Asian countries such as Afghanistan, Pakistan, the Maldives and Bhutan have remained negligible during the last 15 years. Surprisingly, with Pakistan, the second largest South Asian economy, India's pharmaceutical exports account for only 0.50 percent of its overall exports in pharmaceuticals. As per the United Nations' Comtrade data, Pakistan has imported a major chunk of its pharmaceutical requirements from Switzerland and Germany, which respectively account for 12.67 percent and 10.44 percent of its overall pharmaceutical imports in 2020. Qamar (2005) and Chatterjee and George (2013) have opined that if Pakistan imports its medicinal needs from India rather than sourcing from other countries, it could save between US$400 and US$900 million on imports.

---

[10] Pharmexcil (2020). *Annual Report 2020–21*, Pharmaceuticals Export Promotion Council of India, Ministry of Commerce and Industry, Govt. of India. https://pharmexcil.com/annual-report (accessed on 23/07/2022).

**Table 5.1:** India's Pharmaceutical Exports to SAARC Countries
*(Value in US$ Million; Share in %)*

| *Year* | *AFG* | *BAN* | *BHU* | *MAL* | *NEP* | *PAK* | *SL* | *Total Exports to SAARC* | *Share in Total SAARC Export* |
|---|---|---|---|---|---|---|---|---|---|
| 2007 | 39.73 | 36.75 | 0.14 | 3.99 | 63.40 | 21.69 | 80.69 | 246.39 | 5.50 |
| 2008 | 56.82 | 46.99 | 1.60 | 6.19 | 67.71 | 31.65 | 95.29 | 306.24 (24.3) | 5.26 |
| 2009 | 51.45 | 47.94 | 0.76 | 5.85 | 69.73 | 31.70 | 95.94 | 303.37 (–0.9) | 5.12 |
| 2010 | 30.79 | 54.16 | 0.37 | 6.00 | 71.65 | 29.24 | 119.48 | 311.70 (2.7) | 4.38 |
| 2011 | 54.18 | 65.17 | 0.28 | 6.20 | 109.12 | 45.95 | 134.85 | 415.75 (33.4) | 4.38 |
| 2012 | 40.39 | 74.15 | 0.90 | 6.67 | 110.95 | 40.69 | 146.95 | 420.70 (1.2) | 3.87 |
| 2013 | 55.07 | 112.59 | 0.61 | 7.52 | 136.75 | 54.12 | 170.50 | 537.17 (27.7) | 4.08 |
| 2014 | 46.62 | 83.84 | 0.49 | 9.28 | 147.92 | 63.16 | 153.99 | 505.30 (–5.9) | 3.91 |
| 2015 | 46.13 | 79.72 | 2.02 | 10.46 | 133.31 | 47.78 | 187.58 | 506.98 (0.3) | 3.65 |
| 2016 | 66.36 | 95.47 | 1.72 | 10.31 | 192.33 | 63.64 | 202.48 | 632.29 (24.7) | 4.39 |
| 2017 | 80.39 | 87.41 | 2.47 | 13.28 | 197.76 | 79.50 | 200.67 | 661.47 (4.6) | 4.63 |
| 2018 | 84.84 | 111.34 | 4.21 | 15.97 | 212.21 | 89.85 | 199.27 | 717.26 (8.4) | 4.55 |
| 2019 | 76.87 | 167.53 | 6.02 | 19.15 | 222.03 | 83.06 | 202.45 | 777.11 (8.3) | 4.35 |
| 2020 | 85.31 | 138.80 | 4.40 | 24.96 | 192.72 | 83.60 | 248.70 | 778.48 (0.2) | 3.89 |
| 2021 | 65.63 | 218.64 | 8.59 | 25.98 | 285.96 | 211.10 | 227.52 | 1043.42 (34) | 4.97 |
| Avg. Share | 0.53 | 0.75 | 0.02 | 0.09 | 1.18 | 0.50 | 1.39 | 4.46 (11.6) | 4.46 |

*Source:* Authors' estimation based on UN Comtrade Database.

*Note:* Growth rates (%) of India's total pharma exports to SAARC are reported in the parentheses.

**Table 5.2:** India's Pharmaceutical Imports from SAARC Countries *(Value in US$ Thousands Share in %)*

| *Year* | *AFG* | *BAN* | *MAL* | *NEP* | *PAK* | *SL* | *Total Im. from SAARC* | *Share in SAARC Import* |
|---|---|---|---|---|---|---|---|---|
| 2007 | ... | ... | ... | 5509.0 | 10.0 | 213.2 | 5732.3 | 0.35 |
| 2008 | ... | 0.8 | 0.1 | 4445.0 | 1.3 | 187.2 | 4634.3 (–19.2) | 0.25 |
| 2009 | 1.8 | 0.03 | 0.05 | 4573.5 | 12.1 | 261.5 | 4849.1(4.6) | 0.24 |
| 2010 | ... | 17.3 | 0.1 | 5163.6 | 17.9 | 154.8 | 5353.6 (10.4) | 0.22 |
| 2011 | 11.4 | 80.8 | ... | 9486.9 | 99.2 | 1050.1 | 10728.4 (100.4) | 0.39 |
| 2012 | 9.0 | 26.2 | 38.0 | 8674.7 | 72.3 | 1042.2 | 9862.3 (–8.1) | 0.32 |
| 2013 | 2.4 | 2.7 | 10.4 | 8448.6 | 5.3 | 340.0 | 8809.3(–10.7) | 0.29 |
| 2014 | 1.7 | 11.1 | ... | 9168.3 | 6.4 | 456.2 | 9643.7 (9.5) | 0.30 |
| 2015 | ... | 71.6 | ... | 7392.5 | 6.6 | 369.2 | 7839.9 (–18. 7) | 0.25 |
| 2016 | ... | 7.8 | ... | 6090.1 | 49.5 | 555.2 | 6702.5 (–14.5) | 0.21 |
| 2017 | ... | 5.6 | 0.1 | 8261.9 | 59.4 | 566.6 | 8893.5 (32.7) | 0.26 |
| 2018 | ... | 75.6 | ... | 6067.7 | 0.1 | 1392.7 | 8502.1 (–4.4) | 0.21 |
| 2019 | 33.1 | 70.5 | 4.8 | 7465.3 | 47.9 | 3183.8 | 10805.5 (27.1) | 0.24 |
| 2020 | 150.5 | 17.6 | 0.03 | 10595.5 | 41.3 | 2306.2 | 13069.9 (21.0) | 0.29 |
| 2021 | ... | 544.0 | ... | 13667.2 | 34.6 | 1748.9 | 15994.7 (22.4) | 0.29 |
| Avg. Share | 0.00001 | 0.002 | 0.0002 | 0.25 | 0.001 | 0.02 | 0.27 (10.9) | 0.27 |

*Source:* Authors' estimation based on UN Comtrade Database.

*Notes:* ... Data not available; growth rates (%) of total imports from SAARC are reported in the parentheses.

Table 5.2 shows the trends in India's pharmaceutical imports from SAARC countries during 2007–2021. The figures in the table are given in the smallest possible denomination (US$ Thousands) to clearly elucidate the trade patterns among the SAARC countries. Table 5.2 clearly shows that India's dependency on imports from SAARC countries has been quite negligible as far as pharmaceuticals are concerned. Pharmaceutical imports from SAARC countries to India have increased from US$5732.3 thousands in 2007 to US$15994.7 thousands in 2021, registering an average growth of 10.9 percent per year over a period of 15 years. The share of India's imports from SAARC countries in its total pharmaceutical imports has ranged between just 0.21 and 0.39 percent during the same period. Among the SAARC countries, though Nepal is the largest importing partner of India, it accounts for only 0.25 percent of India's total pharmaceutical imports. Sri Lanka and Bangladesh follow Nepal with a share of only 0.02 and 0.002 percent, respectively.

From the analysis it is evident that notwithstanding the creation of regional trading block, India's pharmaceutical trade with SAARC countries is still very low. This could be due to differences in their market sizes. The Maldives and Bhutan, for example, cannot be the key export markets for India's pharmaceuticals. Therefore, expecting more than a modest possibility in trade between a large country like India and smaller South Asian counties like Bhutan and the Maldives, will not be appropriate.

### 5.3.2 *India's Pharmaceutical Contributions to SAARC Countries during COVID-19*

The novel corona virus (COVID-19) pandemic has emerged as a global health crisis with devastating consequences for human lives and economies. As of August 5, 2022, there have been 57,90,92,623 confirmed cases of COVID-19, including 64,07,556 deaths (World Health Organization, 2022). Countries across the world were unprepared to deal with such a huge crisis posed by the pandemic. The South Asian (SAARC) countries are no exception. The region has been caught unaware by the pandemic. During this very difficult time, ensuring the supply of critical healthcare medicine has become a more pressing challenge for the South Asian countries where public health infrastructure is not adequate to care for those affected by the ongoing pandemic. In such circumstances, there has been an overwhelming consensus among the South Asian countries for regional cooperation to ensure the supply of essential medicines/vaccines and other medical instruments critical to the treatment of this pandemic. India, being the largest economy of the region as well as 'the Pharmacy of the World', has taken the lead and supplied essential medicines (Hydroxychloroquine and Paracetamol), vaccine and other healthcare instruments to over 100 countries, focusing on those in its immediate neighbours in sprits of its 'First Responder to a Crisis' and 'Neighbourhood First Policy'. On March 25, 2020, Bangladesh has received the first consignment comprising of 15,000 head caps and 30,000 surgical masks as emergency medical assistance from India. India's second consignment containing 1,00,000 Hydroxychloroquine tablets and 50,000 surgical gloves has been handed over to Bangladesh on April 26, 2020. The third tranche of India's assistance containing 30,000 RT-PCR testing kits has been received by Bangladesh on May 6, 2020[11]. Bangladesh has become the first country to receive RT-PCR testing kits assistance from India as part of India's 'Neighbourhood First Policy'. The President of Afghanistan has also expressed his gratitude to India in a tweet on April 20, 2020, for providing 1,00,000 Paracetamol and 5,00,000 Hydroxychloroquine.[12] During the pandemic, India has provided varied and need-based assistance to Sri Lanka. On April 7, 2020, India has donated a consignment containing 10 tonnes of life-saving drugs to Sri Lanka. An Air India Charter Flight has delivered the consignment to Sri Lanka[13]. In April, 2020, another two consignments of medical gloves and medicines have been delivered. India has also supplied the fourth consignment comprising of 12.5 tonnes of essential medicines

[11] DD News (2020, 6 May). India hands over 3rd tranche of emergency medical assistance to Bangladesh. Retrieved from https://ddnews.gov.in/international/india-hands-over-3rd-tranche-emergency-medical-assistance-bangladesh (accessed on 08/08/2022).

[12] ANI (2020a, 20 April). Afghan President thanks PM Modi for medical supplies to fight COVID-19. https://www.aninews.in/news/world/asia/afghan-president-thanks-pm-modi-for-medical-supplies-to-fight-covid-1920200420185739/ (accessed on 09/08/2022).

[13] The Economic Times (2020, 7 April). India gifts a 10-tonne consignment of medicines to Sri Lanka https://economictimes.indiatimes.com/news/politics-and-nation/india-gifts-a-10-tonne-consignment-of-medicines-to-sri-lanka/articleshow/75030213.cms (accessed on 09/08/2022).

to Sri Lanka on May 8, 2020.[14] On April 22, 2020, India has donated 8, 25,000 doses of life saving drugs including 2,50,000 Hydroxy-chloroquine and 3,20,000 Paracetamol to Nepal to aid the country's fight against the pandemic[15]. In the next month, the second consignment containing 28 ICU ventilators and 30,000 RT-PCR testing kits has been handed over to Nepal. As Part of its on going support, India has also handed over 2,000 vials of Remdesivir injections to Nepal during the Foreign Secretary Harsh Vardhan's visit to Kathmandu on November 26, 2020[16]. On August 26, 2021, India has gifted a 960 Liters Per Minute (LPM) Oxygen Plant, capable of serving 200 patients simultaneously, to Nepal in an effort to assist the country combating the pandemic.[17] In April, 2020, the Maldives has received the first consignment containing 5.5 tonnes of essential medicines from India. In the next month, the Indian Air Force has lifted a second consignment of 6.2 tonnes of medicines to Male as part of *Operation Sanjeevani*. In September, 2020, India has also provided US$ 250 million financial assistance to the Maldives "the single largest financial help from a donor"—to help the country cope with the pandemic.[18] During the pandemic, India has also made it easier for Maldivian patients to travel to the country for emergency medical treatment. Except for the Maldives, no other country has

---

[14] Air News (2020, 8 May). India sends 12.5-tonne gift consignment of essential medicines & medical items to Sri Lanka. https://newsonair.gov.in/News?title=India-sends-12.5-tonne-gift-consignment-of-essential-medicines-%26-medical-items-to-Sri-Lanka&id=388046 (accessed on 09/08/2022).

[15] The Kathmandu Post (2020, 22 April). India gifts 23 tonnes of essential medicines to Nepal to fight Covid-19. https://kathmandupost.com/national/2020/04/22/india-gifts-23-tonnes-of-essential-medicines-to-nepal-to-fight-covid-19(accessed on 09/08/2022).

[16] ANI (2020b, 26 November). India gifts 2,000 vials of Remdesivir, Covid-19 related assistance to Nepal. https://www.aninews.in/news/world/asia/india-gifts-2000-vials-of-remdesivir-covid-19-related assistance-to-nepal20201126191416/( accessed on 09/08/2022).

[17] Firstpost (2020). From COVID-19 vaccines to oxygen, a look at how India helped SAARC countries during pandemic. https://www.firstpost.com/india/from-covid-19-vaccines-to-oxygen-a-look-at-how-india-helped-saarc-countries-during-pandemic-9915941.html (accessed on 09/08/2022).

[18] The Hindu (2020, 30 September). Maldives thanks India for $250 million support amid COVID-19 pandemic.https://www.thehindu.com/news/national/maldives-thanks-india-for-250-million-support-amid-covid-19-pandemic/article32732746.ece (accessed on 09/08/2022).

been granted this privilege.[19] Bhutan has also received three consignments of life saving drugs, including 2,00,000 doses of Hydroxychloroquine, as humanitarian aid from India to combat the outbreak of the pandemic (Pattanaik, 2021). Table 5.3 provides a snapshot of the humanitarian aid that India has extended so far to South Asian countries during the outbreak of COVID-19 pandemic.

**Table 5.3**: A Snapshot of India's COVID-19 Medical Assistance to SAARC Countries

| *Sl.* | *Country* | *Time* | *Medical Assistance* |
|---|---|---|---|
| 1. | Afghanistan | Apr. 2020 | 1,00,000 Paracetamol and 5,00,000 Hydroxychloroquine |
| 2. | Bangladesh | Mar. 2020<br>Apr. 2020<br><br>May 2020 | 15,000 head covers and 30,000 surgical masks<br>1,00,000 Hydroxychloroquine and 50,000 surgical gloves<br>30,000 RT-PCR COVID-19 testing kits |
| 3. | Bhutan | Apr. 2020 | A consignment of essential medicines including Hydroxychloroquine and Paracetamol |
| 4. | Nepal | Apr. 2020<br>May 2020<br><br>Nov. 2020<br><br>Apr. 2021<br><br><br>Aug. 2021 | 8,25,000 doses of medicines comprising<br>2,50,000 Hydroxychloroquine and 3,20,000 Paracetamol<br>28 ICU ventilators and 30,000 RT-PCR testing kits<br>2,000 vials of Remdesivir injections<br>39 Ambulances equipped with emergency facilities<br>A 960 Liters Per Minute (LPM) Medical Oxygen Plant |
| 5. | Maldives | Apr. 2020 | 11.7 tonnes of life saving medicines |
| 6. | Sri Lanka | Apr. 2020<br><br>May 2020<br>Aug. 2021 | 10 tonnes of medicines and one consignment of latex gloves<br>12.5 tonnes of essential life saving medicines<br>280 tonnes of medical grade Oxygen |

*Source:* Authors' compilation from various news papers, articles, reports etc.

[19] ANI (2022, 15 March). Maldives President Solih thanks India for 'generous' COVID, financial aid in last 2 years. https://www.aninews.in/news/world/asia/maldives-president-solih-thanks-india-for-generous-covid-financial-aid-in-last-2-years20220315110200/ (accessed on 09/08/2022).

### 5.3.3 *India's Vaccine Supply to SAARC Countries amid COVID-19*

India is the world's largest producer of generic pharmaceutical products and one of the major providers of low-cost vaccine to various countries across the world. The Serum Institute of India is the largest producer of vaccine globally. It manufactures Covishield (AZD1222) vaccine in collaboration with the United Kingdom's Astra Zeneca and the Oxford University. Other prominent Indian pharma majors engaged in the development of vaccine are Bharat Biotech (Covexin [BBV152] & BBV154), Biological E Limited (JNJ-78436735 & Bio E COVID-19), Gennova Biopharmaceuticals (HGCO19), Indian Immunologicals (SARS-Cov–2), Cadila Healthcare Limited (ZyCoV-D), Aurobindo Pharma (UB-612), Dr. Reddy's Laboratories (Sputnik V) and many others (Sharun and Dhama, 2021; Singh *et al.*, 2022). Thus, India meets approximately 60 percent of the worlds' demand for various vaccines.[20] The country has the capability of manufacturing more than 3 billion doses of COVID-19 vaccine annually (Puranwala, 2020). On January 20, 2021, India has launched its "Vaccine Maitri" initiative to provide vaccine supplies to the needy countries in order to aid them in their fight against the COVID-19 pandemic. Under this initiative, India has committed to assist 101 countries worldwide, including those in its immediate neighbours. As per the "Neighbourhood First Policy", India has dispatched the first consignment of 0.15 million doses of Covishield vaccine to Bhutan on January 20, 2021 (Table 5.4). Thus, Bhutan has become the first South Asian country to receive COVID-19 vaccination (Covishield) gift from India.[21] Similarly, on the same day, India has donated another consignment comprising of 0.1 million doses of Covishield vaccine to the Maldives. In addition to the donated doses, India has also aided these countries in obtaining vaccine supply at reasonable prices from the Indian pharmaceutical companies. On the next day, India has sent another shipment of 2 million doses of Covishield vaccine to Bangladesh. India has made this donation to Bangladesh at a crucial moment when the COVID-19

[20] IBEF (2021). *Indian Pharmaceuticals Industry Report, November, 2021*, India Brand Equity Foundation. https://www.ibef.org/industry/pharmaceutical-india.aspx (accessed on 29/6/2022).

[21] PMO India (2021, 20 January). Press Release. https://www.pmo.gov.bt/press-release-january-20-2021/ (accessed on 12/08/2022).

**Table 5.4:** India's COVID-19 Vaccine Supply to SAARC Countries as of December, 2021 (in Million Doses)

| Sl. | Country | *Grants-in-Aid (Covishield/Covaxin)* | | | *Commercial (Covishield)* | | | *Commercial (Covaxin)* | | | *Total Supply* |
|---|---|---|---|---|---|---|---|---|---|---|---|
| | | *Quantity* | *Date of Dispatch* | | *Quantity* | *Date of Dispatch* | | *Quantity* | *Date of Dispatch* | | |
| 1. | Afghanistan | 1 | 0.5 | 07-Feb-21 | | | | 0.468 | | 06-Mar-21 | 1.468 |
| | | | 0.5 | 31-Dec-21 | | | | | | | |
| 2. | Bangladesh | 3.3 | 2 | 21-Jan-21 | 15.0008 | 5 | 25-Jan-21 | 4.292 | 0.212 | 04-Dec-21 | 22.5928 |
| | | | 1.2 | 26-Mar-21 | | 2 | 22-Feb-21 | | 3.288 | 06-Dec-21 | |
| | | | 0.1 | 02-Apr-21 | | 1 | 09-Oct-21 | | 0.792 | 14-Dec-21 | |
| | | | | | | 4.5006 | 01-Dec-21 | | | | |
| | | | | | | 2.5002 | 07-Dec-21 | | | | |
| 3. | Bhutan | 0.55 | 0.15 | 20-Jan-21 | | | | | | | 0.55 |
| | | | 0.4 | 21-Mar-21 | | | | | | | |
| 4. | Maldives | 0.2 | 0.1 | 20-Jan-21 | 0.1 | | 19-Mar-21 | 0.012 | | 06-Mar-21 | 0.312 |
| | | | 0.1 | 19-Feb-21 | | | | | | | |
| 5. | Nepal | 1.112 | 1 | 21-Jan-21 | 2 | 1 | 20-Feb-21 | 6.387 | 0.348 | 05-Mar-21 | 9.499 |
| | | | 0.1 | 28-Mar-21 | | 1 | 09-Oct-21 | | 0.7255 | 28-Nov-21 | |
| | | | 0.012 | 07-Oct-21 | | | | | 0.972 | 30-Nov-21 | |
| | | | | | | | | | 0.6 | 07-Dec-21 | |
| | | | | | | | | | 1.871 | 14-Dec-21 | |
| | | | | | | | | | 1.8705 | 18-Dec-21 | |
| 6. | Pakistan | - | - | | - | - | | - | - | | - |
| 7. | Sri Lanka | 0.5 | | 28-Jan-21 | 0.5 | | 24-Feb-21 | 0.264 | | 06-Mar-21 | 1.264 |
| India's Total Supply of Vaccine to SAARC Countries | | | | | | | | | | | 35.6858 |
| India's Total Supply of Vaccine to 101 Countries of the World (including SAARC) | | | | | | | | | | | 239.0297 |
| SAARC Countries' Share (%) in India's Total Supply of Vaccine | | | | | | | | | | | 14.93 |

*Source:* Ministry of External Affairs, Govt. of India. (https://mea.gov.in/vaccine-supply.htm)

cases have been rapidly increasing in this country. In late January, Nepal and Sri Lanka have also received one million and 0.5 million doses of Covishield vaccine, respectively, as gifts from India to aid in the fight against the COVID-19 pandemic. Table 5.4 clearly shows that the SAARC countries, barring Pakistan, continue to be India's top priority for COVID-19 vaccine supply and they together account for approximately 15 percent of India's total vaccine supply of about 239 million doses to 101 countries across the world. In February, India has sent a shipment of 0.5 million doses of Covishield vaccine to Afghanistan, a war-torn country. India has donated another consignment consisting of 0.5 million doses of Covaxin to Afghanistan on December 31, 2021. Thus, as of December 31, 2021, India has donated a total of 6.662 million doses of COVID-19 vaccine to SAARC countries as part of its 'Vaccine Maitri' initiative to help them in fighting the pandemic. In addition, India has supplied 17.6008 million doses of Covishield vaccine and 11.423 million doses of Covaxin to SAARC countries as commercial exports. Of the total commercial export supply to SAARC countries, Bangladesh has the largest share (66.47 percent), followed by Nepal (28.90 percent), Sri Lanka (2.63 percent), Afghanistan (1.61 percent) and the Maldives (0.39 percent). It is worth recalling here that Pakistan is the only country that has not received any COVID-19 vaccine from India; instead, it has received it from China. Being the world's vaccine manufacturing hub, India's contribution towards providing COVID-19 vaccine to SAARC countries will not only ensure fair and equitable access to vaccines but will also help strengthen its ties with neighbouring countries.

### 5.3.4 *India-SAARC: Trade Intensity, Comparative Advantage and Complementarity in Pharmaceuticals*

For an expected bilateral trade flow between country *i* and *j*, the share of *i*'s export to *j* should at least be equal to the share of world exports going to country *j*. Otherwise, it indicates that country *i* fails to exploit country *j*'s market and that there is a room for expanding *i*'s exports to country j. Therefore, in order to determine whether India's pharmaceutical trade relation with other SAARC countries is larger or smaller than would be expected, export intensity index (XII) and

**Table 5.5:** India's Pharmaceutical Trade Intensity Indexes with SAARC Countries

| Year | *Export Intensity Index (XII)* | | | | *Import Intensity Index (MII)* | | | |
|---|---|---|---|---|---|---|---|---|
| | *Ind-Ban* | *Ind-Nep* | *Ind-Pak* | *Ind-SL* | *Ind-Ban* | *Ind-Nep* | *Ind-Pak* | *Ind-SL* |
| 2007 | 13.44 | ... | 3.69 | 40.76 | ... | ... | 0.02 | 17.13 |
| 2008 | 14.30 | ... | 4.12 | 35.17 | 0.005 | ... | 0.002 | 14.80 |
| 2009 | 12.58 | 37.43 | 3.40 | 37.34 | 0.0001 | 494.17 | 0.02 | 20.96 |
| 2010 | 10.01 | 21.56 | 2.74 | 35.88 | 0.07 | 135.02 | 0.02 | 10.24 |
| 2011 | 10.26 | 31.43 | 3.30 | 21.32 | 0.28 | 137.50 | 0.11 | 49.12 |
| 2012 | 9.87 | 29.35 | 2.37 | 18.93 | 0.08 | 127.31 | 0.06 | 35.31 |
| 2013 | 14.68 | 34.35 | 2.48 | 18.50 | 0.01 | 149.85 | 0.005 | 18.72 |
| 2014 | ... | 30.98 | 2.76 | 17.79 | ... | 149.30 | 0.005 | 9.53 |
| 2015 | 8.08 | 17.86 | 2.06 | 16.31 | 0.15 | 177.95 | 0.005 | 8.07 |
| 2016 | ... | 29.03 | 2.54 | 15.70 | ... | 128.26 | 0.04 | 14.70 |
| 2017 | .... | 33.41 | 3.32 | 18.06 | ... | 141.13 | 0.04 | 9.34 |
| 2018 | ... | 28.24 | 3.20 | ... | ... | 125.70 | 0.0001 | ... |
| 2019 | ... | 28.99 | 2.99 | 14.92 | ... | 118.19 | 0.03 | 39.76 |
| 2020 | .. | ... | 2.94 | 16.15 | ... | ... | 0.03 | 36.06 |
| 2021 | ... | ... | 1.87 | 9.24 | ... | ... | 0.02 | 20.31 |

*Source:* Authors' computation on the basis of Comtrade data.

*Note:* ...Data not available.

import intensity index (MII) are calculated for the period from 2007 to 2021and the results are reported in Table 5.5. As stated earlier, a trade intensity index greater than unity implies a larger than expected trade flow between two partner countries and vice versa. From the table it is evident that India's export intensity is greater than one for all the South Asian countries considered here, indicating that India's pharmaceutical exports to these countries are more intensive and greater than the expected level.

Export intensity of India is the highest for Nepal as compared to other SAARC countries; however, the index shows a fluctuating trend over the years. India's export intensity with Sri Lanka shows a continuous declining trend. Import intensity of India is well above the expected level for Nepal and Sri Lanka, implying that India has an intense import relationship with these two countries in pharmaceuticals. Import intensity is exceptionally high for Nepal with index value of 494.17 in 2009 which has, however, declined to 118.19 in 2019. Barring a few years, India's import intensity with Sri Lanka shows an overall rising trend, implying thereby a prospect for future bilateral cooperation. Import intensity of India with Bangladesh and Pakistan is smaller than unity throughout the years, indicating that these countries are trading less than they should. There is, thus, a considerable scope for pharmaceutical trade between these countries to expand.

The concept of comparative advantage governs the basic characteristics of international trade. Countries having distinct comparative advantages have more opportunities for mutually beneficial trade than those having a higher degree of similarity (Pitigala, 2005). The index of RCA is a useful indicator of comparative advantage. Table 5.6 shows the indexes of RCA for bulk drugs and drug formulations for India and other major SAARC countries for the period 2007–2021. In case of bulk drugs, none of the SAARC countries has an RCA index greater than one, highlighting the fact that these countries have been at a comparative disadvantage position throughout the years. For India, the index of RCA for bulk drugs shows a declining trend upto 2010, followed by an increasing trend up to 2015, but since 2016 it shows a continuous declining trend. Throughout, the index remains below unity, indicating India's comparative disadvantage in bulk drugs. In case of drug formulations,

**Table 5.6:** RCA Indices of Pharmaceuticals (Bulk Drugs & Formulations) for SAARC Countries

| Year | *India* | | *Bangladesh* | | *Nepal* | | *Pakistan* | | *Sri Lanka* | |
|---|---|---|---|---|---|---|---|---|---|---|
| | *BD* | *F* | *BD* | *F* | *BD* | *F* | *BD* | *F* | *BD* | *F* |
| 2007 | 0.903 | 1.221 | 0.007 | 0.140 | … | … | 0.334 | 0.194 | 0.024 | 0.010 |
| 2008 | 0.788 | 1.367 | 0.007 | 0.119 | … | … | 0.191 | 0.234 | 0.021 | 0.010 |
| 2009 | 0.741 | 1.034 | 0.011 | 0.096 | 0.027 | 0.076 | 0.151 | 0.295 | 0.015 | 0.008 |
| 2010 | 0.706 | 1.356 | 0.006 | 0.105 | 0.049 | 0.360 | 0.168 | 0.253 | 0.012 | 0.010 |
| 2011 | 0.739 | 1.470 | 0.019 | 0.105 | 0.102 | 0.670 | 0.157 | 0.269 | 0.027 | 0.007 |
| 2012 | 0.736 | 1.819 | 0.004 | 0.116 | 0.062 | 0.639 | 0.125 | 0.337 | 0.014 | 0.008 |
| 2013 | 0.796 | 1.909 | 0.007 | 0.142 | 0.002 | 0.581 | 0.074 | 0.362 | 0.015 | 0.008 |
| 2014 | 0.752 | 1.897 | … | … | 0.002 | 0.586 | 0.063 | 0.420 | 0.021 | 0.012 |
| 2015 | 0.840 | 2.264 | 0.002 | 0.112 | 0.002 | 0.483 | 0.055 | 0.470 | 0.014 | 0.011 |
| 2016 | 0.809 | 2.224 | … | … | 0.032 | 0.471 | 0.038 | 0.471 | 0.014 | 0.007 |
| 2017 | 0.683 | 2.050 | … | … | 0.044 | 0.587 | 0.021 | 0.464 | 0.019 | 0.011 |
| 2018 | 0.658 | 2.093 | … | … | 0.071 | 0.407 | 0.019 | 0.416 | … | … |
| 2019 | 0.639 | 2.227 | … | … | 0.081 | 0.381 | 0.017 | 0.424 | 0.024 | 0.014 |
| 2020 | 0.647 | 2.566 | … | … | … | … | 0.018 | 0.426 | 0.015 | 0.015 |
| 2021 | 0.449 | 2.019 | … | … | … | … | 0.008 | 0.413 | 0.011 | 0.018 |

*Source:* Authors' computation on the basis of Comtrade data.

*Note:* …Data not available; BD-Bulk Drugs (SITC 541, Rev. 3); F-Drug Formulations (SITC 542).

the RCA index for India is greater than one throughout the years, indicating the comparative advantage India is enjoying in formulations. The index shows a consistent upward trend, suggesting that India has maintained its progress toward greater competitive advantage in formulations over the years. India's comparative advantage in this high-tech sector reflects the capacity that the industry has built up over the years through the process of reverse-engineering. Despite some progress made by Nepal and Pakistan, all the selected South Asian counties are at comparative disadvantage in this sector, underlining that India can improve its trading relationship with these countries in drug formulations. Bangladesh and Sri Lanka must make significant strides toward developing 'revealed' comparative advantage and exporting pharmaceutical products to other countries. The analysis reveals that India has a good potential for exporting drug formulations to other South Asian countries to meet their medicinal requirements. Thus, India's prospects for benefitting from increased pharmaceutical trade with other low RCA countries of South Asia appear to be quite promising. But the reverse is not true.

In order to investigate the extent of complementarity in trading pharmaceutical products between India and other major SAARC countries, the index of trade complementarity are calculated for the period 2007–2021. The indexes of trade complementarity for India's trade in pharmaceuticals with SAARC countries and SAARC countries' trade with India are reported in Table 5.7. A country-by-country comparison reveals that the complementarity between India's offer and Nepal's demand has been quite strong over the years. On an average, the index has been 0.98. However, there is a clear lack of complementarity between Nepal's offer and India's demand, the index being 0.43, on average. Thus, in the case of bilateral pharmaceutical trade between India and Nepal, there arises a situation of partial complementarity which indicates that India is able to meet the import demands of Nepal, but Nepal has a significant lack of such potential. The same is also true in the case of bilateral trade between India and Pakistan. India's offer matches with Pakistan's demand fairly, but the opposite is not true. Further, the indexes of trade complementarity for both India's offer to Pakistan and Pakistan's offer to India show a gradually declining trend which indicates that the mutual dependency of both the countries on pharmaceutical trade has been declining over time.

**Table 5.7:** Trade Complementarity Indices for Pharmaceuticals among SAARC Countries

| *Year* | *Ind-Ban* | *Ind-Nep* | *Ind-Pak* | *Ind-SL* | *Ban-Ind* | *Nep-Ind* | *Pak-Ind* | *SL-Ind* |
|---|---|---|---|---|---|---|---|---|
| 2007 | 0.460 | ... | 0.742 | 0.969 | 0.388 | ... | 0.757 | 0.829 |
| 2008 | 0.421 | ... | 0.727 | 0.998 | 0.441 | ... | 0.650 | 0.855 |
| 2009 | 0.473 | 0.997 | 0.755 | 0.966 | 0.466 | 0.547 | 0.591 | 0.840 |
| 2010 | 0.445 | 0.970 | 0.715 | 0.994 | 0.427 | 0.459 | 0.636 | 0.765 |
| 2011 | 0.471 | 0.984 | 0.713 | 0.974 | 0.480 | 0.466 | 0.620 | 0.985 |
| 2012 | 0.425 | 0.985 | 0.652 | 0.989 | 0.467 | 0.494 | 0.604 | 0.873 |
| 2013 | 0.416 | 0.977 | 0.652 | 0.987 | 0.412 | 0.391 | 0.483 | 0.877 |
| 2014 | ... | 0.985 | 0.660 | 0.990 | ... | 0.328 | 0.400 | 0.835 |
| 2015 | 0.432 | 0.964 | 0.675 | 0.990 | 0.328 | 0.322 | 0.380 | 0.779 |
| 2016 | ... | 0.983 | 0.702 | 0.994 | ... | 0.396 | 0.402 | 0.859 |
| 2017 | ... | 0.984 | 0.733 | 0.996 | ... | 0.427 | 0.413 | 0.858 |
| 2018 | ... | 0.971 | 0.734 | ... | ... | 0.424 | 0.357 | ... |
| 2019 | ... | 0.962 | 0.705 | 0.972 | ... | 0.491 | 0.399 | 0.890 |
| 2020 | ... | ... | 0.727 | 0.962 | ... | ... | 0.325 | 0.751 |
| 2021 | ... | ... | 0.302 | 0.736 | ... | ... | 0.420 | 0.780 |
| Average | 0.443 | 0.978 | 0.680 | 0.966 | 0.426 | 0.431 | 0.496 | 0.841 |

*Source:* Authors' computation on the basis of Comtrade data.

*Note:* ... Data not available.

In the case of bilateral trade between India-and Sri Lanka, the supply capability of India fairly matches with the demand potential of Sri Lanka. Similarly, the supply capability of Sri Lanka roughly corresponds to the demand potential of India. Thus, in the case of India-Sri Lanka bilateral trade in pharmaceuticals, there arises a situation of what has been described in the literature as 'reciprocal trade complementarity' (Panchmukhi, 1990; Sikdar, 2006). As regards India-Bangladesh bilateral trade, the measure of compatibility between India's offer and Bangladesh's demand is 0.44, while in the case of Bangladesh's offer to India, it is 0.43. Thus, a situation of poor complementarity exists between India and Bangladesh in trading pharmaceutical products.

## 5.4 Conclusion and Policy Suggestions

Pharmaceuticals, as a 'high-social-value' industrial sector with a direct link to human health and well-being, would be a key segment in which South Asian countries can integrate and strengthen their regional trade cooperation. This study is an attempt to investigate the prospects of India's pharmaceutical trade relationship with South Asian (SAARC) countries in the light of some select trade indexes, viz. trade intensity index, revealed comparative advantage index and trade complementarity index. The analysis reveals that India's pharmaceutical trade with other SAARC countries continues to remain very low, accounting for only 3.99 percent of its global pharmaceutical trade. India has a favourable pharmaceutical trade balance with all the other SAARC countries, possibly because their pharmaceutical industries are still in their infancy. An analysis of export intensity index reveals that India has an intense export relationship with all the other South Asian countries, suggesting the possibility of future integration. Further, import intensity of India is found to be well above the expected level for Nepal and Sri Lanka over the years. It is lesser than expected for Bangladesh and Pakistan, underlining an un intense presence of their pharmaceutical products in Indian market. From the calculation of RCA, it is observed that, for bulk drugs, none of the SAARC countries has an RCA index greater than one, highlighting the fact that these countries have been at a comparative disadvantage position throughout the years. In the case of drug formulations, except for India, none of the other South Asian countries enjoys comparative advantage in it. India has maintained its progress toward greater competitive advantage in drug formulations over the years. Moreover, the inference from the computation of trade complementarity index reveals a fair degree of complementarity among the SAARC countries in trading pharmaceuticals. There is, thus, a significant room for pharmaceutical trade between these countries to expand and enormous potentials to be realized. To capitalize on these opportunities, SAARC countries must strengthen their economic cooperation and regional integration.

This study also brings to light the role of India's pharmaceutical industry in ensuring critical medical supplies in the South Asian Region during the outbreak of the COVID-19 pandemic. From the analysis it has been observed that the COVID-19 has aided in bringing the countries of the region together for coordinated efforts to combat the outbreak of the pandemic. Being 'the Pharmacy of the World', India has taken the leadership role and supplied essential medicines, vaccine and other critical healthcare instruments to over 100 countries, including those in its immediate neighbours in sprits of its 'First Responder to a Crisis' and 'Neighbourhood First Policy'. The country has built a development cooperation model through the 'Vaccine Maitri' initiative and has established itself as the first responder to a crisis like COVID-19 which has put the country in more strengthened position for maintaining diplomatic role in South Asia. Therefore, it is possible to argue that India's increased cooperation during the COVID-19 pandemic has been a humanitarian gesture that will not only ensure fair and equitable access to medicine, but will also help strengthen its ties with neighbouring countries.

## References

[1] Ahmad, N., Qayum, A. and Iqbal, A. (2017). Evolving patterns and empirical distribution of normalized revealed comparative advantage: A SAARC countries analysis. *Journal of applied economics and business research*, *7*(1), pp. 59–82.

[2] Ahmed, A., Chakraborty, D. and Bhattacharya, R. (2020). The Recent Coronavirus (COVID 19) Pandemic: A Review of Issues for Indian Pharmaceutical Exports. *Foreign Trade Review*, 55(3), pp. 418–435.

[3] Ahmed, V. and Batool, S. (2014). India-Pakistan Trade: A Case Study of the Pharmaceutical Sector. *Working Paper No. 291*, Indian Council for Research on International Economic Relations, December, pp. 1–27. https://icrier.org/pdf/Working_Paper_291.pdf

[4] Ahmed, V. and Batool, S. (2017). India–Pakistan trade: a case study of the pharmaceutical sector. In *India-Pakistan Trade Normalisation,* Springer, Singapore, pp. 219–244.

[5] Alesina, A., Spolaore, E. and Wacziarg, R. (2005). Trade, growth and the size of countries. In *Handbook of economic growt*h (Vol. 1) Elsevier, Amsterdam, North Holland.

[6] Balassa, B. (1965). Trade Liberalization and "Revealed" Comparative Advantage. *Manchester School of Economic and Social Studies*, 33(2), pp. 99–123.

[7] Banik, N. and Kim, M. (2020). India–ASEAN trade relations: Examining the trends and identifying the potential. *Global Business Review*, pp. 1–19. https://doi.org/10.1177/0972150920953546

[8] Batra, A. and Khan, Z. (2005). Revealed Comparative Advantage: An Analysis for India and China. *Working Paper No. 168, Indian Council for Research on International Economic Relations,* New Delhi, pp. 1–85.

[9] Chatterjee, B. and George, J. (2013). Reforming non-tariff barriers: Case for a participatory approach in South Asia. In *Consumer unity and trust society,* July, pp. 132–138.

[10] Chen, J., Chen, D. and Yao, A. (2020). Trade development between China and countries along the Belt and Road: A spatial econometric analysis based on trade competitiveness and complementarity. *Pacific Economic Review*, *25*(2), pp. 205–227.

[11] Das, S. and Hoque, A. (2023). Firm-level productivity and its determinants in2 the Indian pharmaceuticals industry. Decision 50(4), pp. 439-459.

[12] Das, P. and Das, S. (2015). Competitiveness and its Impact on Research and Development in Indian Pharmaceutical Industry. *Decision*, 42(3), pp. 325–334.

[13] Dennis, A. (2006). The Impact of Regional Trade Agreements and Trade Facilitation in the Middle East and North Africa Region. *World Bank Policy Research Working Paper No. 3837*, pp. 1–24. https://ssrn.com/abstract=922963.

[14] Goyal, K.A. and Vajid, A. (2018). An Analysis of India's Trade Intensity with UAE. *Journal of Commerce and Trade,* April, 13(1), pp. 27–31.

[15] Hassan, M.K. (2000). Trade Relations with SAARC Countries and Trade Policies of Bangladesh. *Journal of Economic Cooperation*, 21(3), pp. 99–132.

[16] Heng, T.M. and Gayathri, V. (2004). Impact of Regional Trade Liberalization on Emerging Economies: The Case of Vietnam. *ASEAN Economic Bulletin*, 21(2), pp. 167–182.

[17] Hoque, A. and Das, S. (2021). Trends in Productivity Growth of Indian Pharmaceutical Industry: A Growth Accounting Analysis. *Journal of Pharmaceutical Research International*, 33 (47A), pp. 437–446.

[18] Hussain, I. (2011). *Prospects and Challenges for Increasing India-Pakistan Trade*. Atlantic Council, Washington DC.

[19] Kojima, K. (1964). The Pattern of International Trade among Advanced Countries, *Hitotsubashi Journal of Economics*, 5(1), pp. 16–36.

[20] Li, W. and Li, C. (2020). The Empirical Study on Potential of Bilateral Trade between China and Kenya in the Context "The Belt and Road". *Theoretical Economics Letters*, 10(1), pp. 119–130.

[21] Ma, S. (2022). Growth Effects of Economic Integration: New Evidence from the Belt and Road Initiative. *Economic Analysis and Policy, Elsevier*, 73, pp. 753–767.

[22] Masood, S., Khurshid, N., Haider, M., Khurshid, J. and Khokar, A.M. (2022). Trade Potential of Pakistan with the South Asian Countries: A Gravity Model Approach. *Asia Pacific Management Review,* Elsevier, North Holland,pp. 1–7, https://www.sciencedirect.com/science/article/pii/S1029313222000070

[23] Michaely, M. (1996). Trade preferential agreements in Latin America: an ex-ante assessment. *Policy Research Working Paper No. 1583*. The World Bank, pp. 1–55. https://core.ac.uk/download/pdf/6645169.pdf

[24] Panchamukhi, V.R. (1990). *Economic Cooperation in the SAARC Region: Potential, Constraints and Policies,* Interest Publication, New Delhi.

[25] Pant, M. and Pande, D. (2014). India-Pakistan Trade: An Analysis of the Pharmaceutical Sector. *Working Paper 275*, Indian Council for Research on International Economic Relations, June, pp. 1–69. http://icrier.org/pdf/working_paper_275.pdf

[26] Pant, M. and Pande, D. (2017). India–Pakistan trade: An analysis of the pharmaceutical sector. In *India-Pakistan Trade Normalisation,* Springer, Singapore, pp. 163–218.

[27] Pattanaik, S.S. (2021). COVID-19 pandemic and India's regional diplomacy. *South Asian Survey*, *28*(1), pp. 92–110.

[28] Pharmexcil (2018). *Regulatory and Market Profile of Sri Lanka*, Pharmaceuticals Export Promotion Council of India, Ministry of Commerce and Industry, Govt. of India. https://pharmexcil.com/uploads/countryreports/Sri_Lanka.pdf (accessed on 14/06/2022).

[29] Pitigala, N. (2005). *What does regional trade in South Asia reveal about future trade integration? Some empirical evidence* (Vol. 3497), World Bank Publications.

[30] Puranwala A. (2020). *Covid-19 vaccine update—The Covid-19 vaccination race has just begun; India aptly placed.* https://images.assettype.com/bloombergquint/2020-12/c8d891f5-e8b7-4ae3-acbd-e6697bcf70a4/Anand_Rathi_Covid_19_Vaccine_Update.pdf (accessed on 08/08/2022).

[31] Qamar, A. (2005). Trade between India and Pakistan: Potential Items and the MFN Status. *State Bank of Pakistan Research Bulletin*, 1(1), pp. 45–57.

[32] Sharun, K. and Dhama, K. (2021). India's role in COVID-19 vaccine diplomacy. *Journal of Travel Medicine*, 28(7), pp. 1–4. https://doi.org/10.1093/jtm/taab064.

[33] Sikdar, C. (2006). Prospects of bilateral trade between India and Bangladesh. *Foreign Trade Review*, 41(1), pp. 27–45.

[34] Singh, B., Singh, S., Singh, B. and Chattu, V. K. (2022). India's Neighbourhood Vaccine Diplomacy during COVID-19 Pandemic: Humanitarian and Geopolitical Perspectives. *Journal of Asian and African Studies*, pp. 1–17. https://doi.org/10.1177/00219096221079310

[35] Srivastava, R.K. and Green, R.T. (1986). Determinants of Bilateral Trade Flows. *The Journal of Business*, University of Chicago Press, 59(4), pp. 623–640.

[36] Taneja, N., Mishita, M., Prithvijit, M., Samridhi, B. and Dayal, I. (2013a). Normalizing India Pakistan Trade. *Working Paper 267*, Indian Council for Research on International Economic Relations, September, pp. 1–44. http://icrier.org/pdf/working_paper_267.pdf

[37] Taneja, N., Prakash, S. and Kalita, P. (2013b). India's role in facilitating trade under SAFTA *Working Paper No. 263*, Indian Council for Research on International Economic Relations, January, pp. 1–19. https://www.econstor.eu/bitstream/10419/176281/1/icrier-wp-263.pdf

[38] Tyagi, S. (2014). Composition, Intensity and Revealed Comparative Advantage in Sino-Indian Bilateral Trade: A Preliminary Study. *ICS*

*Occasional Paper No. 8*, Institute of Chinese studies, September, https://www.icsin.org/publications

[39] Vahalík, B. (2014). Regional bilateral trade analysis of the European Union, China and ASEAN. *Procedia Economics and Finance*, 12, pp. 709–717.

[40] World Health Organization. (2022). *WHO Coronavirus (COVID-19) Dashboard.* https://covid19.who.int/ (accessed on 05/08/2022).

[41] World Integrated Trade Solution (2010). *Trade Indicators*, the World Bank, https://wits.worldbank.org/wits (accessed on 24/6/2022).

[42] Xu, S. (2017). China and South Asia trade competition and complementary: Analysis based on the background of "One Belt and One Road". *Chinese Studies*, 6(2), pp. 108–122.

CHAPTER 6

# An Enquiry into the Dynamics of India's Foreign Trade with SAARC and non-SARRC Nations during the Post-Globalization Period

**Debashish Mazumdar and Mainak Bhattacharjee**

## 6.1 Introduction

The formation of the South Asian Association for Regional Cooperation (SAARC) in December 1985 was hailed as a major diplomatic and economic breakthrough in South Asia. We know that despite a continuous progress of the developed world in terms of capita GNP, share in international trade and commerce etc., the large portion of world population, who lives in less developed or developing regions, were not particularly benefited from this growth process. Regional cooperation in trade and commerce is believed to be a way out from the impasse of development gap between the developed and less developed or developing nations.

SAARC provides a platform for the peoples of the South Asia to work together to solve their common problems in a spirit of friendship, trust and understanding. It aims to improve their quality of life through accelerated economic growth, social progress and cultural development in the region.

This topic has been chosen particularly to indicate the role of regional economic cooperation between the developing countries of the world, particularly between the South Asian nations. It has also been chosen to show how far such cooperation can help these countries in solving their balance of payments problems as well as in helping these nations towards efficient utilization of the regional resources.

## 6.2 Objective of the Study

The objective of the study rests primordially on analysis of the trade dynamics of India with SAARC and the neighbouring non-SAARC nations with respect to the net barter terms of trade and the balance of trade during globalization era. This paper develops a simple macro-theoretical framework to explain the interactive process going into the determination of India's terms of trade with the SAARC and non-SAARC nations under the assumptions of full employment equilibrium in balance of trade, as what can be considered to be significant in terms of long-run situation, more or less. Besides, the study is intended to elicit if there exists a causal relationship between the terms of trade and balance of trade over time.

## 6.3 Literature Survey

The study undertaken by Kaur and Nanda (2010) has shown India's export potential to other SAARC nations using panel data for the period 1981–2005 and the gravity model of exports has indicated that among SAARC countries, India's export potential exists for neighbouring countries like Bhutan, Pakistan, Maldives, and Nepal.

Malik and Mir (2014) have also tried to estimate India's trade potential with Central Asian nations using basic and augmented gravity model employing panel data for the period 2000–2012. This study reveals an enormous trade potential of India with the neighbouring countries despite a few geo-political issues that hinder the pathways of trade in this region.

Some other studies, however, have depicted a dismal picture of India's trade with SAARC nations over the last few decades (Roy, 2016) and an intra-regional trade to the extent of 5 to 6 per cent clearly reveals a failure on the issue of economic integration in this region. This apart, the transition from SAPTA (SAARC Preferential Trading Agreement) to SAFTA (South Asian Free Trade Area) has also failed to make any visible contribution towards improving the trade relations between India and other SAARC countries.

Akram *et al.* (2014) have shown that while India has a favourable balance of trade with all of its neighbouring countries in the South Asian region, it has a huge trade surplus with Bangladesh, Pakistan, Sri Lanka, and Nepal. However, they are of the opinion that the official accounts of South Asia's international trade are flawed by the high incidence of informal trade between India and its neighbours. The data merely captures the formal trade which takes place among the neighbouring countries. Similar opinions are also reflected in the studies of Chaudhury (1995), Bakht (1994), Taneja (2001). All these authors show that apart from official trade, there is a sizeable informal trade between India and Bangladesh. Taneja (2001) shows that India even enjoys a trade surplus with Bangladesh in informal trade account.

Pant and Paul (2018) have indicated that India's Regional Trade Agreements (RTAs) have not generated any significant impact on promoting India's trade particularly because of its limited trade with the RTA partners. In other words, the success of RTAs lies in the substantial trade volume prior to the formation of RTA. So, this study leads to a rather surprising result that India can gain from trade when it negotiates RTAs with its major trading partners such as the USA and China as opposed to its SAARC partners.

That economic integration in South Asia has remained a non-starter even after 22 years of the formation SAARC has been shown in the study of Dubey (2007). He believes that the trade relation between India and Pakistan requires a shift from state security to human security.

## 6.4 Data Source and Methodology

This study is based on secondary data source (DGCI&S) regarding merchandise trade of India with SAARC and the neighbouring Non-SAARC nations, viz. China and Myanmar for the period 1996–2020.A simple macro-theoretic model has been developed to study the trade dynamics of India vis-à-vis her trading partners of SAARC and the two selected non-SAARC nations.

### 6.4.1 *A Simple Macro-Theoretical Model*

The model developed in this paper partly subscribes to the conventional Keynesian framework of macroeconomics, though it comes with a digression to the framework in as much as the assumption of full employment is concerned. Besides, the model draws substantially on the open economy macroeconomics (Dornbusch, 1980). The basic structural frame of the model is built on goods market which is assumed to be full employment as what is theoretically consistent with long-run perspective. Besides the external sector comprising of merchandise trade is assumed to be at equilibrium in as much as the flexibility in the terms of trade (or alternatively real exchange rate) can ensure. Moreover, the model assumes that domestic absorption (or aggregate expenditure in real terms, denoted by D) of the home country (viz. India) depends on aggregate real income at full employment (denoted by $\overline{Y}_I$) and her terms of trade with the SAARC and non-SAARC partner (respectively denoted by $p_s$ and $p_{ns}$), in both of which D is rising vide the well-known 'Laursen-Metzler Effect'. Moreover, the model presented exempts the case of foreign repercussion by assumption. Hence the model has two endogenous variables, namely, $p_s$ and $p_{ns}$ which are determined simultaneously from the equations as given below.

$$\overline{Y}_I = \overline{D} + D(\overline{Y}_I, p_s, p_{ns}) + X_s(Y_s, p_s) + X_{ns}(Y_{ns}, p_{ns}) - p_s M_s(\overline{Y}_I, p_s) - p_{sn} M_{ns}(\overline{Y}_I, p_{ns}) \quad \dots (1)$$

$$X_s(Y_s, p_{ns}) + X_{ns}(Y_{ns}, p_{ns}) - p_s M_s(\overline{Y}_I, p_s) - p_{sn} M_{ns}(\overline{Y}_I, p_{ns}) = 0 \quad \dots (2)$$

Thus, the relationship between the two terms can be seen from two relations – namely the internal balance (as signified by full employment equilibrium) and external balance (signified by balance of trade equilibrium). The natures of the two ends of this relationship are as what have been depicted below [as derived from the total differentiation of equation (1) and (2), holding everything constant except $p_s$ and $p_{ns}$]

$$\frac{dp_{ns}}{dp_s} = -\frac{\left(\frac{\partial D}{\partial p_s}\right) + M_s\left[\varepsilon_s^*\left(1/\alpha_s\right) + \varepsilon_s - 1\right]}{\left(\frac{\partial D}{\partial p_{ns}}\right) + M_s\left[\varepsilon_{ns}^*\left(1/\alpha_{ns}\right) + \varepsilon_{ns} - 1\right]} \quad \dots (3)$$

$$\alpha_i = \frac{X_i}{p_i M_i}, i = s, ns$$

$$\frac{dp_{ns}}{dp_s} = -\frac{M_s\left[\varepsilon_s^*\left(1/\alpha_s\right) + \varepsilon_s - 1\right]}{M_{ns}\left[\varepsilon_{ns}^*\left(1/\alpha_{ns}\right) + \varepsilon_s - 1\right]} \quad \dots (4)$$

Wherein, $\varepsilon_s^*$ denotes the elasticity of import demand of India's SAARC partners taken together and $\varepsilon_{ns}^*$denotes the same in case the non-SAARC partners. Similarly, $\varepsilon_s$ and $\varepsilon_{ns}$ respectively denote India's import demand for the goods exported by SAARC and non-SAARC partners.

Now given, that Lauren-Metzler effect (i.e., $\left(\frac{\partial D}{\partial p_s}\right), \left(\frac{\partial D}{\partial p_{ns}}\right) > 0$ ) and the modified Marshall-Lerner condition (i.e.$M_i\left[\varepsilon_s^*\left(1/\alpha_i\right) + \varepsilon_i - 1\right] > 0$, for all *i*), the expression in the right hand side both equations (3) and (4) are negative. Hence, we have the result, that $p_s$ and $p_{ns}$ move in opposite direction to each other in case of both internal and external balance. Now for the stability of equilibrium, it is required that fall in $p_{ns}$ in response to rise in $p_s$ is higher in magnitude in case of external compared to that in case of internal balance. Thus, the equilibrium terms of trade vis-à-vis SAARC and non-SAARC partners get determined simultaneously as depicted below (Figure 1).

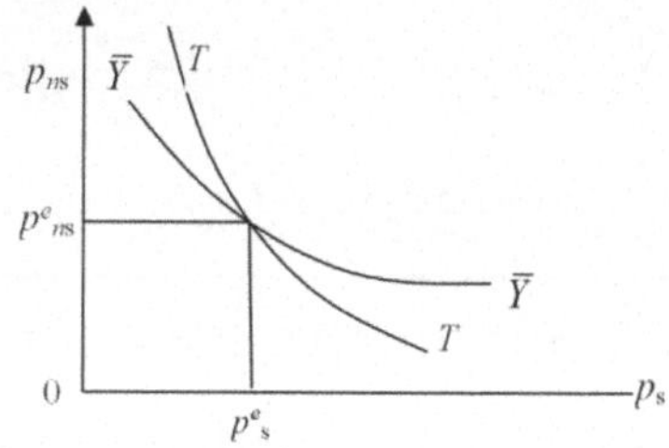


**Figure 6.1**

### 6.4.2 *Outbreak of Pandemic and Terms of Trade*

Here, we shall delve into the potential impact of the outbreak of pandemic on India's terms of trade, vis-a-vis SAARC and non-SAARC countries. To this end, we consider the nature and the significance of India's merchandise trade with the neighbouring countries within SAARC and those outside. It is so because the nature of commodity trade can be crucial to productive capacity of India, in the sense the goods that India obtains from any of her of her trading partners into the production either as intermediate input or as capital. Now as statistics suggest, that India has been the net exporter of finished and semi-finished goods to her neighbours in SAARC, while, a net importer of raw and intermediate inputs from those outside (especially, China). In this backdrop let us assume that, [given the supply-side importance of imports from China (more precisely saying, India's import from China significantly includes intermediate inputs and technology goods, for example, the supply of active pharmaceutical ingredients (API) is sourced to China at large and likewise the devices required for the operation telecommunication system], the potential aggregate output of India is an increasing function the output of her non-SAARC neighbouring trading partners. Thus, following the outbreak of pandemic, which had its epicenter in China, there happened a major setback on production and thereof, an acute disruption of internal and international supply chain. Hence, it is quite obvious that $\mathrm{Y_{ns}}$ got to contract in the aftermath of the pandemic and that had a negative spill-over on $\overline{\mathrm{Y}}_{\mathrm{I}}$. Now the following dispensation intended to elicit the impact of the pandemic-led disruption in production and supply on the equilibrium terms of trade. This analysis is based on comparative static exercise applied to equation (1) and (2), as what follows.

$$\mathrm{dp_{ns}} = \left[\frac{\left(1-\left(\frac{\partial D}{\partial Y_I}\right)(\overline{\mathrm{Y}}_{\mathrm{I}}')-\left(\frac{\partial X_{ns}}{\partial Y_{ns}}\right)+\mathrm{p_{sn}}\left(\left(\frac{\partial M_{ns}}{\partial \mathrm{Y_1}}\right)+\left(\frac{\partial M_{ns}}{\partial \mathrm{Y_1}}\right)\right)(\overline{\mathrm{Y}}_{\mathrm{I}}')\right)\left(M_{ns}\left[\varepsilon_{ns}^*\left(1/\alpha_{ns}\right)+\varepsilon_s-1\right]\right)+\left(\mathrm{p_{sn}}\left(\left(\frac{\partial M_{ns}}{\partial \mathrm{Y_1}}\right)+\left(\frac{\partial M_{ns}}{\partial \mathrm{Y_1}}\right)\right)\right)\left(M_s\left[\varepsilon_s^*\left(1/\alpha_s\right)+\varepsilon_s-1\right]\right)}{\left(\left(\frac{\partial D}{\partial p_s}\right)+M_s\left[\varepsilon_s^*\left(1/\alpha_s\right)+\varepsilon_s-1\right]\right)\left(M_{ns}\left[\varepsilon_{ns}^*\left(1/\alpha_{ns}\right)+\varepsilon_s-1\right]\right)-\left(\left(\frac{\partial D}{\partial p_{ns}}\right)+M_s\left[\varepsilon_{ns}^*\left(1/\alpha_{ns}\right)+\varepsilon_{ns}-1\right]\right)\left(M_s\left[\varepsilon_s^*\left(1/\alpha_s\right)+\varepsilon_s-1\right]\right)}\right] d\overline{\mathrm{Y}}_{ns} \quad \ldots (5)$$

Now, for, $d\overline{\mathrm{Y}}_{ns} < 0$, we get $\mathrm{dp_{ns}} < 0$, given the denominator is positive in sign as what evident from Figure 6.1.

$$\mathrm{dp_s} = -\left[\frac{\left(1-\left(\frac{\partial D}{\partial Y_I}\right)(\overline{\mathrm{Y}}_{\mathrm{I}}')-\left(\frac{\partial X_{ns}}{\partial Y_{ns}}\right)+\mathrm{p_{sn}}\left(\left(\frac{\partial M_{ns}}{\partial \mathrm{Y_1}}\right)+\left(\frac{\partial M_{ns}}{\partial \mathrm{Y_1}}\right)\right)(\overline{\mathrm{Y}}_{\mathrm{I}}')\right)\times\left(\left(\frac{\partial D}{\partial p_{ns}}\right)+M_s\left[\varepsilon_{ns}^*\left(1/\alpha_{ns}\right)+\varepsilon_{ns}-1\right]\right)+\left(\mathrm{p_{sn}}\left(\left(\frac{\partial M_{ns}}{\partial \mathrm{Y_1}}\right)+\left(\frac{\partial M_{ns}}{\partial \mathrm{Y_1}}\right)\right)\right)\left(\left(\frac{\partial D}{\partial p_s}\right)+M_s\left[\varepsilon_s^*\left(1/\alpha_s\right)+\varepsilon_s-1\right]\right)}{\left(\left(\frac{\partial D}{\partial p_s}\right)+M_s\left[\varepsilon_s^*\left(1/\alpha_s\right)+\varepsilon_s-1\right]\right)\left(M_{ns}\left[\varepsilon_{ns}^*\left(1/\alpha_{ns}\right)+\varepsilon_s-1\right]\right)-\left(\left(\frac{\partial D}{\partial p_{ns}}\right)+M_s\left[\varepsilon_{ns}^*\left(1/\alpha_{ns}\right)+\varepsilon_{ns}-1\right]\right)\left(M_s\left[\varepsilon_s^*\left(1/\alpha_s\right)+\varepsilon_s-1\right]\right)}\right] d\overline{\mathrm{Y}}_{ns} \quad \ldots (6)$$

In this case we find, $dp_S > 0$. Thus, it comes forth that the after the onset of the pandemic and resultant fizzling out of production and thereby, the crumbling of the supply, India will have to face worsening of equilibrium terms of trade as against her neighbouring trade partners within SAARC while an improvement in the same as against the those outside SAARC, to keep with the internal and external balance.

## 6.5 Data Analysis

India's export trade with her neighbouring SAARC partners actually reflects her trade with South Asians nations. The share of India's export trade with these countries (viz. Bangladesh, Nepal, Bhutan, Pakistan, Sri Lanka, Afghanistan and Maldives) gradually improved from about 5 per cent in 1996–97 to about 7 per cent of the aggregate export trade with all of her trading partners (Figure 6.2). Despite a declining trend in this regard during 2003–12, the turnaround was substantial during 2012–22 (up to October 2021).

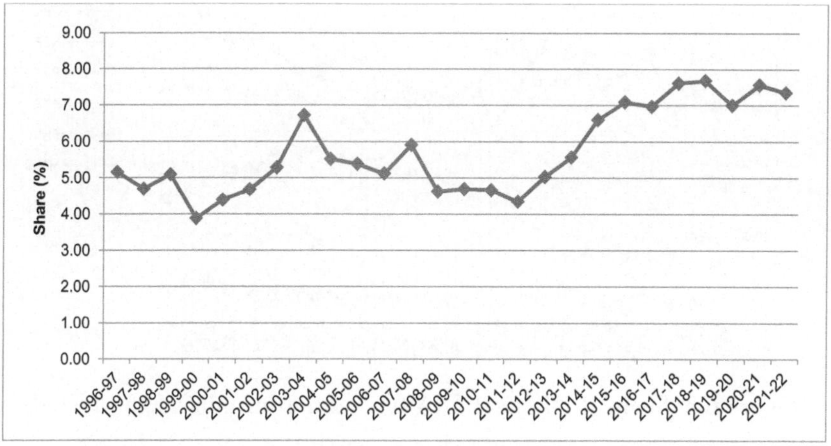


**Figure 6.2:** Share of SAARC Nations in India's Export Trade during 1996–2022

*Source:* Compiled from DGCI&S (Govt. of India). (https://tradestat.commerce.gov.in)

From the analysis of the changing shares of different SAARC partners in India's export trade over this period, a clear indication of a sustained upward trend in the share of Nepal is found during 1996–2022 and that of Bangladesh during 2006–22 (Figure 6.3) clearly reveals that Bangladesh is experienced with a gradual downturn in this share during 1996–2005. Though the share of Sri Lanka in India's export trade was about 27 percent in 1996–97 (much below than that of Bangladesh) it hovered around 30–32 percent on an average during 2000–15 followed by a gradual downturn. Such declining trend is also observed in case of Pakistan whose share in India's export trade has drastically fallen from about 20 percent in 2006–07 to only about 2 percent in 2021–22. The shares of Bhutan and Maldives had always remained insignificant.

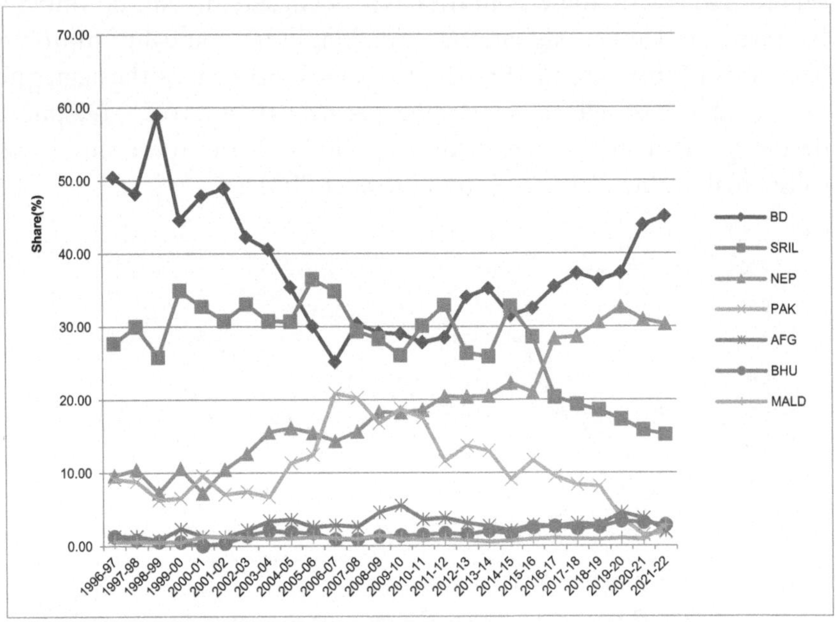


**Figure 6.3:** Share of Different SAARC Nations in India's Export Trade

*Source:* Compiled from DGCI&S (Govt. of India). (https://tradestat.commerce.gov.in)

Let us consider the import trade of India with its SAARC partners (Figure 6.4) and it shows that this share remained mostly below 1 per cent during the period under study. However, a declining trend in this regard during 2002–12 has definitely been followed by an increasing trend during 2012–22.

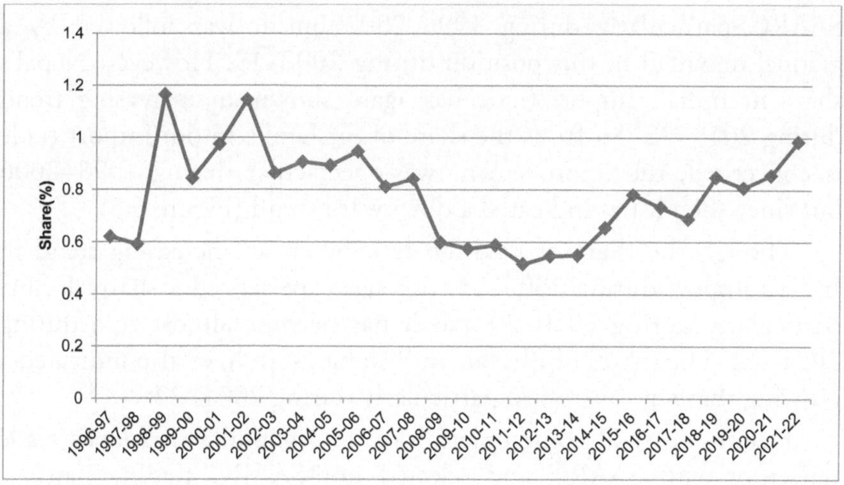


**Figure 6.4**: Share of SAARC Nations in India's Import Trade during 1996–2022

*Source:* Compiled from DGCI&S (Govt. of India). (https://tradestat.commerce.gov.in)

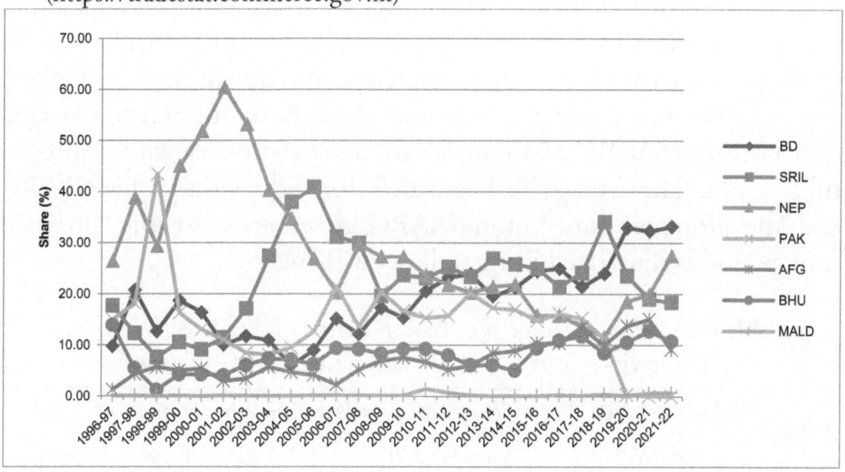


**Figure 6.5:** Share of Different SAARC Nations in India's Import Trade

(*Source:* Compiled from DGCI&S (Govt. of India)) (https://tradestat.commerce.gov.in)

Figure 6.5 suggests that the share of Bangladesh in India's total import from SAARC nations has gradually increased from about 6 per cent in 2004–05 to about 33 per cent in 2021–22. The place of Nepal seems to be most prominent in India's import trade with

SAARC particularly during 1996–2002 but it was followed by a gradual downfall in this position during 2002–19. However, Nepal's share in India's import trade has again shown an increasing trend during 2019–22. So far as the share of Sri Lanka in our import trade is concerned, the improvement was spectacular during 1998–2006 but since then it has indicated a downward trend (Figure 6.5).

Though the share of Pakistan has shown an increasing trend in India's import during 2003–13, this has experienced a sharp decline particularly during 2016–20 and it has become almost zero during 2021–22. The shares of Bhutan and Afghanistan have also indicated a growing share in this regard particularly during 2001–22.

Herein we shall contemplate into the dynamics of India's trade trajectory with SAARC and selected non-SAARC trading partners (which only include China and Myanmar over the period from 1996–2020. To this end we shall refer to two fundamental parameters of trade namely, net barter terms of trade (ToT) (as measured by import to export ratio) and the balance of trade (BoT). The analysis will be embarked on with finding out the nature of the India's terms of trade and balance over time, more specifically we shall be looking into whether the terms of trade and the balance of trade, averaged over both the SAARC and non-SAARC, are stationary with respect to time or not. The average ToT and BoT for India vis-à-vis her SAARC and the aforementioned non-SAARC members over the aforesaid time period is illustrated in the following Table 6.1.

**Table 6.1:** India' Average Net Barter Terms of Trade & Balance of Trade vis-à-vis the SAARC and non-SAARC Nations

| *Year* | *Average Net Barter Terms of Trade* | | *Average Balance of Trade* | |
|---|---|---|---|---|
| | *SAARC* | *Non-SAARC* | *SAARC* | *Non-SAARC* |
| 1996 | 0.35 | 2.58 | 211.73 | –137.06 |
| 1997 | 0.36 | 3.05 | 198.17 | –284.40 |
| 1998 | 0.89 | 4.17 | 171.19 | –406.60 |
| 1999 | 0.75 | 3.71 | 144.16 | –440.67 |
| 2000 | 3.27 | 2.63 | 208.84 | –399.94 |
| 2001 | 0.88 | 4.14 | 208.76 | –698.99 |

| *Year* | *Average Net Barter Terms of Trade* | | *Average Balance of Trade* | |
|---|---|---|---|---|
| | *SAARC* | *Non-SAARC* | *SAARC* | *Non-SAARC* |
| 2002 | 0.33 | 2.94 | 322.07 | –538.77 |
| 2003 | 0.24 | 2.97 | 512.03 | –708.75 |
| 2004 | 0.30 | 2.43 | 515.56 | –887.41 |
| 2005 | 0.34 | 3.22 | 590.62 | –2267.11 |
| 2006 | 0.52 | 3.84 | 709.48 | –4897.69 |
| 2007 | 0.52 | 3.42 | 1074.35 | –8448.94 |
| 2008 | 0.37 | 3.83 | 964.17 | –11925.43 |
| 2009 | 0.34 | 4.43 | 961.91 | –10143.99 |
| 2010 | 0.35 | 3.12 | 1354.74 | –15003.98 |
| 2011 | 0.29 | 2.80 | 1538.82 | –19036.40 |
| 2012 | 0.26 | 3.23 | 1775.82 | –19790.74 |
| 2013 | 0.21 | 2.61 | 2147.27 | –18409.46 |
| 2014 | 0.24 | 3.33 | 2507.02 | –24468.61 |
| 2015 | 0.26 | 3.88 | 2231.31 | –26305.11 |
| 2016 | 0.26 | 3.49 | 2344.11 | –25535.25 |
| 2017 | 0.27 | 3.20 | 2842.61 | –31360.31 |
| 2018 | 0.29 | 2.32 | 2997.97 | –26441.67 |
| 2019 | 0.23 | 2.25 | 2586.54 | –24110.68 |
| 2020 | 0.25 | 1.88 | 2671.52 | –21889.67 |

*Source:* Authors' computation from the reports of DGCI&S, (Govt. of India). (https://tradestat.commerce.gov.in)

A comparative view on India's net barter ToT between the SAARC and non-SAARC nations is depicted in the Figure 6.6.

Herein the above it is well obvious that the evolution of India's ToT with SAARC countries is fairly stable over time except for the time around the year 2000 for which we find an abrupt increase in averaged import-export ratio of India, which in turn is attributable to India's abrupt fall in export to Bhutan. On the other hand, for non-SAARC nations, namely, China and Myanmar, the ToT is fairly unstable over time resembling a random walk in particular.

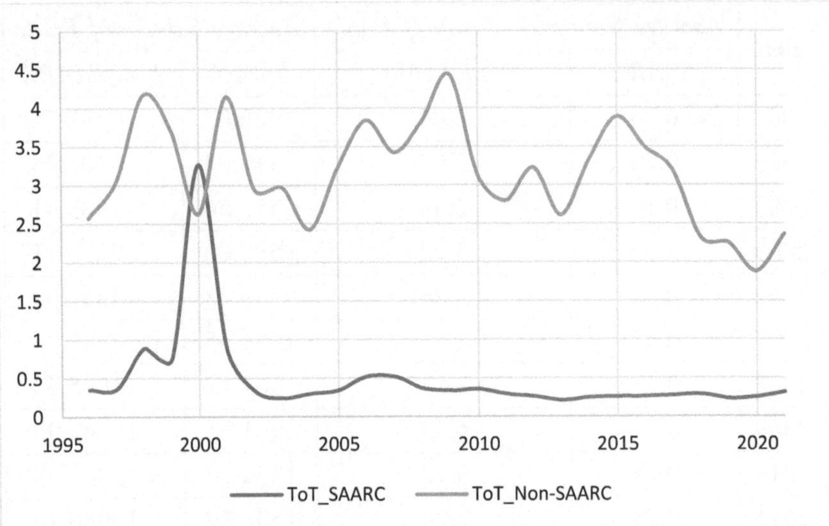


**Figure 6.6:** Over-time Pattern of India's Net Barter Terms of Trade vis-à-vis SAARC and Non-SARRC Nations

*Source:* Computed from DGCI&S, Govt. of India. (https://tradestat.commerce.gov.in)

### 6.6.1 *Dynamic Stability Analysis of India's Average Terms of Trade*

The dynamic stability analysis herein essentially comprises of test for the presence unit root using Dickey-Fuller in the time series on the averaged ToT with the SAARC and the non-SAARC nations.

As evident from Table 6.2, the low Mac-Kinnon p-values in case of both model 1 (with trend and drift) and model 2 (with drift but without trend) as under SAARC confirm the absence of unit root. However, for model 3 (without trend and drift) the absence of unit root is affirmed by the estimated z-statistic (greater than unity in absolute terms) which is significant at 5 per cent. Moreover, the trend coefficients in case of both model 1 and model 2 with high p-values refute the presence deterministic trend. Thus, on over all it is reasonable to conclude that the India's average ToT with the SAARC nation is stationary in nature and hence, dynamically stable. Similar conclusion can be drawn about the India's ToT with selected non-SAARC nations.

**Table 6.2:** Unit Root Test on India's Barter ToT

| | *SAARC* | | | *Non-SAARC* | | |
|---|---|---|---|---|---|---|
| | *Model 1* | *Model 2* | *Model 3* | *Model 1* | *Model 2* | *Model 3* |
| Intercept | 0.8401** (0.04) | 0.3518** (0.033) | – | 2.6932* (0.001) | 1.9553 (0.005) | – |
| Trend | –0.0371*** (0.078) | – | – | –0.0319*** (0.081) | | – |
| Lag Value | –8.679* (0.000) | –0.7197* (0.002) | –0.4247* (0.018) | – 0.7197* (0.001) | –6.452* (0.002) | –0.4247* (0.018) |
| Mac-Kinnon p-value | 0.0047 | 0.0063 | – | 0.0226 | 0.0228 | – |
| z-statistic | – | – | –2.547** | – | – | –2.143** |

*Source:* Computed from DGCI&S, Govt. of India. (https://tradestat.commerce.gov.in)

*Note:* *indicates significant at 1%, **indicates significant at 5% and ***denotes significant at 10%level of significance. Prob. Values are given in the parentheses.

### 6.6.2 *Dynamic Stability Analysis of India's Average Balance of Trade*

Herein we shall look into the nature of India's BoT vis-à-vis the SAARC and the non-SAARC partners over time on average.

As evident from Table 6.3, the high Mac-Kinnon p-values in case of both model 1(with trend and drift) and model 2 (with drift but without trend) as under SAARC confirm the presence of unit root. However, for model 3 (without trend and drift) the absence of unit root is affirmed by the estimated z-statistic (less than unity in absolute terms) which is significant at 5 per cent. Moreover, the trend coefficients in case of both model 1 and model 2 with high p-values refute the presence deterministic trend. Besides the intercept estimates are also insignificant in as much as there are associated high p-value. Thus, on over all it is reasonable to conclude that the India's average BoT with the SAARC nation are non-stationary in nature and hence dynamically unstable, in particular it resembles a random walk process without drift. Similar conclusion can be drawn about the India's ToT with selected non-SAARC nations. Given this we shall proceed to determine the order of integration of the BoT series in each case. To this end we shall consider the first order differenced version of BoT series to check for the presence of unit root, as what has been articulated in Table 6.4.

As evident from Table 6.4, the low Mac-Kinnon p-values in case of both model 1(with trend and drift) and model 2 (with drift but without trend) as under SAARC confirm the absence of unit root. However, for model 3 (without trend and drift) the absence of unit root is affirmed by the estimated z-statistic (greater than unity in absolute terms) which is significant at 5 per cent. Moreover, the trend coefficients in case of both model 1 and model 2 with high p-values refute the presence deterministic trend. Besides, the coefficient on lagged differenced value is less than unity in absolute terms and highly significant in each model. Thus, on overall it is reasonable to conclude that the India's differenced BoT with the SAARC nations are stationary in nature and hence dynamically stable with the order the integration being unity. Similar conclusion can be drawn about the India's differenced BoT with selected non-SAARC nations.

**Table 6.3:** Unit Root Test on India's Balance of Trade

| | *SAARC* | | | *Non-SAARC* | | |
|---|---|---|---|---|---|---|
| | *Model 1* | *Model 2* | *Model 3* | *Model 1* | *Model 2* | *Model 3* |
| Intercept | – 2.8595<br>(0.983) | 133.26<br>(0.131) | – | –542.59<br>(0.728) | –1328.04<br>(0.123) | – |
| Trend | 34.3533<br>(0.210) | – | – | –141.4678<br>(0.549) | – | – |
| Lag | – 0.2928<br>(0.150) | –0.0487<br>(0.367) | 0.1711<br>(0.622) | – 0.1398<br>(0.38) | –0.0504<br>(0.342) | 0.0112<br>(0.76) |
| Mac-Kinnon p-value | 0.8314 | 0.7825 | | 0.9566 | 0.7642 | – |
| z-statistic | – | – | 0.514** | | | 0.309** |

*Source:* Authors' computation from DGCI&S, Govt. of India. (https://tradestat.commerce.gov.in)

*Note:* *indicates significant at 1%, **indicates significant at 5% and ***denotes significant at 10% level of significance. Prob. Values are given in the parentheses.

**Table 6.4:** Unit Root Test on India's BoT (Differenced)

| | *SAARC* | | | *Non-SAARC* | | |
|---|---|---|---|---|---|---|
| | *Model 1* | *Model 2* | *Model 3* | *Model 1* | *Model 2* | *Model 3* |
| Intercept | 138.74 (0.244) | 71.42 (0.257) | – | –1563.26 (0.226) | –714.59 (0.267) | – |
| Trend | –5.5766 (0.498) | – | – | 67.3379 (0.445) | –0.9515* (0.000) | – |
| Lag | –0.9436* (0.002) | –0.9669 (0.002) | –0.8285* (0.002) | –0.9500* (0.000) | | –0.8690* (0.000) |
| Mac-Kinnon p-value | 0.0430 | 0.0053 | | 0.0038 | 0.0005 | – |
| z-statistic | | | –3.442** | | | –4.079*** |

*Source:* Authors' computation from DGCI&S, Govt. of India, (https://tradestat.commerce.gov.in)

*Note:* *indicates significant at 1%, **indicates significant at 5% and ***denotes significant at 10% level of significance. Prob. Values are given in the parentheses.

### 6.6.3 *Causality between the Net Barter ToT and BoT*

Herein we shall investigate into the potential causal relationship between India's ToT and Bot with the SAARC and non-SAARC nations. These have been dealt with the help of vector auto regression (VAR) analysis and Granger-Causality test, depicted in the table given below. It is to be noted at this juncture that both the parameter of India's regional trade in tryst with SAARC and non-SAARC nations have been taken in logarithmic form.

As evident from Table 6.5, in case of both SAARC and non-SAARC countries, the coefficient of lag1- ln(ToT) in the regression of ln(D1_BoT) is positive and statistically significant indicating any improvement in barter ToT or real exchange rate amounting to improvement in BoT. However, in case SAARC nations in particular, the statically significant negative coefficient on lag2- ln(D1_BoT) implies an escalation of BoT is associated with fall in barter ToT. Similarly finding has been obtained for the non-SAARC countries as well. Finally, the Granger Causality Chi-square is statistically significant.

**Table 6.5:** VAR and Granger Causality Test

| *Variable* | *SAARC* | | *Non-SAARC* | |
|---|---|---|---|---|
| | *Ln(ToT)* | *Ln(D1_BoT)* | *Ln(ToT)* | *Ln(D1_BoT)* |
| **Ln(ToT)** | | | | |
| Lag 1 | 0.7201*<br>(0.0015) | 4.5895**<br>(0.0246) | –1.3653*<br>(0.002) | 3.2617*<br>(0.0195) |
| Lag 2 | –0.0296 | –6.8020 | – | – |
| **Ln(D1_BoT)** | | | | |
| Lag 1 | –0.0552 | | 0.2939*<br>(0.0026) | 1.2045**<br>(0.0206) |
| Lag 2 | –0.1151*<br>(0.0000) | | – | – |
| Intercept | 0.3778 | –2.1048 | –0.5432 | –2.413 |
| Granger Causality Chisquare | 16.042*<br>(0.0001) | | 17.089*<br>(0.0022) | |

*Source:* Authors' computation from DGCI&S, Govt. of India, (https://tradestat.commerce.gov.in)

*Note:* *indicates significant at 1%, **indicates significant at 5% and ***denotes significant at 10% level of significance. Prob. Values are given in the parentheses.

## 6.7 Conclusion

The present study can be concluded on the following points.

(a) The dynamics of India's ToT, in net barter form, is same in nature for the both the SAARC and the non-SAARC nations during the post globalization period, in the sense that both are stationary, meaning that the evolution of ToT is headed towards the constant mean over time reflecting dynamic stability.

(b) The dynamics of India's BoT is same in nature for the both the SAARC and the non-SAARC nations during the post globalization in the sense that both are non-stationary, meaning that the evolution the BoT is heading away from the mean over time, which in turn is time variant reflecting dynamic instability.

(c) There is no contemporaneous correlation between the ToT and BoT, instead there is significant evident correlation between these two parameters of trade across time.

## References

[1] Akram, Hafiz Wasim, Ciddiekie, M.D. and Khan, M. Altaf (2014). India's Trade Relationship with SAFTA Countries: A Review, *Journal of Indian Research*, Vol. 2, No. 1, January–March, pp. 46–58.

[2] Chaudhary, S.K. (1995). Cross Border Trade between India and Bangladesh, *NCAER*, Working Paper, 58, New Delhi.

[3] Dubey, Muchkund (2007). SAARC and South Asian Economic Integration, *Economic & Political Weekly*, April 7, Vol. 42, No. 14, 7 April, pp. 1238–1240.

[4] Kaur, Sandeep and Nanda, Paramjeet (2010). India's Export Potential to Other SAARC Countries: A Gravity Model Analysis, *Journal of Global Economy*, Research Centre for Social Sciences, Mumbai, India, June, Vol. 6(3), pp. 167–184.

[5] Malik, IshfaqAhamd and Mir, M. Afzal (2014). India's Trade Potential with Central Asia: An Application of Gravity Model Analysis, *International Journal on World Peace*, September, Vol. 31, No. 3, pp. 53–69.

[6] Roy, Suparna (2016). Review of Trade Relations between India and Other SAARC Nations and Its Challenges, *Proceedings of the Indian History Congress*, Vol. 77, pp. 799–807.

[7] *Reports of DGCI&S*, (Directorate General of Commercial Intelligence and Statistics, Ministry of Commerce and Industry, GOI (Available at https://tradestat.commerce.gov.in).

[8] Zaki Eusufzai (2000). Liberalisation in the Shadow of a Large Neighbour: A Case of Bangladesh-India Economic Relations, University Press Limited, Dhaka.

[9] Taneja, N. (2001). Informal Trade in SAARC Region, *Economic and Political Weekly*, March 17, Vol. 36, No. 11, pp. 959–964.

[10] Pant, Manoj and Paul, Anusree (2018). The Role of Regional Trade Agreements: in the Case of India, *Journal of Economic Integration*, Vol. 33, No. 3, September, pp. 538–571.

CHAPTER 7

# Evaluating E-commerce as the Future of India's Trade with SAARC Countries

**Dukhabandhu Sahoo, Suryakanta Nayak and Jayanti Behera**

## 7.1 Introduction

The broader objective of SAARC (South Asian Association for Regional Cooperation) was to boost the social, cultural, and economic cooperation between the affiliated countries. Like the European Union (EU), the members of the SAARC share a lot of similarities, but they too have much dissimilarity. The member nations of the EU are mostly developed, whereas the member counties of SAARC are either developing or underdeveloped. Another distinct difference between EU and SAARC is that while most of the members in the former case are homogeneous in their economic structure and development process, in SAARC, India is a very large economy. In contrast, the economy of the other members is relatively smaller. Further, India has been on the higher path of the growth trajectory than its counterparts in SAARC. All these uniqueness of SAARC makes it an interesting area of research in comparison to other regional blocks.

Unfortunately, the economic cooperation (especially cross border trade) between the SAARC countries is very limited, like other regional unions of South-Asia. In addition to the geopolitical conditions, the extent of the knowledge gap and lack of knowledge transfer could be accounted for such poor performance of these nations in economic cooperation. The use of technology can work towards this, and E-commerce is an area that can boost economic cooperation among these countries. The emergence of E-commerce towards the late 1990s' has been a very highly successful business plan that has reduced the cost of many business organizations that had earlier used their intranets (which were costly and required a large number of the workforce for maintenance). The use of E-commerce in the form of Business-to-Business (B2B) can directly reduce the cost of the transaction of trade (International Trade Statistics 2015). Therefore, the pertinent question that can be raised is whether E-commerce could be used as a means to promote trade of India with the members of the SAARC. Under this backdrop, the broad objective of this research is to find out the impact of E-commerce on the international trade of India with the member countries in SAARC by using the Gravity model of international trade. The rest of the paper is organized as follows: the next section gives some facts about SAARC, followed by the performance of the SAARC countries in the third section. The fourth section describes the empirical framework with some relevant literature. The fifth section discusses the results of the empirical examination, while the paper concludes in the sixth section.

### 7.1.1 *The Genesis of SAARC and India's Position*

The brainchild of late president of Bangladesh, Ziaur Rehman, SAARC, is an economic and geopolitical association of eight South Asian nations with the largest geo-economic block of the world and around 2 billion populations. SAARC Chamber of Commerce and Industry (SCCI) has been formed to accelerate trade and industry in the region and to promote and achieve common objectives in the areas of trade and industry. Though South-Asia houses 22 percent of the world population in its three percent of the world's surface, it only shares one percent of the world trade. South-Asia was looking for an Economic union and towards this, the South-Asia Preferential Trade Agreement (SAPTA) has been converted into the South-Asia Free Trade Agreement (SAFTA) in 2006. Most of the countries of South-Asia are now the members of the World Trade Organization (WTO) and are in the practice of Most Favoured Nation (MFN). It was estimated that SAFTA would help in raising the formal trade in the region from US$11 billion in 2007 to US$40 billion by 2015. But it failed dismally in its set goal. The major stumbling blocks are poor and unorganized institutions, insufficient infrastructure to promote trade through E-commerce, and lack of skilled manpower to execute the existing infrastructure (Das and Pohit 2006; Taneja 2007). The economic performance of all the member countries of SAARC is presented in Table 7.1.

**Table 7.1:** Economic Performance of the SAARC Countries (2001–2020)

| *Country*[1] | *Annual Average Growth Rates (AAGR)* | | | | | | |
|---|---|---|---|---|---|---|---|
| | *Afghanistan* | *Bangladesh* | *Bhutan* | *India* | *Nepal* | *Pakistan* | *Sri Lanka* |
| Population (No. in Millions.) | 2.28 | 1.34 | 0.16 | 1.6 | –4.5 | 2.1 | 0.8 |
| GDP at Market Prices (Current Prices) | 12.5 | 10.8 | 11.5 | 11 | 3.5 | 10 | 10 |
| GDP at Market Prices (Constant Prices) | 4.61 | 8.17 | 5.73 | 9.4 | –3.8 | 5 | 4.7 |
| Agriculture (Current Prices) | 7.57 | 7.3 | 6.67 | 7.9 | 2.6 | 11 | 7.3 |
| Agriculture (Constant Prices) | –0.6 | 4.29 | –0.16 | 1.37 | –4.4 | 4 | 9.1 |
| Industry (Current Prices) | 12.9 | 11.3 | 13.8 | 12 | 1.7 | 7.3 | 14 |
| Industry (Constant Prices) | 5.68 | 8.82 | 8 | 11 | –5.3 | 3.4 | 19 |
| Mining & Quarrying (Current Prices) | 35.3 | 14.6 | 17.2 | 13 | 4.6 | 11 | 17 |
| Mining & Quarrying (Constant Prices) | 24 | 13.3 | 9.41 | 12 | –5.3 | 8.1 | 20 |
| Manufacturing (Current Prices) | 9.62 | 11.6 | 13 | 12 | 0.4 | 9 | 15 |
| Manufacturing (Constant Prices) | 0.5 | 9.93 | 7.22 | 11 | –6.1 | 3.2 | 21 |
| Electricity, Gas & Water Supply (Current prices) | 17 | 10.9 | 18.3 | 12 | –0.9 | 9.8 | 11 |
| Electricity, Gas & Water Supply (Constant prices) | 2.71 | 7.1 | 14 | 11 | –3 | 2.4 | 18 |
| Services (Current Prices) | 16.3 | 11.7 | 12.6 | 12 | 4.3 | 7.9 | 14 |
| Services (Constant Prices) | 8.02 | 9.37 | 7.02 | 9.6 | –3.1 | 6.6 | 20 |
| Construction (Current Prices) | 20.7 | 10.4 | 11.7 | 15 | 3.8 | 9.3 | 14 |
| Construction (Constant Prices) | 15.1 | 6.37 | 3.72 | 13 | –4.7 | 6.2 | 17 |

*Source:* Calculated by the authors from Reserve Bank of India Bulletin, 2020.

[1] Maldives is removed from the Table as data on most of the variables were missing.

Analysis of macroeconomic variables of all the eight SAARC countries shows that India is economically the most powerful member of the association (Table 7.1). India has fared well ahead of its other member countries in almost all the parameters. The annual average growth rate of the Gross Domestic Product (GDP) of India is at a staggering high (9.4 percent), followed by Bangladesh (8.17 percent) during 2001–2015. However, Nepal has experienced a negative AAGR during the same period, which may be attributed to the frequent natural calamities, Nepal had to face. The AAGR of India's Trade (export, import, and total trade, Table 7.2) with other SAARC Countries during 2001–2015 has been very high that goes with the postulation of the gravity model of international trade.

**Table 7.2:** Annual Average Growth Rates (AAGR) of India's Trade with other SAARC Countries during 2001–2020

| *Countries* | *AAGR of Export* | *AAGR of Import* | *AAGR of Total Trade* |
|---|---|---|---|
| Afghanistan | 34.69 | 33.67 | 31.12 |
| Bangladesh | 19.51 | 20.07 | 16.53 |
| Bhutan | 47.12 | 16.94 | 23.63 |
| Maldives | 11.89 | 59.31 | 12.07 |
| Nepal | 25.21 | 401.84 | 26.67 |
| Pakistan | 20.02 | 15.45 | 17.82 |
| Sri Lanka | 10.78 | 18.60 | 10.55 |

*Source:* Calculated by the authors from Reserve Bank of India Bulletin, 2020.

All SAARC countries have varying levels of infrastructure related to E-commerce. India has the largest number of Secure Internet servers (254032), followed by Pakistan (23161), while Bhutan (134) in 2020. This is inevitable, as the size of these countries is hugely different, and the degree of heterogeneity is different in different counties. This is justified from the analysis of the table as the internet users per 100 people is higher in Bhutan (48.11) in comparison to countries like India (34.45), Sri Lanka (34.11), Pakistan (15.51), Nepal (34), Bangladesh (15) and Afghanistan (13.5) in 2020. Internet users per 100 people are highest in Maldives (63.18) in 2020. This may be

**Table 7.3:** Internet-related Indicators in SAARC Counties During 2001–2020 (per million)

| *Countries* | *Indicators* | *2001* | *2010* | *2015* | *2020* | *AAGR* |
|---|---|---|---|---|---|---|
| Afghanistan | IU*** | 0.00 | 3.55 | 6.39 | 13.5 | 200.03 |
| | SIT** | | 9.00 | 32.00 | 1965 | 124.63 |
| | SINTP* | | 0.33 | 1.01 | 52.86 | 118.17 |
| Bangladesh | IU*** | 0.13 | 3.70 | 9.70 | 15 | 45.68 |
| | SIT** | | 47.00 | 212.00 | 18712 | 208.47 |
| | SINTP* | | 0.31 | 1.32 | 115.97 | 205.08 |
| Bhutan | IU*** | 0.40 | 7.17 | 34.37 | 48.11 | 30.84 |
| | SIT** | | 3.00 | 13.00 | 134 | 106.49 |
| | SINTP* | | 4.17 | 16.78 | 177.63 | 104.05 |
| Maldives | IU*** | 2.20 | 24.80 | 49.28 | 63.18 | 20.77 |
| | SIT** | | 17.00 | 42.00 | 270 | 60.64 |
| | SINTP* | | 46.32 | 102.65 | 523.56 | 53.88 |
| Nepal | IU*** | 0.20 | 1.97 | 15.44 | 34 | 45.37 |
| | SIT** | | 31.00 | 84.00 | 5126 | 156.06 |
| | SINTP* | | 1.17 | 2.98 | 182.5 | 154.00 |
| Pakistan | IU*** | 0.06 | 7.50 | 13.80 | 15.51 | 19.57 |
| | SIT** | | 169.00 | 448.00 | 23161 | 167.86 |
| | SINTP* | | 0.99 | 2.37 | 109.14 | 162.31 |
| Sri Lanka | IU*** | 0.65 | 8.78 | 25.80 | 34.11 | 31.32 |
| | SIT** | | 92.00 | 290.00 | 8937 | 104.66 |
| | SINTP* | | 4.57 | 13.83 | 412.41 | 102.81 |
| India | IU*** | 0.53 | 5.12 | 18.00 | 34.45 | 31.15 |
| | SIT** | | 2601.00 | 8944.00 | 254032 | 95.73 |
| | SINTP* | | 2.11 | 6.82 | 187.81 | 93.53 |

***,**and *imply Internet users, IU, (per 100 population), Secure Internet servers, SIT, and Secure Internet servers, (per 1 million people), SINTP, respectively.

*Source:* World Development Indicator, CD ROM (2020).

because a large section of the Maldives population is concentrated in small pockets leading to higher urbanization and availing of urban amenities by these people. This result is corroborated with the fact that the Secure Internet servers per 1 million people are highest in Maldives (523.56). If we look at the growth rate of these indicators, Maldives lag behind the other countries probably because the availability of these facilities is higher initially for the Maldives than the other countries. The AAGR of internet users per 100 population, secure internet servers, and secure internet servers per 1 million people of India is 31.15, 95.73, and 93.53, respectively. The same for the Maldives is 20.77, 60.64, and 53.88, respectively.

## 7.2 Review of Literature

The regional blocks formed to accelerate trade among the members stem from the concept of free trade which was first postulated by Adam Smith in 1776 in his book "The Wealth of Nation" where he argued that countries should specialize in the production and export of those commodities and/or service in which they have an absolute advantage. This argument of Smith was further taken to another level by Ricardo and Hecksher and Ohlin. For the Ricardian theory, Linder mentioned that "A nation, like a person, gains from trade by exporting the goods or services in which it has its greatest comparative advantage in productivity and importing those in which it has the least comparative advantage". On the Hecksher and Ohlin gave, an explanation for the pattern of trade between the two countries. According to the Hecksher-Ohlin theory, a country will specialize in the production and export of that commodity and/or services to produce which it intensively uses the abundant factor(s) of production available in that country and import that commodity and/or services for the production of which the required factor(s) of productions are scarce in that country. This indicates that the classical theories of international trade advocated for trade between countries with different factor endowments and distinct economic structures. Such a postulation goes against the spirit of regional trading blocs like SAARC, as most of these blocks are formed by counties with similar economic structures. The formation of regional trading blocs like SAARC to accelerate regional trade could be explained by the new trade theory.

The new trade theories relax the restrictive assumptions of the classical trade theories and state that trade between countries could be explained by product differentiation, imperfect completion, and economies of scale (Krugman and Obstfeld, 2005).

Of late, the gravity model (as per Newton's law of gravitation) is used frequently to explain the bilateral trade. Tinbergen was the first economist to use a gravity model to explain the flow of goods and/or services to other countries, where distance was used as one of the explanatory variables and was supposed to have a negative effect on trade flows. Krugman and Obstfeld (2005) also provided a general form of the gravity model of international trade that can be explained as follows:

$$T_{ij} = A\left(\frac{Y_i \times Y_j}{D_{ij}^2}\right) \quad \ldots (1)$$

Where, $T_{ij}$ is the total trade flows from the country "i" to country "j", "A" is a constant term, "$Y_i$" and "$Y_j$" are some measure of the size of the country "i" and "j" respectively, "$D_{ij}$" is the distance between country "i" and "j". However, in empirical research, economists have tried to use other explanatory variables to explain trade flows (e.g., Martínez-Zarzoso and Nowak-Lehmann (2004) have used infra-structure, exchange rates, and income differentials to explain the Mercosur-EU trade; Rahman (2009) showed that trade openness and cultural factors are also the determinants of Australia's bilateral trade). Similarly, other economists also have tried to explain the bilateral as well as multilateral trade flows across the globe [Sohn*et al.* (2010) for Korea; Ranajoy and Tathagata (2006) for India and Alberto (2009) for Africa; Do (2006); Nguyen (2010) and Binh, *et al.* (2011) in Vietnam].

Intra-regional trade among the SAARC countries has been evaluated in parallel not with its potential. Accordingly, South Asian countries have seen inadequate gains from intraregional trade which varies across countries, although many efforts to promote regional cooperation and integration have been implemented. Hassan (2000) investigates that Bangladesh's trade with the SAARC countries and find that benefits from intraregional trade are modest while trade with developed countries is more considerable. Moreover, Chowdhury (2005) finds that Bangladesh may gain benefits from both intraregional and international trade whereas this is not completely true for a bigger country Pakistan. While the trade performance of Sri Lanka become better only in the case of trade with neighboring countries, India may take increased advantages of international trade. In a recent study, Zaheer (2013) finds that intraregional integration has significant and positive effects on the economic development of four countries—Pakistan, India, Bangladesh, and Sri Lanka in the SAARC in terms of market expansion, technology transfer, scale economies and among others. Khandare and Babar (2012) argue that although there exists an impressive increase in the share of intraregional trade in GDP in the SAARC countries, a rise of around 35 per cent for the period 1970s–2008, it was still lower compared to the East Asia and Pacific countries.

The slow growth in intraregional trade derives from barriers existing in trade flows. Apart from political conflicts over the past decades, the similarity in factor endowments and socio-economic structure is another important reason. Therefore, it could be suggested that more attention should be paid to restructure the industrial sector, improve vertical and horizontal linkages and this, in turn, takes advantage of economies of scale so that intraregional trade in the SAARC is cultivated and facilitated (Hasan, 2000). Meanwhile, some studies, instead, have emphasized trade facilitation as a determining factor of cross-border trade within the SAARC region. A study by Wilson and Otsuki (2007) using gravity models show that the improvement in trade facilitation may lead to larger benefits in terms of trade for countries in South Asia. Similarly, Weerahewa (2009) confirms the role of trade facilitation on food and agricultural trade. In particular, cutting down costs of trade and improving the Logistic Performance Index, as proxies of trade facilitation, result in the significant rise of agricultural trade within the South Asian countries. Hertel and Mirza (2009), using data on agricultural and manufacturing goods in 95 countries and accounting for endogeneity and spurious correlation, find that trade facilitation has a larger influence on trade than efforts to reduce tariff barriers do.

Further, with respect to the trade of India with SAARC countries, considerable literature is available (Venketesh 2006; Vadra 2011; Ambrose and Sundaral 2014; Akram*et al.* 2014; Mahaswararao 2015). All these studies on the trade of India with SAARC countries have tried to explain the bilateral and/or multilateral trend, pattern, and growth. These studies have concluded that trade of India with the SAARC countries has increased in volume as well as in diversification over a period. However, using the gravity model, Kaur and Nanda (2010) found that the actual export flows from India to the SAARC countries converge with the potential export for the period 1981 to 2005. Thus, the study concluded that it is in India's interest to back the SAARC. Another study is done by Sultan and Munir (2015) that used gravity the model to explore the trade potential of Pakistan and concluded that Pakistan has not been successful in exploiting the trade potential with India. The review of the literature shows that there is hardly any study to analyze India's trade with the SAARC countries in the era of E-commerce when it has really facilitated cross border trade through the reduction in transaction costs. To that extent, there lies a vacuum in the literature, and this study will fill the gap. The following section explains the empirical methods for analyzing data so that relevant conclusions could be drawn in the last section.

## 7.3 Empirical Methods

The present study is totally carried out on SAARC countries by using secondary data. The secondary data have been sourced from the World Development Indicator of the World Bank and the Reserve Bank of India (RBI) for a period of 20 years (2001 to 2020). For data on distance, the distance of Indian capital (New Delhi) to the capitals of other SAARC countries, was considered and it was retrieved from www.chemical-ecology.net.

### 7.3.1 *Variables Used in the Study*

In this study, the gravity model is used for three dependent variables. Therefore, there are three different models in the study. The dependent variables for the three models are the total trade of India (TTI), total exports of India (TEI), and total imports of India (TII) to each county of the SAARC. The independent variables in all three models are the same. The independent variables included in the models are, the per capita Gross Domestic Product of India (PGDPI), the per capita Gross Domestic Product of other SAARC countries (PGDPO), a distance from New Delhi to the capitals of other SAARC countries (DIST), exchange rate in Indian rupee with the currency of other SAARC countries (ERI)[1], internet users per 100 people in India (INI) and other SAARC countries (INO), and taxes on international trade (% of revenue) of India (TXI) and other SAARC countries (TXO)[2]. The descriptive statistics of all these variables are presented in Table 7.4.

For the empirical purpose, the present study has made some variation in the gravity model of Krugman and Obstfeld (2005) due to the additional independent variables. Further, the model is estimated in double log so that the co-efficient will be interpreted in elasticity. The estimable equation for the present study is stated as follows:

$$Log(Y_{ijt}) = \propto + \beta_1 Log(PGDP_{it}) + \beta_2 Log(PGDP_{jt}) + \beta_3 Log(DIST_{ij}) + \beta_4 Log(ERI_{ijt}) + \beta_5 Log(INI_{it}) + \beta_6 Log(INO_{jt}) + \beta_7 Log(TXI_{it}) + \beta_8 Log(TXO_{jt}) + e_{ijt} \quad \ldots (2)$$

Where i = 1 (India), j = 2, 3, 4, 5, 6, 7, 8 (other SAARC countries like Bangladesh, Bhutan, Maldives, Nepal, Pakistan, Sri Lanka, and Afghanistan), t = 2001 ... 2020.

Y = Either TTI, TEI, or TII and all other variables are as explained in sub-section 7.3.1.

Equation (2) could have been empirically estimated in three ways: the Pooled Regression model (PRM), the Fixed Effect Model (FEM), and the Random Effect Model (REM). However, the FEM requires that all variables must change over a period of time, but in this case,

---

[1] Studies by Bergstand (1985) has concluded that inclusion of bilateral exchange rate (BER) in the gravity model would explain the variation in trade among the countries. Therefore, in the present study, BER of Indian rupee vis-a-vis the currency of other SAARC counties is considered. However, the data on BER of Indian rupee vis-a-vis the currency of other SAARC counties was not available. Thus, the BER of Indian rupee vis-a-vis the currency of other SAARC counties is calculated as: $BER_{ijt} = \frac{\text{BER of Indian rupee with US\$ in period } t}{\text{BER of country j with US\$ in period } t}$, "i" is country India.

[2] These are the variables for E-commerce. As Panagariya (2000) reports "Access to e-commerce, which in the WTO parlance often means access to e-exports, has two components that must be distinguished sharply: access to Internet services and access to services that can be traded electronically. The former deals with access to Internet infrastructure while the latter relates to specific commitments in electronically tradable services". Therefore, in the present study internet users per 100 people and taxes on international trade (% of revenue) are considered in this study.

Table 7.4: Descriptive Statistics of the Variables

| *Variables* | *Descriptive Statistics* | | | | | | |
|---|---|---|---|---|---|---|---|
| | *Minimum* | *Maximum* | *Mean* | *Std. Deviation* | *Variance* | *Skewness* | *Kurtosis* |
| TEI | 3623.63 | 4103801.13 | 756376.25 | 9.71836.00 | 9.445E11 | 1.88 | 3.22 |
| TII | 161.00 | 485357.89 | 133084.09 | 1.24018E5 | 1.538E10 | 0.94 | .14 |
| TTI | 13006.43 | 4568077.03 | 889460.34 | 1082089.40 | 1.171E12 | 1.80 | 2.88 |
| GDPI | 560304.30 | 1822936.20 | 1052385.53 | 441225.39 | 1.947E11 | 0.59 | –1.1 |
| PGDPI | 818.50 | 1805.57 | 1246.48 | 312.61 | 97731.15 | 0.23 | –1.2 |
| GDPO | 493.3 | 142052.4 | 32759.239 | 40481.77 | 1.639E9 | 1.12 | –.04 |
| PGDPO | 355 | 7197 | 1888.66 | 1867.89 | 3489031.75 | 1.56 | 1.42 |
| DIST | 687.35 | 2999.20 | 1518.20 | 795.14 | 632248.04 | 0.80 | –.75 |
| ERI | 0.37 | 4.17 | 1.15 | 1.03 | 1.07 | 1.96 | 2.25 |
| INI | 0.52 | 18.00 | 5.88 | 5.39 | 29.12 | 1.02 | –.24 |
| INO | 0.004 | 49.28 | 7.92 | 9.98 | 99.62 | 2.09 | 4.47 |
| TXI | 11.41 | 20.77 | 15.50 | 2.55 | 6.54 | 0.97 | .18 |
| TXO | 0.69 | 33.36 | 15.47 | 10.35 | 107.31 | 0.16 | –1.2 |

*Source:* Calculated by the authors.

the variable "DIST" does not change at all. Therefore, using FEM to estimate equation (2) is ruled out, and thus, in the present study, both REM and PRM were used for empirical estimation. However, the Breusch-Pagan LM test confirmed that, in this case, the PRM should be preferred over the REM.

A PRM that pools the time series data across cross-section units may have the presence of heteroscedasticity and autocorrelation. Such an issue could be addressed by making certain assumptions on heteroscedasticity and autocorrelation. These assumptions can be stated as follows:

Homoscedasticity & no autocorrelation; homoscedasticity & common autocorrelation; homoscedasticity & specific autocorrelation; group-wise hetroscedasticity & no autocorrelation; group-wise hetroscedasticity & common autocorrelation; group-wise hetroscedasticity & specific autocorrelation; cross group hetroscedasticity & no autocorrelation; cross group hetroscedasticity & common autocorrelation; and cross group hetroscedasticity & specific autocorrelation

The key validation for the postulation of heteroscedasticity in the pooled regression estimation is the specific countries. Since the variables of the respective country are not homogenous, the difference in the error variances is expected. The literature on empirical econometric studies with respect to cross-sectional data also supports this view. Similarly, the problem of autocorrelation in the error term of a given cross-section unit may be present in a PRM. Therefore, while estimating such models, the appropriate correction has to be made so that the coefficients are consistent. The procedure is explained in the following paragraphs.

The panel data regression is different from a regular time series or cross-section regression as it has a dual subscript on its variables which indicates changes over time and across units/countries, which may be written as:

$$Y_{it} = (X_{it}) \times \beta + \varepsilon_{it} \qquad \ldots (3)$$

I = 1, 2 …, N

t = 1, 2 …, T

Where "i" indicates the cross-section units, i.e., the different countries (N = 7[3], in this case) and "t" indicates the period (T = 20 here, as the study period, is from 2001 to 2020[4]), $\beta$ is K×1 and $X_{it}$ is the $i^{th}$ observation on the $K^{th}$ variable. The error term $\varepsilon_{it}$ supposed to be homoscedastic and non-auto correlated, i.e.,

$$Var[\varepsilon_{it}] = \sigma_{\varepsilon}^{2} \text{ and } E[\varepsilon_{it}] = 0$$

If we violate the assumption of homoscedasticity and auto-correlation, then it may give rise to alternative possibilities, that includes: (1) Group-wise heteroscedasticity, $E[\varepsilon_{it}^{2}] = \sigma_{ii}$, (2) Cross group correlation, $Cov(\varepsilon_{it}, \varepsilon_{jt}) = \sigma_{ij}$, for $i \neq j$, (3) Within-group autocorrelation, i.e., $\varepsilon_{it} = \rho_i \varepsilon_{i,t-1} + U_{it}$. These three cases could be explained as follows:

Let $\Sigma$ be an N×N, period-specific covariance matrix, i.e., $\Sigma = \{\sigma_{ij}\}I$, j = 1, 2, ..., N.

Some restrictions can be imposed on $\Sigma$, which may provide three possible cases. The first one denotes the classical homoscedastic regression, which represents a naïve condition where in:

$S_0$: $\Sigma = \sigma^2 I$, where I is an identity matrix.

It stands for group-wise heteroscedasticity in the second case and thus:

$S_1$:$\Sigma = diag[\sigma_{11}, \sigma_{22}, \ldots, \sigma_{NN}]$

In the third case, $\Sigma$ is understood to be a positive definite matrix which signifies cross-group correlated errors aside from group-wise heteroscedasticity, i.e.,

$S_2$:$\Sigma$ = N×N positive definite matrix.

An alike set of assumptions could be considered for auto-correlation. Let $\rho$ be an N×1, vector of group-specific autocorrelation coefficients. Three meaningful restrictions that could be imposed on

[3] Seven SAARC countries (excluding India) are taken for estimation of the modified gravity model.

[4] Data for estimation is taken from 2001–2020 as E-commerce in international trade took off during the new millennium.

the ρ vector can be visualized. In the first case, $R_0$:ρ=0, representing a situation where disturbances are non-auto correlated. In the second case, R1:ρ = {ρ, ρ, …, ρ}, where all the units have a common autocorrelation coefficient. In the third case, $R_2$: ρ = $\{\rho_1, \rho_2, ..., \rho_N\}$, where individual units have specific coefficients.

If we combine both the restrictions on Σ and ρ, we will have nine different combinations. These nine combinations will give nine different models, which could be specified as [$S_0R_0$, $S_1R_0$, $S_2R_0$, $S_0R_1$, $S_1R_1$, $S_2R_1$, $S_0R_2$, $S_1R_2$, and $S_2R_2$]. The last model (i.e.$S_2R_2$) is a special case of all the other eight models. Thus, it could be said that once we correct for Cross group heteroskedasticity and specific auto-correlation, the parameters may become consistent, allowing us to go ahead with the Pooled Regression model (PRM).

## 7.4 Result and Discussion

Since the FEM could not be used here, the Breusch-Pagan LM test was conducted to choose between PRM and REM, and the results are presented in Table 7.5. The result of the test confirmed that in this case, the PRM should be preferred over the REM.

**Table 7.5:** Breusch-Pagan LM Test Result for PRM

| *Model* | *$\chi^2$-value* | *P-value* |
|---|---|---|
| PRM | 1271.64* | 0.000 |

*Source:* Authors' estimation.

*Note:* *implies significant at 1% level.

After confirming that the gravity models could be estimated through PRM through the Breusch-Pagan LM test, three models are estimated (for three dependent variables) with correction for Cross group heteroscedasticity and specific autocorrelation ($S_2R_2$), and the results are presented in Table 7.6 through Table 7.8.

The perusal of Table 7.6 provides some interesting results. Though the elasticity of PGDPI shows the predicted sign (0.66), the result indicates that a one percent increase in the PGDPO brings about a 0.44 percent decline in the trade of India to the SAARC countries. This may be because of the fact that with the increase in income of the people of other SAARC countries than India, the people there are interested either to import from other countries than India or they might be resorting to a policy of import substitution. This is also corroborated with the fact that as BERI increases, the trade of India with these countries declines. Distance, as predicted, shows a negative effect on the trade of India to the SAARC countries.

**Table 7.6:** PRM Results for Dependent Variable-LTTIO ($S_2R_2$)

| *Independent Variables* | *Dependent Variable: LTTIO* | | | |
|---|---|---|---|---|
| | *Coefficient* | *Standard Error* | *Z Value* | *Prob. Z* |
| Constant | 2.33** | 1.09 | 2.14 | 0.032 |
| LPGDPI | 0.66*** | 0.36 | 1.85 | 0.064 |
| LPGDPO | –0.41* | 0.09 | –4.23 | 0.000 |
| LDIST | –0.34** | 0.14 | 2.31 | 0.020 |
| LERI | –1.83* | 0.05 | –36.51 | 0.000 |
| LINI | 0.42* | 0.09 | 4.66 | 0.000 |
| LINO | 0.20* | 0.02 | 7.03 | 0.000 |
| LTXI | 0.43* | 0.18 | 2.37 | 0.017 |
| LTXO | 0.41* | 0.02 | 17.01 | 0.000 |

$R^2$ = 0.94, Adjusted $R^2$ = 0.94, Model test F[8,96] = 222.86*

LR statistic = 36.74, Log-likelihood function = 93.66.

*Source:* Authors' estimation.

*Note:* *, **and ***imply that the coefficients are significant at 1%, 5% and 10% respectively.

However, the variables of interest here are INTI and INO. The results indicated that with the increase in the infrastructure for E-commerce in India and other countries, India's trade also goes up. This may be because the available infrastructure towards E-commerce in India and other SAARC countries reduces the transaction cost of international trade and thereby induces the B2B activities across countries. On the other hand, the positive effect of TXI and TXO may be due to the fact that with the increase in the volume of trade in the region, the tax revenue for all the countries has been rising.

**Table 7.7:** PRM Results for Dependent Variable-LEXI ($S_2R_2$)

| *Independent Variables* | *Dependent Variable: LEXI* | | | |
|---|---|---|---|---|
| | *Coefficient* | *Standard Error* | *Z Value* | *Prob. Z* |
| Constant | 7.18* | 2.05 | 3.50 | 0.000 |
| LPGDPI | –1.58** | 0.70 | –2.27 | 0.023 |
| LPGDPO | –0.47* | 0.13 | –3.47 | 0.000 |
| LDIST | –0.55* | 0.19 | 2.78 | 0.005 |
| LERI | –1.91* | 0.06 | –28.73 | 0.000 |
| LINI | 1.05* | 0.17 | 5.93 | 0.000 |
| LINO | 0.23* | 0.05 | 4.29 | 0.000 |
| LTXI | 1.22* | 0.37 | 3.31 | 0.000 |
| LTXO | 0.64* | 0.04 | 15.24 | 0.000 |

$R^2$ = 0.93, Adjusted $R^2$ = 0.93, Model test F[8,96] = 185.48*
LR statistic = 33.21, Log-likelihood function = 81.55.

*Source:* Authors' estimation.

*Note:* * and ** imply that the coefficients are significant at 1% and 5% respectively.

Analysis of Tables 7.7 reveals a similar result except for the fact that as PGDPI increases by one percent, India's export to SAARC countries declines by 1.58 percent. This indicates that as the purchasing power of the people of India increases, the domestic production caters to the domestic consumption, leaving the export to the SAARC nation lower. But the infrastructure for E-commerce in India promotes the export to the SAARC countries more than proportionately (elasticity of INI is 1.05) though the infrastructure in the trading partner country has a positive but proportionately lower effect on the export of India (elasticity of INO is 0.23). On the other hand, table 7.8 shows that with a one percent increase in TXI, the import of India declines by 0.48 percent. This may be due to the fact that the government of India has followed some restrictive policy when it comes to importing from SAARC countries. The impacts of all other explanatory variables are in line with the prediction of the theory (though some of them are insignificant).

**Table 7.8:** PRM Results for Dependent Variable-LIMO ($S_2R_2$)

| *Independent Variables* | *Dependent Variable-LIMO* | | | |
|---|---|---|---|---|
| | *Coefficient* | *Standard Error* | *Z Value* | *Prob. Z* |
| LPGDPI | 2.19* | 0.13 | 15.77 | 0.000 |
| LPGDPO | –0.08 | 0.16 | –0.54 | 0.588 |
| LDIST | –0.42** | 0.20 | –2.07 | 0.038 |
| LERI | –2.30* | 0.11 | –19.36 | 0.000 |
| LINTI | 0.09 | 0.07 | 1.25 | 0.210 |
| LINTO | 0.02 | 0.06 | 0.44 | 0.660 |
| LTXI | –0.48*** | 0.28 | –1.67 | 0.094 |
| LTXO | –0.02 | 0.02 | –0.79 | 0.431 |

$R^2$ = 0.93, Adjusted $R^2$ = 0.92, Model test F[8,96] = 192.73*
LR statistic = 21.98, Log-likelihood function = 72.24

*Source:* Authors' estimation.

*Note:* *, ** and ***implies that the coefficients are significant at 1%, 5%, and 10% respectively.

## 7.5 Conclusion

To conclude, it could be said that the regional trading bloc in the form of SAARC has not been that successful in its objective of greater economic cooperation by promoting cross border trade among the member countries. The share of the trade in SAARC is a meager one percent of the world trade. The expectation of the economically biggest member of the association, i.e., India, is also not met with. The higher economic growth rate of India is associated with higher trade with the SAARC countries (since the elasticity of total trade of India with the SAARC countries with respect to the per capita GDP of India is positive, it is 0.66). On the other hand, the growth of the other SAARC member countries has a negative effect on the total trade of India (the elasticity is negative, and it is 0.44). This implies that with the increase in income of the people of other SAARC countries than India, the people there are interested in importing from other countries than India. This may also be because of the import (from India) substitution policy of other SAARC countries. Even the decline of the bilateral exchange rate of Indian rupee vis-a-vis the currency of the other SAARC countries is not good enough to give the boost to the Indian export to the SAARC countries.

However, the silver lining for India lies with E-commerce. The study shows that with the increase in the infrastructure for E-commerce in India and other countries, India's trade with the SAARC nations also increases. This may be because the available infrastructure towards E-commerce in India and other SAARC countries reduces the transaction cost of international trade and thereby induces the B2B activities across countries. Infrastructure for E-commerce in India also promotes the export to the SAARC countries more than proportionately (elasticity is 1.05), but the infrastructure in the trading partner country has a positive but proportionately lower effect on the export of India (elasticity is 0.23). Similarly, the restrictions on E-commerce by the Indian government is not helping the Indian importer to raise the import with the SAARC countries (the elasticity of Indian import with respect to the taxes on international trade as a percentage of revenue is negative, it is 0.48). Thus, to sum up, it could be said that all the members of the SAARC have to promote E-commerce in the form of providing E-commerce infrastructure and reducing the tariff rates on E-commerce so that the cherished dream objective of SAARC is achieved.

## References

[1] Akram, H.W., M.D. Ciddikie and Khan, M.A. (2014). India's Trade relationship with SAFTA Countries: A Review. *Journal of Indian Research*, Vol. 2(1), pp. 46–58.

[2] Alberto, B. (2009). De Bonus Vetus OLS: Approximating the international trade-cost effects of red tape (unpublished paper). Available at https://works.bepress.com/alberto_behar/11/

[3] Ambrose, B. and Sundarraj, P. (2014). A Brief Analysis on India's Trade with SAARC Countries: Recent Trends. *Global Journal of Social Science, Economics,* Vol. 14(6), pp. 26–30.

[4] Bergstrand, J.H. (1985). The gravity equation in international trade: Some microeconomic foundations and empirical evidence. *The Review of Economic and Statistics,* Vol. 67, pp. 474–481.

[5] Binh, D.T.T., Doung, N.V. and Coung, H.M. (2011). Applying Gravity Model to analyse trade activities of Vietnam, pp. 1–24.

Available at http://www.freit.org/WorkingPapers/Papers/TradePatterns/FREIT639.pdf.

[6] Chowdhury, M.B. (2005). Trade Reforms and Economic Integration in South Asia: SAARC to SAPTA. *Applied Econometrics and International Development*, Vol. 5(4), pp. 23–40.

[7] Das, S. and Pohit, S. (2006). Quantifying transport, regulatory and other costs of Indian overland exports to Bangladesh. *WORLD ECONOMY-LONDON,* Vol. 29(9), pp. 1227–1242.

[8] Do, T.T. (2006). A gravity model for trade between Vietnam and twenty-three European countries (Thesis). Department of Economics and Society, Dalarna University, Sweden, pp. 1–26.

[9] Hassan, M.K. (2000). Trade Relations with SAARC Countries and Trade Policies of Bangladesh. *Journal of Economic Cooperation*, Vol. 21(3), pp. 99–151.

[10] Hertel, T.W. and Mirza, T. (2009). The Role of Trade Facilitation in South Asian Economic Integration. In *Study on Intraregional Trade and Investment in South Asia*. Manila: Asian Development Bank, pp. 12–39.

[11] International Trade Statistics (2015). World Trade Organization, Centre William Rappard.

[12] Kaur, S. and Nanda, P. (2010). India's Export Potential to Other SAARC Countries: A *Gravity Model Analysis. Journal of Global Economy,* Vol. 6(3), pp. 167–184.

[13] Khandare, V. and Babar, S.N. (2012). Trade among SAARC Countries: With Special Reference to India. *IJIBF*, Vol. 2(1), pp. 127–137.

[14] Krugman, P.R. and Obstfeld, M. (2005). International economics: Theory and Practice (7th ed.). Boston, MA: Addison-Wesley.

[15] Mahaswararao, K. (2015). Growth of India's trade with individual SAARC Countries. *International Journal of Academic Research,* Vol. *2*(1), pp. 102–110.

[16] Martínez-Zarzoso, I. and Nowak-Lehmann, D.F. (2004). MERCOSUR-European Union Trade: How important is EU Trade Liberalisation for MERCOSUR's Exports? In Center for European, Governance and Economic Development Research Discussion Papers, Göttingen, Germany: University of Gottingen, Department of Economics, pp. 1–30.

[17] Nguyen, B.X. (2010). The Determinants of Vietnamese Export Flows: Static and Dynamic Panel Gravity Approaches. *International Journal of Economics & Finance,* Vol. 2(4), pp. 122–129.

[18] Panagariya, A. (2000). E-commerce, WTO and Developing Countries. Policy issues in International Trade and Commodities, Study Series, No. 2, UNCTAD, UN, Geneva 21, Switzerland.

[19] Rahman, M.M. (2009). A panel data analysis of Bangladesh's trade: the gravity model approach. University of Sydney, pp. 1–54. Retrieved from: http://www.etsg.org/ETSG2003/papers/rahman.pdf

[20] Ranajoy and Tathagata (2006). Does the Gravity Model Explain India's Direction of Trade? A Panel Data Approach, Working Paper No. 2006–09–01, IIM, Ahmedabad, pp. 1–18.

[21] Reserve Bank of India Bulletin (2016). Reserve Bank of India, Mumbai.

[22] Sohn, Chan-Hyun and Lee, Hongshik (2010). Trade Structure, FTAs, and Economic Growth. *Review of Development Economics,* Vol. 14(3), pp. 683–698.

[23] Sultan, M. and Munir, K. (2015). Export, Import and Total Trade Potential of Pakistan: A Gravity Model Approach. *MPRA Paper No. 66621*, pp. 1–34. Available at https://mpra.ub.uni-muenchen.de/66621/.

[24] Taneja, N. (2007). India's Informal Trade With Sri Lanka. *Working Papers id:953, eSocial* Sciences, pp. 1–25.

[25] Vadra, R. (2012). A study on India's trade relationship with SAARC countries. *International Journal of Indian Culture and Business Management*, Vol. 5(1), pp. 15–36. https://doi.org/10.1504/IJICBM.2012.044016

[26] Venketesh, M. (2006). A Study on India's Trade relationship with SAARC Countries with special reference to SAPTA, pp. 1–207. Available at https://dyuthi.cusat.ac.in/jspui/bitstream/purl/47/3/Dyuthi-T0281.pdf.

[27] Weerahewa, J. (2009). Impact of Trade Facilitation Measures and Regional Trade Agreements on Food and Agricultural Trade in South Asia, Working Paper Series, (No. 69), pp. 1–39.

[28] Wilson, J.S. and Otsuki, T. (2007). Regional Integration in South Asia: What Role for Trade Facilitation? Policy Research Working Paper, (No. 4423), pp. 1–37.

[29] World Development Indicator CD ROM (2020). World Bank, Washington DC.

[30] www.chemical-ecology.net.accessed on 25th January 2021.

[31] Zaheer, R. (2013). The Economic Performance of SAARC Member Countries. *Research on Humanities and Social Sciences*, Vol. 3(5), pp. 201–214.

CHAPTER 8

# Impact of Indian Power Sector Reform on the Economy of North-Eastern Region

**Sanjukta Niyogi and Soumyananda Dinda**

## 8.1 Introduction

Power sector becomes a vital input for economic growth and development. Energy plays a major role for betterment of the economic condition in the initial period. Since before liberalisation the Govt. of India undertakes most important part of economy such as industrial sectors, telecommunications, and as well as electricity and created "natural monopoly". Energy plays the role of golden thread to grow up an economy. Vital issues in electricity market were excess demand over supply. Since pre liberalisation era India suffered from widespread shortage of electricity supply hence insufficient generation capacities of State Electricity Boards (SEBs) units. The Govt. initiates to expand the generation capacity which face resource constraint that sluggish whole system.

In global scenario worldwide power sector undergo with a radical restructuring change. UK and USA are the pioneer and most highlighted example in radical changes. After that some developing countries such as Chile, Brazil, Pakistan Argentina, Philippines etc. follow restructuring of change in power sector. After economic liberalisation in 1991, the Govt. of India welcomes private sectors to electricity generation and distribution sector to encouraged greater private investments for increasing efficiency. Electricity is included in the concurrent list III under seventh schedule. The basic concerns of Power Ministry are policy formation, investment projection, implementation of such policies, creation proper human capital and finally administering the thermal hydro power plant generation, transmission, and its distribution. The section 66(178) of the Indian Electricity Act 2003, states that it is responsibility of a regulatory body to develop a market for electricity. Accordingly, EA2003, CERC took an initiative to develop a common market for electricity trading. Electrical energy market enables us to buy and sold electrical energy alike any other commodities.

In India two power exchanges namely Indian Energy Exchange (IEX) and Power Exchange of India Ltd. (PXIL) are functioning with the regulation of Central Electricity Regulatory Commission (CERC). Power Exchange market: Indian Power exchange started his journey from 2008. Generally, Nord Pool power exchange (Elspot) is the standard power exchange design. Electricity traded through two power exchange market such as Indian Energy Exchange Ltd. (IEX) and Power Exchange India Ltd. (PXIL). Power exchange pattern varies country to country or between different market designs depending on market structures. In the case of Indian power market, it is mostly excess demand and deficient supply in nature. In India power sector generation mainly mixed in nature and Power exchange (PX) is a trading centres where various power suppliers submit their most suitable price and submit their saleable quantity bids. Similarly, buyers are submitted their willingness to purchases. Trading of electricity unlike the others commodity trading efficiency of the market mainly depends on transparency and liquidity power trading via exchange enables the traders to compare all demand price situations and choose the optimum price quantity situations. In electricity market transacting power over gird and all technical clearances are done by Transaction System Operator (TSO). Power exchange trading directly operates day-ahead market or hour-ahead market.

North East region in India has very unique strategic nature, and the borders with neighbouring countries such as Nepal, Myanmar, China, Bangladesh, Bhutan etc. North Eastern part of India is much enriched in natural resources and biodiversity. Since from independence the North eastern region faces various challenges such as very low stagnant growth rate, low economic political development etc. As a result, Govt. of India has taken several economic policies such as Look East Policy, in later period it is Act East Policy etc. The SDG 7 focuses that an economy should have to ensure access to affordable, reliable, sustainable, and modern clean energy for all. To achieve this target Govt. has taken various power reform policies through which renewable energy generation take place and very slowly a clean energy trading market established over the world. More over cross border energy trading gives a chance to neighbouring South Asian countries to integrate their markets which provide a possibility to be facilitated with reliable lower cost electricity consumptions.

India's Look East Policy is an initiative to build extensive socio-economic and strategic relationships others and increasing cooperation with Southeast Asia in post-Cold war period. In 1992 former Prime Minister of India P.V. Narasimha Rao has been launched the Look East policy to achieve some targets such as increasing political contacts, economic integration as well as foreign security cooperation with countries of Southeast Asia. The Look East policy has some several major objectives with in which fourth objective is development of North-eastern region. One major Goal of Look East policy is reducing regional disparity in India. Since independence North-Eastern states were lag behind in respect of economic development. As a result, various unrest happened there. Through Look East policy India represent that region not like *cul-de-sac* rather as a gateway to East. There by various policy have been taken to link between North-Eastern region with Southeast Asia. Such as other development policies electricity reform Policies have very negligible impact on some states in North-Eastern region whereas in some states in North-East region also have a significant impact. This study focuses on the impact of power sector reform in North-east part of India; however, we are looking for analyse impact of power sector reform in overall India. As a result of power reform policies, a very potential energy market is emerging across the five regions especially North-Eastern region. This paper attempts to investigate whether energy sector reform and Look-East policy interlinked or not.

## 8.2 Objective of the Study

The basic objective of this paper is to examine whether the economy significantly changed or not in North-Eastern region of India after implementation of various reform policies in Indian Power sector.

## 8.3 Literature Review

Bhattacharyya (2005) has highlighted evaluation of this act. This act has been enacted to increasing efficiency through competitive structure that consists of multi-buyers and multi-sellers and some sort of retail competition and provides consumers certain supply choice. This act has tried to reduce cross-subsidy through promoting captive generators. Captive power act as a potential threat to maintaining cross-subsidies, hence for cross-subsidies customer it seems cheaper to build own captive station. Agrawal *et al.* (2017) focus on effects of Electricity Act (EA) on distribution, generation as well as transmission sectors. In case of power generation sector delicensing was started through this act thus any private company can generate electricity without any license if the company fulfils technical code as mention in grid system. In transmission sector has National Load Dispatch Centres, Regional Load Dispatch centres, State Load Dispatch Centres mainly to control grid system when intra and interstate transmission occurred. To ensure efficient inter-state transmission system Central Transmission Utility was provisioned. The main role of transmission utility played was to maintain the coordination between state transmission utilities and generation companies and other stock holders. To increase private participation in distribution segment this act introduces distribution franchises as well as multiple licensees, wholesale markets. Later section of their paper they are analysis the importance of implementing Electricity Amendment Bill, 2014. This bill consolidates all the previous acts such as Electricity Act (1910), Electricity (supply) Acts, 1948 and Electricity Regulatory Commission Act (1998), Electricity Act (2003). This bill implemented mainly to introduce competition in distribution segment through bifurcation of carriage and content. Whereas carriage is physical distribution network through which electricity flows from one point to another for end use while content implies the electricity which comes through distribution channel for our end use.

The renewable sources of energy are promoted in India through various govt. fiscal policies accordance to Singh (2007) in fiscal policies tax incentives promote purchase of electricity generation through renewable energy sources. The enactment of Electricity Act (2003) has further support to renewable energy by mentioning state should declared own renewable portfolio obligation accordance to their renewable capacity. A market for national tradable renewable energy should form alike some developed countries that includes green certificates, renewable energy credits etc. India has set a gigantic target in National Action Policy on Climate Change (NAPCC) 15 percent of electricity via renewable energy sources by 2020. Shrimali and Tirumalachetty (2013) show in their paper to achieve these targets Govt. has launched Energy certificates which has a market-based mechanism main goal was encourage renewable investments and developments of renewable energy market.

The worldwide increased use of fossil fuel over the green energy has led to enhance greenhouse gas emission which leads to climate change. Chandel *et al.* (2015) has studied mainly the immediate issues in energy sector is supply shortage, that deficient supply may fulfil with renewable energy and through the condition of renewable sector under the nation action plan on climate change (NAPCC). Under this plan eight different "National Mission" was taken such as National Solar Mission, National Mission for Enhanced Energy Efficiency, National Mission on Sustainable Habitat, National Mission on Strategic Knowledge for Climate Change etc. The study shows solar energy has potential capacity 30–40 $km^2$, high-quality wind potential at 80 m turbine hub and 19.7 GW small hydro. To reduce dependency from fossil fuel and decrease carbon emission these vast potentials should be exploited effectively. To promote electricity generation from renewable sources, Government of India has taken various fiscal policies and preferential tariff and also implement various tax incentives.

NAPCC envisages renewable energy to constitute approximately 15 percent of the energy mix of India by 2020. In November 2010, to achieve this gigantic target, Indian Ministry of Power launched Renewable Energy Certificates (REC). Gupta and Purohit (2013) mainly investigate mechanism and overview of REC market in India. REC is mainly a market-based instrument. REC is designed to meet up mismatch between availability of renewable electricity and the requirement of the obligated entities to meet their renewable purchase obligation (RPO). RECs trading has been happened in India till from 2011. In India performance of RECs measured by cost competitiveness, decentralized distributed generation. Data of geographical distribution of registered capacity is skewed towards some limited state other hand some state such as Maharastra (23 percent), Tamil Nadu (27 percent), Uttar Pradesh (22 percent) and other some state should review their policies. At present 3.4 percent only of estimated potential is registered under REC.

To address inadequacy, inequity, and climate change issues of energy sector, India should move through a energy-efficient pathway. According to Balachandra (2009), India has substantial progress in improving energy efficiency that showed reduction of energy intensity of GDP.

## 8.4 Background

In 2003 for over come under performing sectors a new act come into force Electricity Act (EA), a single market oriented progressive movement mainly taken for generating more competition, accountability commercial viability in the electricity market. After this bold activity several further policies followed such as National Electrification Policy in 2005, national tariff policy integrated energy policy, Rural electrification policy, Integrated Energy Policy, 2006, Hydro Power Policy, 2008. Energy Conservation Act on 2001 focused on clean energy as well as central govt introduce a very important investment scheme in this year Accelerated Power Development Programme and after this a more incentives-based programme Accelerated Power Development and Reform Programme (APDRP) in 2003. APDRP has several targets such as strong financial viability, aggregate technical and commercial loss reduction up to 15%, increasing customer satisfaction, improve reliability and quality of power supply, through computerised make system more transparent.

The Rural electrification Policy (2006) launched with a goal quality and reliable power supply for all household by the year 2009 at a reasonable rates and minimum lifeline consumption of 1 unit per household per day as by year 2012.

### 8.4.1 *Recent Reform Policy*

In 2015, the Govt. of India has taken a new scheme Integrated Power Development Scheme. The main motive behind this scheme was increasing strengthen of sub transmission network through metering,

IT application, customer care services, provisioning of solar panel. In that year another policy 'Prakash Path'—'Way to Light'—The National Led Programme was launch; the main objective of this programme was distributing LED bulbs and decrease both power consumption and cost. Ujwal Discom Assurance Yojana (UDAY) was started in November, 2015. The objective of this policy was improved operational and financial condition of State-owned Power Distribution Companies (DISCOMs) through reduce the interest burden, reduce power loss in distribution sector, reduce cost of power and lastly through increase efficiencies of DISCOMs.

In 2016, Ministry of Power, Govt. of India has taken another policy Pradhan Mantri Jan Ujjwala Yojana to distribute free LPG connections to the women belonging to 5 crore BPL families across the whole country with EMI facility will also be available for stove and refill cost.

In 2017 through Pradhan Mantri Sahaj Bijli Har GharYojana 'Saubhagya' scheme main target was provide electricity to all households in India by December 2018. Rural Electrification Corporation proposed Power Asset Revival through Warehousing and Rehabilitation (PARIWARTAN) which is one of resolution routes of Scheme of Asset Management and Debt Change Structure (SAMADHAN).

In 2018, Govt. of India has taken Kisan Urja Surakshaevam Utthaan Mahabhiyan (KUSUM) Scheme for farmer. In this scheme Govt. provides subsidy on setting up solar power plants on their barren land and use that generated energy as well as farmer call sell excess power to distribution companies through grid set up and, in this way, they can earn additional income.

The gains from trade theory are also applicable in case of power trading. In the case of electricity trading, with in India North-East and their neighbouring Asian countries have huge unused potential energy trading hub. In recent times North Eastern region eight states including neighbouring Asian countries start increasing economic growth in energy sector as a result of improving connectivity network(infrastructure), rapid growth in supply chain as well as production sectors, with this a trending heightened demand for clean renewable source of energy. In the demand supply scenario near North Eastern Region Bangladesh is the country which has largest population with combining highest gross domestic product (GDP), over exceed the combining sum of Bhutan, Nepal, Myanmar, and the North Eastern Region. Since the North Eastern Region has a very low per capita income in respect to other region in India, this region has a huge potential to grow and increasing economic activities as well as energy consumption. In Bhutan there is abundant hydro power and consumption on electricity per capita was 3,415 kilowatt-hours (kWh) per person in 2015, recently India starts importing power from Bhutan through synchronise transmission line.

## 8.5 Data Sources and Methodology

In this paper we are considering secondary data from EPW research Foundation. The panel data for seven states such as Assam, Arunachal Pradesh, Manipur, Meghalaya, Mizoram, Nagaland, Tripura are being analysed in this study. The data from the year 1990 to 2018 has been considered in this study. Here the total data set are divided in to two parts. First part is Pre-reform era, from the year 1990 to 2004. Second part is Post reform era from the year of 2005 to 2018. Since in the history of power sector reform policies, the Electricity Act (2003) have led the role of a significant instigator of major changes in the power sector. Hence to capture the real changes in this study the total time period is segregated in two parts first before implication of this policy (National Electrification Policy in 2005) since from initial time period i.e., 1990 and the second part is after implementation of this policy from the year of 2005 to 2018.

For analysis purpose this study uses the following model:

$$y_t = \alpha + \beta x_t + \varepsilon_t$$

Where $y$ and $x$ are dependent and independent variables, and $\varepsilon$ is the disturbance term, suffix $t$ denotes time (year). Now, $x_t$ could be a dummy variable and it can be defined as $x_t = 1 \text{ for } t \geq 2005,$ zero, otherwise.

For the study purpose, this paper has considered five variables such as Installed capacity (in MW), generation (in GWh), Transmission (ckt KMs), Energy Sold (in GWh), Per capita energy Consumption (in GWh).

For Panel data analysis this study uses the following model:

$$y_{it} = \alpha + \beta x_{it} + \varepsilon_{it}$$

Where $y$ and $x$ are dependent and independent variables, and $\varepsilon$ is the disturbance term, suffix $t$ denotes time (year) and $i$ denotes the cores sectional ID. Now, considering Electricity Act 2010, $x_{it}$ could be a dummy variable and it can be defined as $x_{it} = 1 \text{ for } t \geq 2011$; zero, otherwise.

For the study purpose, this paper has considered five variables such as Installed capacity (in MW), generation (in GWh), Transmission (ckt KMs), Energy Sold (in GWh), Per capita energy Consumption (in GWh).

Table 8.1 shows the descriptive statistic of all variables in North-Eastern region during post reform period. In the case of installation capacity mean is 1664.94 MW. Installation capacity reaches highest in the year of 2017 that is 2141.38 MW and it goes lowest in the year of 2007 that is 1380.49 MW. Standard Deviation of installation capacity is 214.57 MW. Mean of generation, transmission and energy sold lastly per capita consumption are 4743.89 GWh, 267389.2 cktkms, 7535.34 GWh, 13127.98 GWh respectively. North-Eastern region has achieved highest generation during 2013 that is 5761.97 GWh. Both installation capacity and generation have very negligible growth rate such as 2.18 percent, 4.97 percent. Whereas average per-capita growth rate is 7.06 percent, and average growth rate of energy sold is 8.42 percent. Transmission also has a very significant average growth rate (6.93 cktkms). Average annual growth rate during post reform is shown in Figure 8.1.

All variables in horizontal axis and average growth rate in vertical axis are being measured in the above chart. Here the post reform growth rate is being presented through bar diagram. Energy sold has largest percentage growth rate in post-reform era where as installation capacity has lowest percentage growth rate among five variables.

In the Table 8.2, Pre-reform (1990–2004) and post-reform (2005–2018) scenario are visible. To examine whether mean difference significant or not paired t-test is used. From Table 8.2, it is observed that mean difference of all variables between two periods are positive and significant. Hence, it is found that all variables are increased rapidly during post-reform period.

**Table 8.1:** Descriptive Statistics of the Variables in North-Eastern Region During 2005 to 2018

| *Summary Statistics* | *Installation Capacity (MW)* | *Generation (GWh)* | *Transmission (ckt*. Kms)* | *Energy Sold (in GWh)* | *Per capita Consumption (GWh)* |
|---|---|---|---|---|---|
| Mean | 1664.94 | 4743.89 | 267389.2 | 7535.34 | 13127.98 |
| Standard Deviation | 214.57 | 832.88 | 85603.56 | 2734.45 | 3020.79 |
| Minimum | 1380.49 | 2981.79 | 168616 | 3927.72 | 9214.41 |
| Maximum | 2141.38 | 5761.97 | 404674 | 11475.11 | 18127.3 |
| Range | 760.89 | 2780.18 | 236058 | 7547.39 | 8912.89 |
| Post reform Average growth rate (%) | 2.18 | 4.97 | 6.93 | 8.42 | 7.06 |

*Source:* Author's calculation. *Note:* * denotes cktkms in length of the circuit.

**Table 8.2:** Statistical Analysis Both of Pre-Reform Period and Post-Reform Period

| *Variables* | *Pre-reform Mean* | *Post-reform Mean* | *Mean Difference* | *Pre-reform SD* | *Post-reform SD* | *t-Stat.* |
|---|---|---|---|---|---|---|
| Installed Capacity (MW) | 1270.69 | 1664.94 | 394.25 | 130.59 | 214.57 | 5.76 |
| Generation (GWh) | 2785.321 | 4743.89 | 1958.57 | 214.49 | 832.88 | 8.24 |
| Transmission (ckt. Kms) | 140787.9 | 267389.2 | 126601.2 | 18195.46 | 85603.56 | 5.23 |
| Energy Sold (GWh) | 2950.633 | 7535.34 | 4584.71 | 516.04 | 2734.45 | 5.95 |
| Per-capita consumption (GWh) | 7860.81 | 13127.98 | 5267.17 | 2361.84 | 3020.79 | 5.08 |

*Source:* Author's calculation.

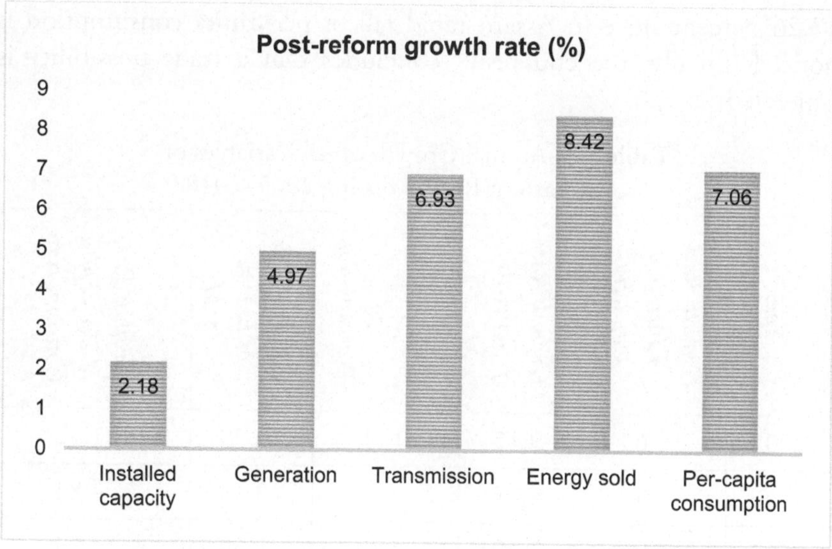


**Figure 8.1:** Post-reform Growth Rate of the Variables in North-Eastern Region during 2005–2018

*Source:* Author's own chart.

Since, in post-reform period all five variables in North Eastern region are increased significantly, which indicates the better performance in power sector during post-reform period in North Eastern region.

Growth rate of all variables over the year is shown in Table 8.3. It is observed that the growth rate of installation capacity is highest in the year of 2017 that is 21.34 percent. But growth rate of generation tends to decline after 2010; whereas per-capita consumption increases at higher rate. The average growth rate of per capita consumption is 7.095 percent which is much higher than other variables. The average growth rate of generations and installed capacity are 2.84 percent and 2.30 percent, much lower than per-capita consumption. The average growth rate of transmission and energy sold are 5.24 percent and 6.089 percent, both are very high in respect to generations and installed capacity. In post-reform period (2005–2018) generation all variables grow more than pre-reform period except installed capacity and consumption. Generation sector grows highest almost 4.10 percent higher than previous period. In the case of Consumption highest growth rate is 40.47 percent in 2017 but in 2018 it falls rapidly

13.26 percent since in Assam rapid fall of per-capita consumption is noticed. Finally, the end result concludes that a trade possibility is generated.

**Table 8.3:** Annual Growth of All Variables of North-Eastern Region during 2005–2018

| *Year* | *Growth Rate of Installed Capacity* | *Growth Rate of Generation* | *Growth Rate of Transmission* | *Growth Rate of Energy Sold* | *Growth Rate of Per-capita Consumption* |
|---|---|---|---|---|---|
| 2005 | 6.69 | 9.15 | 1.46 | 5.39 | 21.12 |
| 2006 | 7.46 | 4.73 | 0.376 | 12.18 | –4.84 |
| 2007 | –17.04 | 47.49 | 8.39 | 3.60 | 14.89 |
| 2008 | 1.81 | 3.38 | 0.58 | 9.99 | 5.48 |
| 2009 | 2.36 | 3.17 | –3.019 | 11.49 | 21.73 |
| 2010 | 2.66 | –0.94 | 29.72 | 9.96 | 16.03 |
| 2011 | NA | NA | NA | NA | NA |
| 2012 | NA | NA | NA | NA | NA |
| 2013 | 4.22 | 8.20 | 5.85 | 9.59 | 0.75 |
| 2014 | 1.00 | –1.24 | 0.95 | 11.74 | –38.31 |
| 2015 | –5.19 | –9.04 | 2.24 | 7.11 | 3.72 |
| 2016 | 3.86 | –10.48 | 0.23 | 2.30 | 19.22 |
| 2017 | 21.34 | 6.38 | 23.04 | 8.30 | 40.47 |
| 2018 | –13.33 | –0.51 | 2.38 | 3.23 | 13.27 |

*Source:* Author's calculation.

From this analysis it is concluded in North-Eastern region energy demand increases more than the power generation. Hence, there is an import possibility. That means a nascent tradable energy market generated there.

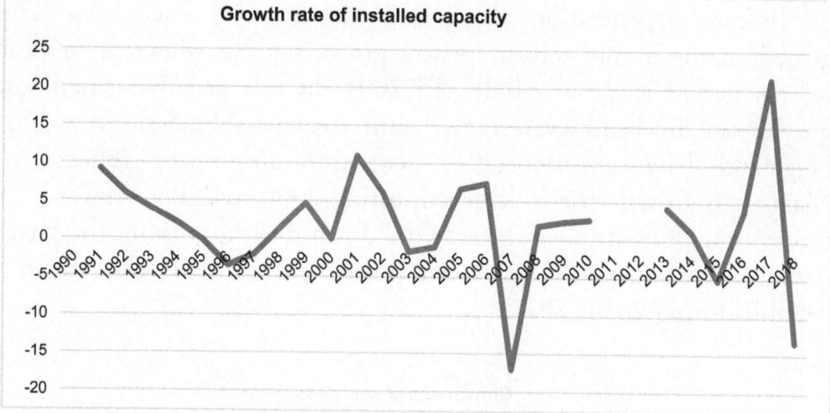


**Figure 8.2:** Growth Rate of Installed Capacity During 1990 to 2018
*Source:* Author's own chart.

In above diagram growth path of installed capacity is depicted. In the case of installed capacity pre reform period growth rate goes downward and fluctuating. But after 1996 it starts increasing. In 2007 installation growth rate goes to negative since from 2006 to 2007 with in the 7 States. Assam and Arunachal Pradesh have experienced slight reduction in installation capacity while in rest 5 states it was remains constant. Maximum growth is achieved during post reform period and in 2016–2017 it achieves maximum growth.

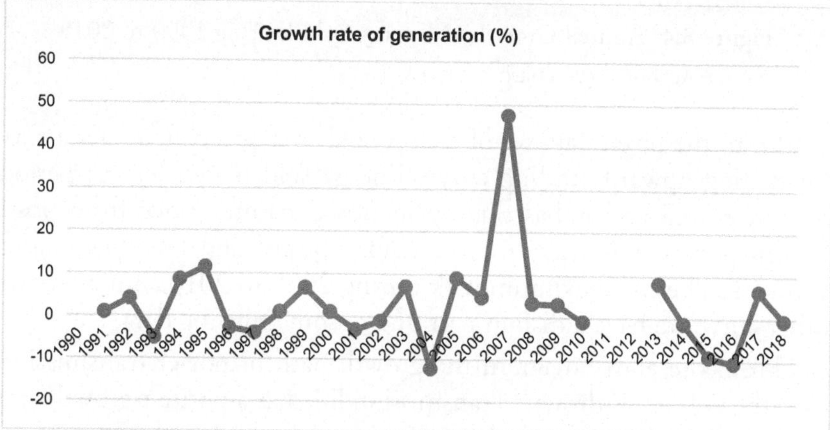


**Figure 8.3:** Growth Rate of Generation during 1990 to 2018
*Source:* Author's own chart.

In case of generation, the growth curve is very fluctuating. The growth paths in pre reform period grows slightly where as in post reform period its grow rapidly. In 2004 there is negative generation growth rate due to in seven states Assam, Arunachal Pradesh, Mizoram, Nagaland have experienced a reduction in power generation. Maximum growth rate is achieved during 2006 to 2008. However in recent time growth move towards the down direction. From the given data we have a disjoined generation growth curve due to some missing variable during 2011–2012.

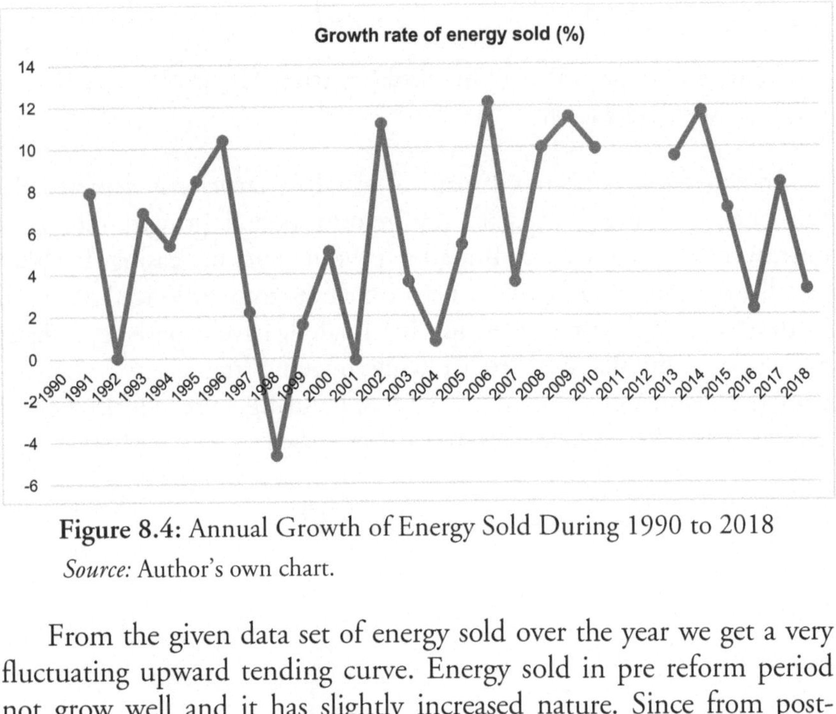


**Figure 8.4:** Annual Growth of Energy Sold During 1990 to 2018

*Source:* Author's own chart.

From the given data set of energy sold over the year we get a very fluctuating upward tending curve. Energy sold in pre reform period not grow well and it has slightly increased nature. Since from post-reform period, the growth curve tends upward and less fluctuations and its reaches its maximum pick during 2005 to 2015. But alike the other curve we have a disjoin part due to some missing data.

From the above diagram the growth path of power transmission over the year are is drown. Transmission line has a positive growth rate in the initial period up to 1998. In post reform period transmission growth line moves upward and again it become negative in the year of 2009 and in later period it moves upward.

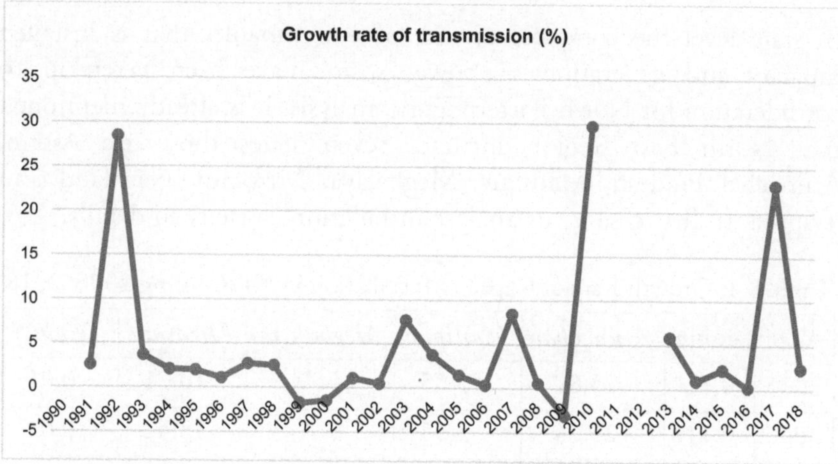


**Figure 8.5:** Annual Growth of Transmission During 1990 to 2018

*Source:* Author's own tabulation.

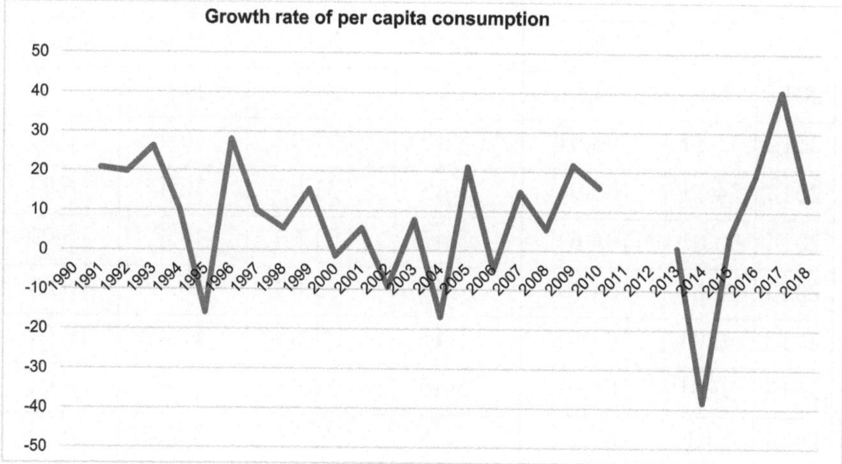


**Figure 8.6:** Annual Growth of Per-capita Consumption During 1990 to 2018

*Source:* Author's own chart.

In the case of per capita consumption growth rate is very fluctuating in pre reform period. Per-capita energy consumption goes upward in post reform period and its reached highest in the period of 2015 to 2017.

### 8.5.1 *State Level Analysis in the North-Eastern Region*

In state level the complete picture of two variables that is installed capacity and generation of power sector have been taken in to consideration for North Eastern Zone analysis. It is already mentioned that North East Region includes seven states those are Assam, Arunachal Pradesh, Manipur, Meghalaya, Mizoram, Nagaland and Tripura. In first case let us analyse installation capacity in details.

**Table 8.4:** Growth Rate of Capacity Installation in NER during 2005–2018

| *Year* | *Assam* | *Arunachal* | *Manipur* | *Meghalaya* | *Mizoram* | *Tripura* |
|---|---|---|---|---|---|---|
| 2005 | 0.11 | 25.8 | 3.95 | NA | 10.71 | 0.01 |
| 2006 | 0.11 | 26.74 | 3.95 | NA | 13.42 | 0.01 |
| 2007 | 2.11 | 45.24 | 5.45 | NA | 17.47 | 16.01 |
| 2008 | 27.11 | 45.24 | 5.45 | NA | 17.47 | 16.01 |
| 2009 | 27.11 | 67.42 | 5.45 | NA | 28.47 | 16.01 |
| 2010 | 27.11 | 78.83 | 5.45 | NA | 36.47 | 16.01 |
| 2011 | NA | NA | NA | NA | NA | NA |
| 2012 | 31.11 | 103.91 | 5.45 | 31.02 | 36.47 | 16.01 |
| 2013 | 34.11 | 103.9 | 5.45 | 31.03 | 36.47 | 16.01 |
| 2014 | 30.01 | 104.61 | 5.45 | 31.03 | 36.47 | 16.01 |
| 2015 | 30.01 | 104.61 | 5.45 | 31.03 | 36.47 | 16.01 |
| 2016 | 30.01 | 104.61 | 5.45 | 31.03 | 41.47 | 16.01 |
| 2017 | 30.01 | 104.61 | 5.45 | 31.03 | 36.47 | 16.01 |
| 2018 | 5.01 | 107.11 | 5.45 | 32.53 | 36.47 | 16.01 |

*Source:* Author's own tabulation.

In NER, among seven states Assam has highest installed capacity that is average capacity is 928.15 MW (from appendix) and followed by Meghalaya. Meghalaya has average installation capacity 243.51 MW. Nagaland has the lowest average installed capacity. Average Installed capacity of Nagaland is 22.54 MW. Tripura has third largest average installation capacity, that is 123.82 MW. In 2017, Assam has achieved highest average installation capacity in compare to others year that is 1300.48 MW. In Assam, installation capacity grows significantly after 2008 and its reached highest rate in 2013. In case of Meghalaya, installation capacity starts its growth journey after 2011 and reaches highest rate in 2018 that is 32.53 percent. In the case of Tripura Installation capacity growth rate is not changes from 2007 to 2018. Therefore, it is concluded that Nagaland, Manipur, Mizoram have to grow more in respect to installation capacity.

In case of power generation, Assam is the leading state in North-Eastern Zone. Assam has average power generation 2882.305 GWh as shown in Figure 8.7. Manipur has lowest average generation that is 10.67 GWh. In 2014 Assam and Arunachal Pradesh have achieved their highest average power generation such as 3378.85 GWh and 292.96 GWh. Meghalaya has second largest average power generation, that is 884.09 GWh.

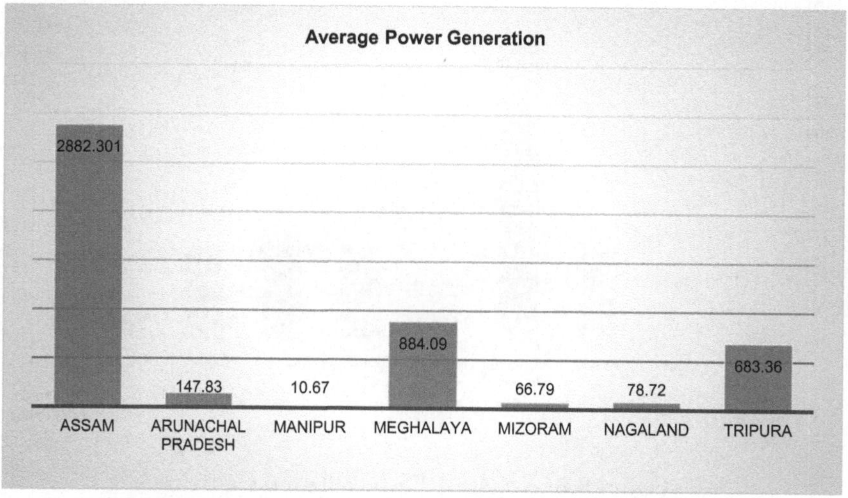


**Figure 8.7:** Average Generation During 2005 to 2018

*Source:* Author's own chart.

From Figure 8.7, it is observed that Assam has highest average power generation that is 2882.30 GWh whereas Manipur has lowest. Average power generation in Manipur is 10.67. Assam generate 388 times more than Manipur, which has smallest power generation. After Assam Meghalaya has second largest power generation just followed by Mizoram. Among all seven states, Assam, Meghalaya, Tripura have high power generation than others.

### 8.5.2 *State Level Analysis in The Case of RES*

After implementation of EA2003, in all over India generation of renewable Energy started. In later period September 2015 SDGs Goal #7 implemented. Our one major objective is analysing RES Power status in North-Eastern Zone. Hence in this section the study has taken the actual situation of RES generation and installation capacity in seven states separately. First, we will analyse installation scenario then generation scenario in seven states. After implementation of EA2003 in North Eastern Region renewable capacity installation starts from 2004–2005.

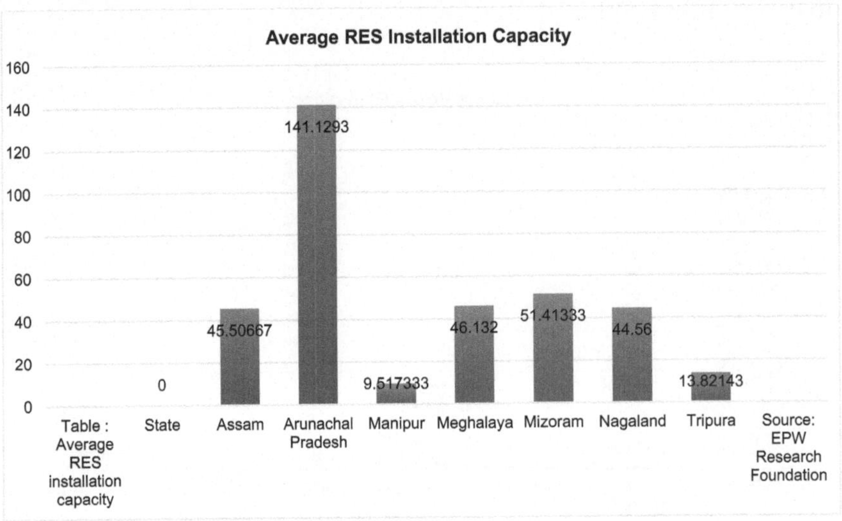


**Figure 8.8:** Average RES Installation Capacity

*Source:* Author's own chart.

From the above Figure 8.8, it is concluded that Arunachal Pradesh has the highest average installation capacity of RES, 141.1293 MW followed by Mizoram, Meghalaya and lastly Assam. Manipur has lowest average rate of RES installation capacity that is 9.517 MW.

It is found that Arunachal Pradesh has highest average RES generation units in compare to others since in Arunachal Pradesh huge hydro energy (153.75 GWh) is being generated after implementation of EA 2003, (Figure 8.8). Arunachal Pradesh has highest RES generation in 2014–2015 which is 292.96 GWh. Manipur has the lowest average RES generation rate (10.89 GWh). After Arunachal Pradesh, Nagaland has largest average generation of RES that is 89.52 GWh. Meghalaya has third highest average generation of RES that is 83.30 GWh. In the case of Tripura average generation growth rate is very poor that is 47.36 GWh. Hence, it is concluded that in respect to RES generation Arunachal Pradesh has very impressive picture. After Arunachal Pradesh, Nagaland, Meghalaya, Mizoram have moderate rate of average generation. Lastly, Manipur and Tripura have very poor scenario.

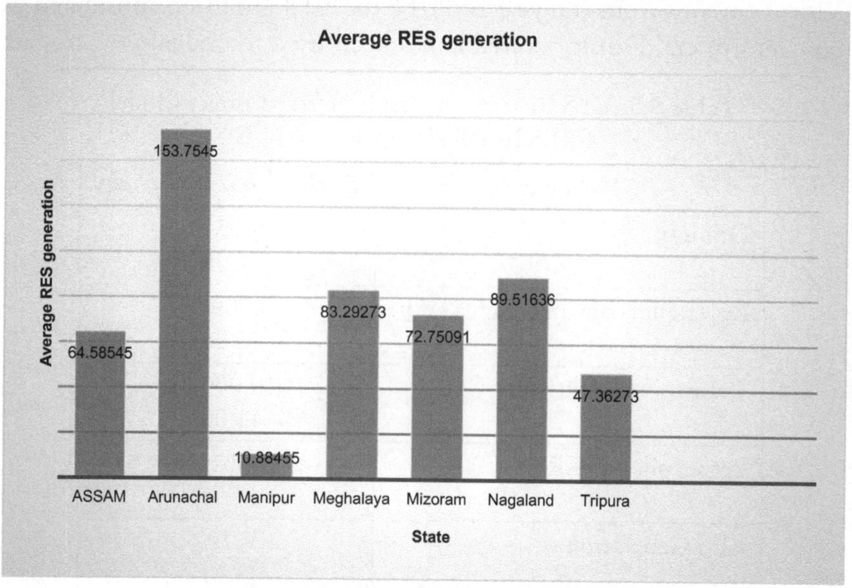


**Figure 8.9:** Average RES Generation

*Source:* Author's own chart.

Figure 8.9 shows a clear picture of average RES generation in NER seven states. Arunachal Pradesh has highest average generation of RES that is 153.76 GWh just followed by Nagaland. Meghalaya and Mizoram also have very impressive rate of average RES generation. Manipur has lowest rate of average RES generation that is 10.88 GWh just followed by Tripura.

### 8.5.3 *Panel Regression*

This study consists of total 97 observations for seven different states. Since this study has the Characteristic of cross-section and time-series, longitudinal/panel data analysis has to be implemented. Here for examine second phase of reforms in power sector the time series runs from 2000 to 2018. Another major reform policy is the Electricity Act (2010), which was implemented in 2010. Now the study attempts to identify its impacts. Before implementation of this policy the time periods are considered to be pre reform and after implementation the time period is to be considered as post reform time period. For the sake of simplification as well as for better measurement of effects of reform on economy from the year 2000 to 2010 are to be considered as pre-reform era and from the year of 2011 to 2018 are to be considered as post-reform era. Dummy variable has been used to evaluate the impact

**Table 8.5:** GLS Regression Result of Fixed Effect Model of RES Installed Capacity in N-E

| *Variables* | *RES_ installed_capacity* |
|---|---|
| Dummy | 8.2713<br>(1.08) |
| Per Capita consumption (GWh) | 0.009***<br>(6.98) |
| Transmission(cktKms) | 0.0001<br>(1.06) |
| Per Capita SDGRS | 0.001***<br>(3.95) |
| RES Generation | 0.107<br>(1.61) |
| Constant | –30.915**<br>(–1.97)) |
| Within $R^2$ | 0.7561 |
| Between $R^2$ | 0.9866 |
| Overall $R^2$ | 0.8410 |

*Note:* Figures in parentheses are t-values. '***', and '**' denote level of significance at 1% and 5% respectively.

*Source:* Author's own Tabulation using STATA software.

of specific energy policy related to power sector reform in India. Dummy variable takes the value one for the years of post-reform period and the value zero for the years of pre-reform era.

The panel regression has been done and represented in the tabular form. The result of Hausman $\chi^2$ Test suggests Fixed Effect Model for panel regression (see Table A8.1 in Appendix) and this study continues itas a preferred model for analysis purpose.

Table 8.5 The table represent the model of random effects GLS regression result where RES installed capacity is dependent variable and dummy, per capita consumption, transmission, per capita SDGRS, RES generation are independent variables. In this model with in all independent variable Per Capita consumption GWh per capita SDGRS, Constant are significant.

**Table 8.6:** GLS Regression Result of Fixed Effect Model of Per-Capita SDGRS Capacity in N-E

| *Variables* | *Per_Capita_SDGRS* |
|---|---|
| Dummy | 14890.09***<br>(6.65) |
| Per Capita consumption (GWh) | 0.7606<br>(1.50) |
| RES Installed Capacity (GWh) | 145.8321***<br>(5.33) |
| Constant | 37172.26***<br>(22.64) |
| Within $R^2$ | 0.6617 |
| Between $R^2$ | 0.5049 |
| Overall $R^2$ | 0.6197 |
| Prob.>F | 0.000 |

*Note:* Figures in parentheses are t-values. '***', and '**' denote level of significance at 1% and 5% respectively.

*Source:* Author's own Tabulation using STATA software.

Table 8.6 represents random effect GLS regression result where per capita SDGRS dependent variable and dummy, per capita consumption and RES installed capacity are independent variables.

**Table 8.7:** GLS Regression Result of Fixed Effect Model where Dummy is the Independent Variable N-E

| *Variables* | *Installed capacity)* | *Generation* | *Transmission* | *Energy Sold* | *per capita Consumption* | *RES Installation* |
|---|---|---|---|---|---|---|
| Dummy | 5.75*** (2.64) | 220.68** (2.93) | 22883.58*** (4.66) | 789.92*** (0.000) | 626.31 (1.52) | 39.98 (4.14) |
| Constant | 207.673 (15.75) | 518.842*** (11.06) | 24500.17 (1.60) | 611.549*** (6.34) | 1643.74*** (6.39) | 33.204 (4.88) |
| Within $R^2$ | 0.0556 | 00679 | 0.1556 | 0.1809 | 0.0192 | 0.1612 |
| Between $R^2$ | 0.0000 | | 0.0000 | 0.0000 | | 0.0786 |
| Overall $R^2$ | 0.0074 | 0.0134 | 0.0568 | 0.0735 | 0.0055 | 0.1244 |
| F Statistics | 6.95*** | 8.60*** | 21.74*** | 26.07*** | 2.31 | 17.11*** |
| Prob>F | 0.0095 | 0.0040 | 0.0000 | 0.0000 | 0.1314 | 0.0001 |

*Note:* Figures in parentheses are t-values. '***' and '**' denote level of significance at 1% and 5% respectively.

*Source:* Author's oḌwn Tabulation using STATA software.

The above table showed that all independent variables except Per Capita consumption GWh all are significant with dependent variables.

Table 8.7 represents GLS regression fixed effect model where dummy is the independent variable. For M1 column installed capacity of energy is dependent variable and reform has significantly positive effects on this. Power generation has played the role of dependent variable in M2 column. M2 shows that reform has significantly positive effect on power generation. In the case of M3 column, Transmission is dependent variable whereas reforms also have positively significant effects on power transmission. M4, M5 and M6 presents as energy sold, per-capita energy consumption and RES installation capacity treated as dependent variables as well. M4, M5, M6 show that reforms have significant effects on energy sold, per-capita energy consumption and RES installation capacity.

## 8.6 Major Findings

After completing the whole analysis, we want highlighted some major issues let us explain in details below:

1. After implementation of various power sector reform policies in north-eastern region have measurable changes. Installation capacity, generation, transmission, energy sold and lastly per capita consumption increased.
2. Energy Sold and Per capita Energy consumption grow much higher approximately 6.09% and 7.095%. Whereas power generation grows only 2.84%. Installation capacity grows 2.30%. Both generation and installation capacity are lower. Transmission also grows rapidly 5.24%.
3. Within north-eastern region among seven states impacts of power sector reform distributed unevenly. Arunachal Pradesh has the maximum positive changes. whereas Nagaland Tripura couldn't response significantly.
4. After the implementation of EA2003 renewable power generation started in NER from 2004–2005 onward.
5. After implementation of power sectors reform policies some variables are positively significant that means due to reform policies these sectors thrive. But some of sectors are not influenced by power sector reform policies.

6. In regional analysis our second variable is Power generation. Among all the 7 states Arunachal Pradesh has highest RES Power generation and RES Installation capacity whereas Manipur has lowest RES Power generation and RES installation capacity. After Arunachal Pradesh in Meghalaya, Mizoram, Assam Nagaland RES power generation and installation capacity moderately grow. But, in Manipur and Tripura growth rate of RES generation and installation capacity is triable. Since in respect of power generation regional disparity occur there is some possibilities of regional power trading of NER or nearing South Asian countries.

## 8.7 Conclusion

This study analyses the impact of power reform policies and energy market integration of NER of India with neighbouring state and countries. From this study it is found that in NER there is demand-supply unbalancing in respect to power. To mitigate increasing demand for power importation of power can take place from intra trading or inter trading. To improving energy connectivity and facilitating cross-countries energy trade depending on more improved and stable transmission ways and powergrides. The cross- border energy trading mainly depends on hydropower and gas pipelines. Within neighbouring state Myanmar has played vital contribution in energy trading since its significant reserve of potential natural gas and hydro power. To close coordination and reliable trade partnership among NER states and neighbouring South Asian and ASEAN countries it required firstly more stable efficient transmission lines and grides, secondly more stable efficient clean energy trading market. From 1st January 2022 Bhutan has taken initiative to trade in Day Ahead market through Durk Green Power. Recently in India through synchronise transmission power is imported from Bhutan. Power is exported from India to Nepal and Bangladesh through using of asynchronies transmission.

## References

[1] Agrawal, A. (2020). A Proposed Framework for Introduction Retail Competition in Indian Power Sector. *The Electricity Journal* 33, https://doi.org/10.1016/j.tej.2020.106786s

[2] Agrawal, A., Kumar, A. and Rao, T.J. (2017). Future of Indian Power Sector Reforms: Electricity Amendment Bill 2014. *Energy Policy,* 107, pp. 491–497.

[3] Ahma, F. and Alam, M.S., Assessment of Power Exchange Based Electricity Market in India. *Energy Strategy Reviews* 23, pp. 163–177.

[4] Balachandra, P., Ravindranath, D. and Ravindranath, N.H. (2009). Energy efficiency in India: Assessing the policy regimes and their impacts. *Energy Policy* 38, pp. 6428–6438.

[5] Bhatt, B. and Singh, A. (2020). Power Sector Reforms and Technology Adoption in the Indian Electricity Distribution Sector. *Energy*, pp. 1–42.

[6] Bhattacharyya, S.C. (2004). The electricity act 2003: will it transform the Indian Power Sector? *Utility Policy* 13, pp. 260–272.

[7] Cheng, C.Y., L, Y.J., Murray, G., Noh, Y. and urpelation J. (2020). Vested Interests: Examining the Political Obstacles to Power Sector Reform in Twenty Indian States. *Energy Research and Social Science,* 70, pp. 1–12.

[8] Chandel, S.S., Shrivastva, R., Sharma, V. and Ramasamy, P. (2015). Overview of initiative in renewable energy sector under the national action plan on climate change in India. *Renewable and Sustainable Energy Reviews* 54, pp. 866–873.

[9] Dubash, N.K. and Rajan, S.C. (2001). Power Politics: Process of Power Sector Reform in India. *Economic and Political Weekly,* Vol. 36(35), pp. 3367–3390.

[10] Gotzens, F., Heinrichs, H., Horsch, J. and Hofmann, F. (2019). Performing Energy Modelling Exercise in a Transparent Way- The Issue of data Quality in Power Databases. *Energy Strategy Reviews* 23, pp. 1–12.

[11] Goyal, M. and Jha, R. (2008). Introduction of renewable energy certificates in the Indian scenario. *Renewable and Sustainable Energy Review* 13, pp. 1395–1405.

[12] Goyal, M. and Jha, R. (2009). Introduction of Renewable Energy Certificates in The Indian Scenario. *Renewable and Sustainable Energy Reviews* 13, pp. 1395–1405.

[13] Gupta, S.K. and Purohit, P. (2013). Renewable Energy Certificates Mechanism in India: A Preliminary Assessment. *Renewable and Sustainable Energy Reviews,* 22, pp. 380–392.

[14] Harmsen, R., Moth, L. and Kumar, A. (2014). Applicability of Energy Saving Obligation to India Electricity Efficiency Efforts. *Energy Strategy Reviews,* pp. 298–306.

[15] Jahangiri, M., Haghani, A., Shamsabadi, A.A. and Mostafaeipour, A. (2019). Feasibility Study on the Provision of Electricity and Hydrogen for Domestic Purpose in the South of Iran Using Grid-Connected Renewable Energy Plants. *Energy Strategy Reviews* 23, pp. 23–32.

[16] Kishore, L. and Kumar, S. G.V. (2018). Operational and Financial Performance Optimization of Power Distribution Utilities in India. *International Journal of Pure and Applied Mathematics*, Vol. 119(15), pp. 1559–1566.

[17] Lal, S. (2019). Can Good Economics Ever Be Good Politics? Case Study of the Power Sector in India. Economic and Political weekly, Vol. 40, 7, pp. 649–656.

[18] Makhijani, A. (1977). Energy Policy for Rural India. *Economic and Political weekly*. 33/34, Vol. 12, pp. 1451–1464.

[19] Narula, K. (2013). Renewable Energy Certificates (Res) in India—A Performance Analysis and Future Outlook. *Renewable and Sustainable Energy Reviews* 27, pp. 654–663.

[20] Singh, A. (2009). A market for renewable energy credits in the Indian Power Sector. *Renewable and Sustainable Energy Reviews* 13, pp. 643–652.

[21] Shrimali, G. and Tirumalachetty, S. (2013). Renewable Energy Certificates Markets in India- A Review. *Renewable and Sustainable Energy Reviews* 26, pp. 702–716.

[21] Tishler, A., Newman, J., Spekterman, I. and Woo, C.K. (2006). Cost-benefit analysis of reforming Israel's electricity industry. *Energy Policy* 34, pp. 2442–2454.

[22] Upadhyaya, A.K. (2000). Power Sector Reforms: India Experience and Global Trends. *Economic & Political Weekly*, Vol. 35(12), pp. 1023–1028.

# Appendix

**Table A8.1:** Hausman Test

| *Variable* | *(b) Fixed Effect* | *(B) Random Effect* | *(b-B) Difference* | *Sqrt (diag(V_b-V_B))* |
|---|---|---|---|---|
| Dummy | 8.918385 | 9.064027 | –.1456425 | 3.594982 |
| Per Capita-s | .0092316 | .0079455 | .0012861 | .0010286 |
| Transmission-s | .0001089 | .0001125 | –3.57e–06 | .0000863 |
| Per capita SDGRS | .0010926 | .1022564 | .0047531 | .0425416 |

*Source:* Author's own tabulation using STATA software.

Table A8.1 represents the result of Hausman $\chi^2$ Test for the underlying model (i.e., for Model 4). This test assists researchers to determine whether to keep Fixed Effect Model or Random Effect Model as a preferred model for the model as generated in this study. The respective result demonstrated that chi2(3) = 1.95 which is insignificant. Since Chi 2 insignificant in this study the null hypothesis is rejected and alternative hypothesis is accepted. Thus, Random Effect Model is to be considered a good fit for this study.

SECTION – III

# Demography & Social Sector Issues

CHAPTER 9

# Health and Educational Performance: A Comparative Analysis between India and China

**Salim Shah, Pubali Das and Banalata Saikia**

## 9.1 Introduction

Health and education are the major social indicators in the economy which help to improve the human capital formation. Both the indicators have major role in achieving country's economic growth. In last three decades with increasing globalization, across developing countries, we can find an increase of interest in studying health and education system, comparing and contrasting their outcomes and interventions. Economic, political, social and cultural histories influence the way countries perceive, organize, and plan their systems like health and education. India and China, the world's two most populated countries, since their independence are experiencing significant demographic, social, and economic transformations. Both the countries have achieved their independence almost at the same time and were poor in terms of economic development consisting of higher levels of poverty, under nutrition, high mortality, and morbidity. Also, the literacy rate was very low in both the countries at the time of their independence. After independence, India adopted both socialistic and capitalistic approach, whereas China was totally socialistic in nature. The differences in the politico-administration of both the countries led in different trajectories for addressing the different vulnerabilities. Currently both the countries – India and China, which are equally large nations is going through rapid economic growth, urbanization and widening inequalities between rich and poor. However, India and China do not have similar political and administrative structure. Also, they are dissimilar in terms of the policies taken for population growth; heterogeneity and ethnic composition (Dummar & Cook, 2008).

The outcomes of the diverse approaches resulted in histrionic improvements in under nutrition, mortality and morbidity in the case of China, whereas, it was much more slow in the case of India. To meet a country's health needs in the most equitable and efficient manner, while remaining financially sustainable must be the basic objective of healthcare systems (Bhat & Jain, 2006). The far reaching changes employed by China to deal with socio-economic inequalities through radical land reforms and the guarantees for livelihood, food and housing, that were important determinants of health, was reflected in their advance in health status. India, on the other hand, did not address the question of inequality in a bigger way as China did. However, in China, during post 1979 there were reforms for which much of the social welfare system was dismantled. In case of routine services, the money charges consistently increased, but the trend was less in lower-income communities. The quality of care improved in wealthier rural areas, but not in poorer villages (Akin *et al.*, 2005). Also, India and China during their rapid social and industrial transformation faced similar challenges in education. During the late 1940s both the countries started building their national education systems under comparable conditions but differences owing to their historical perspectives, policy and strategies at the later phases have led them through different routes. China's achievements in improving basic educational attainment have been impressive. China has performed better than India in primary and secondary education along a broad range of access, quality, and delivery indicators. However, India though started late but has made great paces in basic education during the last few years. In case of secondary enrolments, both countries are far from 100 percent. In case of tertiary enrolment, the result shows a reverse observation as China exceeding India's enrolment ratios by the early 2000s (Goldman, *et al.*, 2008). Though, both the countries follow a general pattern for their education level but, these two countries differ a lot regarding their overall education structure, duration of different level, accessibilities of higher education, affiliation of institutions and so on (Palit & Guha, 2018). The Human Development Index (HDI), which measures the average achievements of a country in three basic aspects of human development i.e., health, knowledge and standard of living for India and China is shown in Table 9.1.

**Table 9.1:** Human Development Index for China and India; 1980–2020

| *Year* | *India* | *China* | *Disparity Index* | *World* |
|---|---|---|---|---|
| 1980 | 0.32 | 0.37 | –0.05 | 0.45 |
| 1990 | 0.39 | 0.46 | –0.07 | 0.53 |
| 2000 | 0.44 | 0.57 | –0.13 | 0.57 |
| 2010 | 0.52 | 0.66 | –0.14 | 0.62 |
| 2020 | 0.65 | 0.76 | –0.11 | – |

*Source:* World Development Indicators, World Bank Database.

Table 9.1 indicates that India had low human development till 2010, whereas China had low human development till 1990. China had medium human development till 2010 and had high human development in 2020, whereas India had medium human development in 2020. Out of 189 countries, India ranked 131 and China's ranked 85 in HDI 2020. It can be seen that the gap between human development index of India and China has been increasing up to the year 2010, which again slightly decreased in the year 2020.

Given the aspirations of India and China for becoming world class economies, it was imperative for them to have a world class health and education systems. Therefore, a study comparing the health and education systems of India and China with dissimilar politico-administrative structure along with varied achievements and challenges felt very useful. The present study attempts to make a comparative analysis of these two countries in the context of their health and educational performance by taking both the input and output indicators. As overtime the performance of China got better than India, the study tries to examine the reasons for such deviations observed in respect of health and educational performance over time in India and China. It also tries to examine whether the deviation is due to their differences in economic structure or not. India adopted a system of mixed economy after independence but was more socialistic in nature at the initial phases but went on approaching towards a capitalistic economy over time, especially after adopting neo-liberal economic policies in 1990s. In this context, the objective of the paper is to analyze and compare the health and education performance of India and China in terms of health and educational outcomes. Also, it analyzes and compares the health and education performance in terms of availability of health and educational infrastructure in India and China. The present study is descriptive in nature and based on secondary data, collected from World Bank Database, OECD Stat, China Statistical Year book, EPWRF etc. The study is expected to provide valuable insights into the forces shaping the inputs and outcomes of health and education of the two countries focusing their future needs and challenges.

## 9.2 A Demographic Overview of India and China since Independence

India and China have many things in common, having rapid economic development together with huge population. Besides, they cover one-third of the total world population. Prior to comparing health and educational performance of India and China, it is necessary to observe their respective demographic profile for understanding relevant social and economic issues for the countries concerned (Table 9.2). There is high transition in case of all the indicators over time and also there is high variation between the countries. The GDP growth rate in China is increasing though it was in negative trend in 1960. However, in 1990, India's GDP growth rate is more than that of China but it started decreasing again from 2000 and it is negative in 2020. Also, the gap of GDP growth rate between India and China which was highest in 1970 started decreasing from 1980 but again started increasing from 2000. However, in 2010 the gap was little less which again was huge in 2020. The gap of gross capital formation between both the countries also gradually increased and were quite high in 2020. It is worthy to note that India is having a larger share of younger population with a faster growth rate of the same. Before the year 2000, India's per capita income is more than China but after that China's per capita income increased at a double than India. In case of the urban population, the rate is higher in India than in China in 1960 and 1970. But it is less than China from 1980 and again it declined. Though, the dependency ratio of both the countries seems quite similar but after 1990, there is huge reduction in case of China. The total dependency ratio comprising of the number of working age individuals to non-working age individuals (i.e., children and the elderly) remains to be quite high for India over a long span of time from 1960 to 2010 (over and above 50 percent). However, the dependency ratio for China was also high till 2000 at more than 50 percent and after 2000, China could drastically reduce its dependency ratio in comparison to India. In this regard, the gap in dependency ratio between the two countries started increasing from 1970. It is only in 2020, when the gap started comes closer. From Table 9.2, it can be seen that this high ratio is primarily due to the high proportion of younger population of the age of below 15 years, which can be considered as potentially good for India as they join the labour force in near future.

China was having the largest share of world's population at 1.3 billion, in the year 2004 which was more than four times of the population of United States, the third populated country in the world. However, China's population growth rate has come down at only 0.8 percent between 1994 and 2004 and as per the Population Reference Bureau (PRB) projection, India is estimated to surpass China in total population by 2050. In case of sectoral composition, the countries perform well, but in India, agriculture and service sector is comparable with China and its performance is better in some of the years. In case of industrial sector, China's performance is significant, but India's performance is lower than China though it increased over time. The gap between India and China in case of contribution of industrial sector in GDP though decreased overtime but still is quite high. Fertility rate is declined in both the countries but it is more rapid in case of China. Thus, it is observed that in case of India though their performance in agriculture and service sectors are better in comparison to China but performance in industrial sector is worse in case of India with increasing youth population. So, India needs to pay attention to improving the industrial sector by utilizing the country's massive youth population.

**Table 9.2:** Demographic Profile of India and China; 1960–2020

| Years | Country | GDP | GDP Growth Rate | Per Capita Income (current US$) | Gross Capital Formation (% GDP) | Fertility Rate, Total (births per woman) | Population | Urban Population Growth | Dependency Ratio | Population Ages < 15 (% of total population) | Population Ages 15–64 (% of total population) | Population Ages > 64 and above (% of total population) | Agriculture Sector | Industry Sector | Service Sector |
|---|---|---|---|---|---|---|---|---|---|---|---|---|---|---|---|
| 1960 | India | 37029883875 | 3.72 | – | 15.69 | 5.9 | 450547675 | 2.6 | 77 | 41.042 | 55.807 | 3.15 | 41.31 | 20.83 | 38.78 |
| | China | 59716467625 | –27.27 | – | 22.81 | 5.75 | 667070000 | 2.05 | 77.02 | 39.822 | 56.489 | 3.689 | 23.18 | 44.39 | 32.43 |
| | Disparity Index | –22686583750 | 30.99 | – | –7.12 | 0.15 | –216522325 | 0.55 | –0.02 | 1.22 | –0.68 | –0.54 | 18.13 | –23.56 | 6.35 |
| 1970 | India | 62422483054 | 5.16 | 104.07 | 16.65 | 5.58 | 555189797 | 3.21 | 79.27 | 40.914 | 55.782 | 3.305 | 39.93 | 21.73 | 35.05 |
| | China | 92602973434 | 19.3 | 103.52 | 32.87 | 5.72 | 818315000 | 2.03 | 79.07 | 40.407 | 55.845 | 3.748 | 34.8 | 40.27 | 24.93 |
| | Disparity Index | –30180490380 | –14.14 | 0.55 | –16.22 | –0.14 | –263125203 | 1.18 | 0.20 | 0.51 | –0.06 | –0.44 | 5.13 | –18.54 | 10.12 |
| 1980 | India | 186325345089 | 6.74 | 241.68 | 21.08 | 4.82 | 698952837 | 3.89 | 75 | 39.248 | 57.143 | 3.609 | 33.06 | 25.34 | 33.81 |
| | China | 191149211575 | 7.83 | 151.51 | 34.61 | 2.61 | 981235000 | 5.16 | 68.38 | 35.936 | 59.39 | 4.674 | 29.63 | 48.06 | 22.31 |
| | Disparity Index | –4823866486 | –1.09 | 90.17 | –13.53 | 2.21 | –282282163 | –1.27 | 6.62 | 3.31 | –2.25 | –1.07 | 3.43 | –22.72 | 11.50 |
| 1990 | India | 320979026419 | 5.53 | 320.71 | 28.62 | 4.04 | 873277799 | 3.03 | 71.73 | 37.966 | 58.23 | 3.804 | 26.9 | 27.45 | 37.04 |
| | China | 360857912565 | 3.92 | 271.29 | 34.16 | 2.3 | 1135185000 | 4.31 | 52.02 | 28.59 | 65.78 | 5.63 | 26.58 | 41.03 | 32.38 |

| Years | Country | GDP | GDP Growth Rate | Per Capita Income (current US$) | Gross Capital Formation (% GDP) | Fertility Rate, Total (births per woman) | Population | Urban Population Growth | Dependency Ratio | Population Ages < 15 (% of total population) | Population Ages 15–64 (% of total population) | Population Ages > 64 and above (% of total population) | Agriculture Sector | Industry Sector | Service Sector |
|---|---|---|---|---|---|---|---|---|---|---|---|---|---|---|---|
| | Disparity Index | –39878886146 | 1.61 | 49.42 | –5.54 | 1.74 | –261907201 | –1.28 | 19.71 | 9.38 | –7.55 | –1.83 | 0.32 | –13.58 | 4.66 |
| 2000 | India | 468394937262 | 3.84 | 387.13 | 26.68 | 3.31 | 1056575548 | 2.54 | 64.18 | 34.726 | 60.909 | 4.366 | 21.61 | 27.33 | 42.73 |
| | China | 1211346869600 | 8.49 | 797.8 | 33.57 | 1.59 | 1262645000 | 3.65 | 46.2 | 24.789 | 68.399 | 6.812 | 14.68 | 45.54 | 39.79 |
| | Disparity Index | –742951932338 | –4.65 | –.410.67 | –6.89 | 1.72 | –206069452 | –1.11 | 17.98 | 9.94 | –7.49 | –2.45 | 6.93 | –18.21 | 2.94 |
| 2010 | India | 1675615335600 | 8.5 | 1170.08 | 40.22 | 2.58 | 1234281163 | 2.47 | 55.99 | 30.81 | 64.108 | 5.082 | 17.03 | 30.73 | 45.03 |
| | China | 6087163874510 | 10.64 | 3512.38 | 46.56 | 1.62 | 1337705000 | 3.26 | 36.49 | 18.66 | 73.266 | 8.074 | 9.33 | 46.5 | 44.18 |
| | Disparity Index | –4411548538910 | –2.14 | –2342.30 | –6.34 | 0.96 | –103423837 | –0.79 | 19.50 | 12.15 | –9.16 | –2.99 | 7.70 | –15.77 | 0.85 |
| 2020 | India | 2660245248867 | –7.25 | 1678.71 | 29.28 | 2.18 | 1380004385 | 2.3 | 48.66 | 26.161 | 67.265 | 6.574 | 18.32 | 23.52 | 48.89 |
| | China | 14722730697890 | 2.35 | 7556.25 | 43.54 | 1.7 | 1410929362 | 2.07 | 42.21 | 17.712 | 70.32 | 11.968 | 7.65 | 37.82 | 54.53 |
| | Disparity Index | –12062485449023 | –9.60 | –5877.54 | –14.26 | 0.48 | –30924977 | 0.23 | 6.45 | 8.45 | –3.05 | –5.39 | 10.67 | –14.30 | –5.64 |

*Source:* World Development Indicators, World Bank Database.

## 9.3 Dynamics of Health Performance in India and China

Both the countries India and China has implemented various health policies to improve the health system at their level. However, China is doing better for improving healthcare system than India over time. It may be due to their innovative techniques towards all the services in the economy. The deviation in health performances between both the countries was due to different policies, strategies, and historical circumstances. However, India's Health system has also improved since its independence but it was not up to the mark.

### 9.3.1 *Overview of Health System in India and China*

The current health policy in India originated on the pursuit of nation building which occurred during the independence in 1947 and in the idea manifested in the 1946 Report on the Health Survey and Development Committee or the Bhore Committee Report. According to the report, the insufficiency in medical as well as preventive health organizations, lack of health awareness, defective nutrition, unsanitary conditions etc resulted in the poor health conditions in India. The committee recommendations include limiting of the private practitioners, emphasizing on preventive healthcare and controlling communicable diseases. The committee also recommends for introduction of the three-tier health care system at the district level to provide preventive and curative health care for both the rural and urban areas. However, majority of the recommendations were not taken care of by the Government of India. The principle that it is a basic right to have access to primary care irrespective of any socioeconomic conditions was given by the Bhore Committee. Accordingly, primary health care as the foundation of the national health care system was established and public health care service was prioritized. However, the elimination of privatization of health care was never the intension of the Indian Government. China which on the other hand was experiencing both internal conflicts and conflict with Japan gained its independence in 1949 when the People's Republic of China was established. As the country was recovering from this chaos, health conditions of the people then declined hugely with health indicators at lowest level. The politico- administration of the country resulted in owning all means of production by the people which was represented by the government and there was no role of private sector. Thus, from the beginning of 1949, in China, all the health care facilities i.e., large hospitals and small township clinics was owned, funded and ran by the government. The first National Health Work Conference was held in 1950 in China where four fundamental principles were announced by the central government of China for improving medical and healthcare such as health services for workers, peasants and soldiers; greater emphasis on preventive care; proper combination of Chinese and Western medicines; and also mass campaign for health awareness.

India adopts different modes of operation for providing health care services in rural and urban areas. In India a three-tier hierarchical system of providing health care is adopted in case of rural areas. Primary healthcare is provided through a network of Sub-Centres (SC), Primary Health Centres (PHC) and Community Health Centres (CHC). Sub-Centres for provision of basic health care i.e., nutritional advice, immunization, controlling basic infectious diseases, providing basic drugs, etc are established for per 5000 population which for hill and tribal areas is per 3000 population. Primary Health Centres for providing preventive and curative care, which is the point of contact between rural population and doctors or physicians, is established per 30,000 populations which are per 20,000 populations for hill and tribal areas. And Community Health Centres for provision of emergency specialist health care are established per 120,000 populations which is per 80,000 population for hill and tribal areas. Also, for providing specialist, acute health care in both rural and urban areas, there are number of District Hospitals. On the other hand, in India, there is the existence of large and unregulated private sector health care provisions on payment basis. Private sector health care infrastructure includes: Private Hospitals, Nursing Homes and Dispensaries; General Practitioners and Clinics. Additionally, India has some indigenous medicine systems such as Homeopathy, Ayurveda, Siddha, Unani, etc. China also adopted a three-tier hierarchical system of providing health care but in case of both rural and urban areas. Rural areas include Rural Clinics or Health Stations, operated by numerous part time staff for providing basic health care services in almost all the villages at the bottom level; Township Health Centres for provision of primary health care and supervision of public health and health care services which were provided by the clinics at the next level of hierarchy; County Hospitals, the larger medical centres which provides specialist health care and referral services. Urban areas include Street Health Stations which provides the basic level of health care and functions similarly like rural clinics or health stations; District Hospitals for provision of primary health care and administrative organisation at the next level of urban hierarchy; and the Municipal or Provincial Hospital i.e., final tier in urban hierarchy for providing referral and specialist health care. Also initially, there exist unique dual economic and social structures in China because of which the healthcare delivery mechanism happens to be quite different across its urban and rural areas. Government plans and controls all expenditures and revenues; organize and almost completely funds health services in the cities. In case of rural areas in China, there exist Communes i.e., the institutes which represents the peasants, owns the land, organize all activities such as farming, distribution of products and social services like education and health care. Health care was provided in Cooperative Medical System (CMS) in China. In the form of low-priced equipment and medicines central government minimally supported CMS. The Communes supported the CMS mostly by financing through their collective revenue. Village and town health clinics were operated by CMS and were mostly staffed by practitioners with basic health care training (Ma & Sood, 2008).

In India, the responsibility of the delivery of health care is largely of the state governments and the central government defines policies, provide the national framework, and financial resources. The 1983 National Health Policy was influenced by Bhore Committee Report and Alma Ata Declaration of Health for All by the Year 2000 (WHO and United Nations' Children's Fund, 1978), which basing on foundation of decentralized primary health care services, stressed on establishing a well-built national public health services system. However, the states in reality became dependent over time for financial assistance, implementation of disease control on Central Government and failed in maintaining and administering health care facilities. The five-year planning process which was used by India, however resulted a top to down process of making decisions about setting priorities, implementing centrally sponsored programmes for disease control, and creating plans for healthcare workers and facilities

(Peters, Rao, & Fryatt, 2003). In spite of the slow economic growth, the health and health care in China improved significantly between 1950 and 1990. This is remarkable that the life expectancy at birth gets doubled from 35 to 69 years during 1950 to 1990. Also, through a highly centralized governmental agency, major investments were made in public health. China experienced an epidemiological transition by early 1980s and the prevalence of infectious diseases decreased significantly, and chronic diseases like cardiac problems, cancer, stroke etc. lead as the major cause of illness and death. The government focused on preventive rather than curative health care and also emphasized on public health approach and cost-effective approaches to improve population health (Ma & Sood, 2008). Also, health status is not only dependent on health care facilities. Educational attainment, hygiene, nutrition, living standards etc which significantly improved between 1950 and 1990 may have positive impact on health status. However, the inadequacies of the highly centralized system might have been concealed owing to lack of information.

India experienced changes in the health system for different reasons since 1980. Health care system was pushed towards privatization with emerging middle class and private practitioners working with international donors such as International Monetary Fund (IMF) and World Bank. These were the donors who supported reforms which included cutting investments in health sector, increasing private sector operations along with higher fees in public hospitals. In 1990s this resulted in a setback which the PHCs suffered. The PHCs reduced their services due to the decline in funds meant for programmes on controlling infectious disease and the focus shifted to family planning (Dummer & Cook, 2008). Since the second National Health Policy in 2002, there have been few changes in the general health scenario of India. First, India has achieved slow improvement in the Infant Mortality Rate (IMR) and Maternal Mortality Rate (MMR) along with control of infectious diseases to a larger extent but the burden of non-communicable diseases is showing an upward trend. The emergence of private sector as robust healthcare industry is the second discernible feature. Also, the rising cost of medical care pushes more and more people into poverty due to catastrophic out of pocket expenditures. Against this backdrop, the last National Health

Policy 2017 aims at providing good quality healthcare services in an assured manner to all by addressing current and emerging challenges arising from the ever changing socio-economic, epidemiological and technological scenarios. Among the key policy principles, equity, affordability, accountability, inclusive partnership and decentralization are worth mentioning. The policy recognizes the pivotal importance of Sustainable Development Goals (SDGs). China experienced fundamental societal transformation and economic reforms since early 1980s. The health care system with many other public services underwent changes that are often been characterized as privatization. Chinese Ministry of Health also recommended to legalize private medical practice with strict regulation during 1980s. Thus, in this context, decision makers made some crucial decisions at the national level about not ownership but to partially privatize the delivery of some health care services. Healthcare financing structure dramatically changed and shifted a larger share from the central government to individual consumers and also provincial and local authorities through local taxation. Subsequently, government share of national health care spending decreased and individual out-of-pocket payment increased. However, for controlling healthcare costs for individuals and ensuring access to basic healthcare to individuals, tight price regulations on medicines and procedures was imposed by the government. The rural health care system also experienced significant changes as the rural economic system, after 1982, changed from the collective economy (under the communes) to one based on individual household decisions. As a result, CMS lost its institutional fund rising base and therefore collapsed rapidly. Many doctors became unemployed and were forced to practice privately and their interest of providing a public service shifted to making a profit (Ma & Sood, 2008). There were increase in inequalities in access to healthcare services as public health resources were redirected away from rural areas. Recognizing these unintended consequences, more recently, China has launched several programs to reform its healthcare system, which include strengthening its public health systems (Bangdiwala, *et al.*, 2011). Also, government of China proposed a social medical-insurance system comprising both the urban and rural insurance components. Urban Employee Basic Medical Insurance was launched in 1998 which was made mandatory for urban residents with formal jobs. In 2003, the voluntary Newly Cooperative Medical Scheme was offered to rural population. Also, to cover urban population without formal jobs, including children, the elderly, and the self-employed, voluntary Urban Resident Basic Medical Insurance was launched in 2007. With these three-insurance programmes, in 2011, China largely achieved universal insurance coverage.

However, the out-of-pocket expenditure (percentage of current health expenditure) for both the countries- India and China has been shown in Figure 9.1.

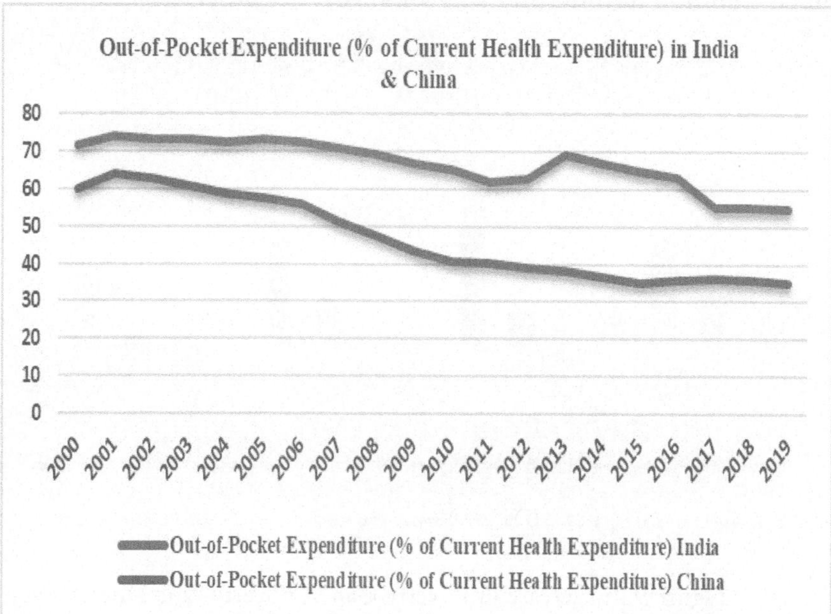


**Figure 9.1:** Out-of-Pocket Expenditure (% of Current Health Expenditure) in India and China from 2000–2019

*Source:* World Development Indicators, World Bank Database.

The out-of-pocket expenditure is the expense which is directly paid to the health care providers by the patients where the insurance does not cover the full cost of the health goods or services. In both the countries—India and China, out-of-pocket expenditure declined from 2000 to 2019 but not significantly. Comparing the countries i.e., India and China from the Figure 9.2, we can see that China is in better condition than India. In India percentage of health expenditure directly borne by the patient was 71.7 percent in the year 2000 which declined to just 54.8 percent in 2019. Whereas in China the percentage was much lower than India in the year 2000 that is 60.1 percent and it declined to 35.2 percent in the year 2019 which is also much lower than India. The reason of this may be because China largely achieved universal insurance coverage by 2011 as mentioned above. In India health insurance system still not developed significantly.

The out-of-pocket health expenditure driven poverty is very much common in India and also somewhat in China too.

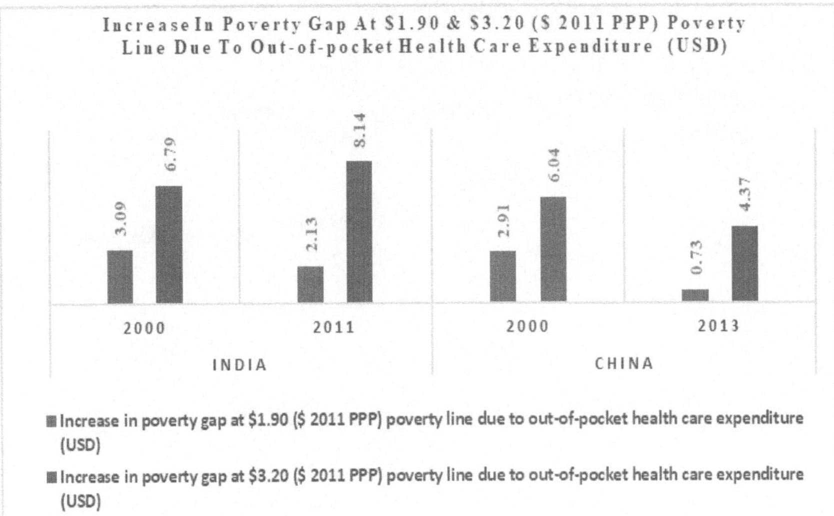


**Figure 9.2:** Increase in Poverty Gap at Poverty Line Due to Out-of-Pocket Health Expenditure (USD)

*Source:* World Development Indicators, World Bank Database.

From Figure 9.3, it can be seen that in India, the poverty gap i.e., the average shortfall of total population from minimum income $1.90 per day declined from 3.09 in 2000 to 2.13 in 2011 and that for minimum income $3.20 per day increased from 6.79 in 2000 to 8.14 in 2011. In China, the poverty gap both for minimum income $1.90 and $3.20 per day declined from 2000 to 2013. This shows that India experiences much more out-of-pocket health expenditure driver poverty than China.

## 9.4 Health Status in India and China

Some of the key health outcome indicators taken in this study are Life Expectancy (LE) at Birth, Infant Mortality Rate (IMR) per 1000 live births, Under 5 Mortality Rate (U5MR) per 1000 live births, Crude Death Rate (CDR) per 1000 people. Health status of India and China has been compared in Table 9.3.

From Table 9.3, it can be seen that the average Life Expectancy at Birth in India was 43.26 years during 1961–65 while that in China was 46.39 years which gradually increased over the years but it is much higher in China than that in India. The average Life Expectancy at Birth in India was 69.40 years during 2016–20 while that in China was 76.68 years. The gap between the Life Expectancy at Birth in India and China increased from 1961–65 to 1976–80, which started decreasing from the year 1981–85 until 2016–20. The gap between female Life Expectancy at Birth in India and China is more than that of male Life Expectancy at Birth.

Average of Infant Mortality Rate (Per 1000 Live Births) and Under 5 Mortality Rate (Per 1000 Live Births), both declined over the years 1961–65 to 2016–20 in India and China. But the position of China is better in both the case. During 1966–70, 81.55 out of every 1000 infants died before their first birthday in China whereas in India, 146.40 out of every 1000 infants died before their first birthday, which decreased to 6.48 and 29.92 respectively during 2016–20. Similarly, during 1966–70, 115.45 out of every 1000 in China and 219.12 out of every 1000 in India died before reaching the age of 5 Years, which decreased to 8.56 and 36.58 respectively in 2016–20. The gap between India and China's Infant Mortality Rate (Per 1000 Live Births) and Under 5 Mortality Rate though decreased over the years but still in 2020, it is quite high. Also, Crude Death Rate (Per 1000 People) in both the countries gradually declined over the years but the position of China is better than India. The difference between two countries also decreased over the years. Also, comparing India and China's health status across sex composition, it is found that the variations in life expectancy, Infant mortality and Under 5 Mortality Rate for India and China is greater for female than male throughout the period 1961–65 to 2016–20.

**Table 9.3:** Health Status of India and China, 1961–2020

| *Year* | | *1961–65* | *1966–70* | *1971–75* | *1976–80* | *1981–85* | *1986–90* | *1991–95* | *1996–00* | *2001–05* | *2006–10* | *2011–15* | *2016–20* |
|---|---|---|---|---|---|---|---|---|---|---|---|---|---|
| Life expectancy at birth, total (years) | India | 43.26 | 46.43 | 49.71 | 52.75 | 55.05 | 56.99 | 59.34 | 61.66 | 63.7 | 65.8 | 67.9 | 69.4 |
| | China | 46.39 | 55.61 | 62.2 | 65.8 | 67.91 | 68.93 | 69.53 | 70.75 | 72.37 | 73.84 | 75.32 | 76.68 |
| | Disparity Index | –3.13 | –9.18 | –12.49 | –13.05 | –12.86 | –11.94 | –10.19 | –9.09 | –8.67 | –8.04 | –7.42 | –7.28 |
| Life expectancy at birth, female (years) | India | 42.39 | 45.71 | 49.29 | 52.73 | 55.21 | 57.26 | 59.89 | 62.44 | 64.55 | 66.75 | 69.07 | 70.68 |
| | China | 47.94 | 57.47 | 63.73 | 67.21 | 69.43 | 70.63 | 71.64 | 72.88 | 74.25 | 75.86 | 77.62 | 79.02 |
| | Disparity Index | –5.55 | –11.76 | –14.44 | –14.48 | –14.22 | –13.37 | –11.75 | –10.44 | –9.7 | –9.11 | –8.55 | –8.34 |
| Life expectancy at birth, male (years) | India | 44.08 | 47.12 | 50.13 | 52.81 | 54.93 | 56.75 | 58.84 | 60.93 | 62.9 | 64.91 | 66.82 | 68.23 |
| | China | 44.98 | 53.84 | 60.69 | 64.41 | 66.45 | 67.35 | 67.64 | 68.86 | 70.67 | 72.02 | 73.25 | 74.53 |
| | Disparity Index | –0.9 | –6.72 | –10.56 | –11.6 | –11.52 | –10.6 | –8.8 | –7.93 | –7.77 | –7.11 | –6.43 | –6.3 |
| Death rate, crude (per 1,000 people) | India | 20.61 | 18.13 | 15.85 | 13.92 | 12.57 | 11.39 | 10.07 | 9.02 | 8.31 | 7.72 | 7.27 | 7.24 |
| | China | 11.06 | 8.22 | 7.33 | 6.58 | 6.69 | 6.69 | 6.61 | 6.5 | 6.43 | 7 | 7.12 | 7.07 |
| | Disparity Index | 9.55 | 9.91 | 8.52 | 7.34 | 5.88 | 4.7 | 3.46 | 2.52 | 1.88 | 0.72 | 0.15 | 0.17 |
| Mortality rate, infant (per 1,000 live births) | India | 155.42 | 146.4 | 136.22 | 121.3 | 106.02 | 93.44 | 82.12 | 71.22 | 60 | 49.36 | 38.9 | 29.92 |
| | China | – | 81.55 | 68.86 | 52.12 | 43.04 | 42.36 | 40.64 | 33.56 | 23.52 | 14.96 | 9.84 | 6.48 |
| | Disparity Index | – | 64.85 | 67.36 | 69.18 | 62.98 | 51.08 | 41.48 | 37.66 | 36.48 | 34.4 | 29.06 | 23.44 |
| Mortality rate, infant, female (per 1,000 live births) | India | 150.84 | 142 | 132.38 | 117.46 | 102.58 | 90.94 | 80.68 | 71.08 | 60.78 | 50.2 | 39.38 | 29.9 |
| | China | – | 77.7 | 65.44 | 49.32 | 40.74 | 40.12 | 38.46 | 31.68 | 22.04 | 13.96 | 9.16 | 6.1 |
| | Disparity Index | – | 64.3 | 66.94 | 68.14 | 61.84 | 50.82 | 42.22 | 39.4 | 38.74 | 36.24 | 30.22 | 23.8 |

| *Year* | | *1961–65* | *1966–70* | *1971–75* | *1976–80* | *1981–85* | *1986–90* | *1991–95* | *1996–00* | *2001–05* | *2006–10* | *2011–15* | *2016–20* |
|---|---|---|---|---|---|---|---|---|---|---|---|---|---|
| Mortality rate, infant, male (per 1,000 live births) | India | 159.76 | 150.6 | 139.86 | 124.96 | 109.32 | 95.82 | 83.52 | 71.36 | 59.22 | 48.6 | 38.42 | 29.94 |
| | China | – | 85 | 72.08 | 54.72 | 45.28 | 44.46 | 42.74 | 35.36 | 24.96 | 15.92 | 10.48 | 6.88 |
| | Disparity Index | – | 65.6 | 67.78 | 70.24 | 64.04 | 51.36 | 40.78 | 36 | 34.26 | 32.68 | 27.94 | 23.06 |
| Mortality rate, under–5 (per 1,000 live births) | India | 233.04 | 219.12 | 202.86 | 179 | 154.08 | 133.88 | 116.02 | 98.88 | 81.18 | 64.64 | 49.14 | 36.58 |
| | China | – | 115.45 | 95.74 | 70.5 | 56.48 | 53.9 | 50.62 | 41.26 | 28.94 | 18.66 | 12.58 | 8.56 |
| | Disparity Index | – | 103.67 | 107.12 | 108.5 | 97.6 | 79.98 | 65.4 | 57.62 | 52.24 | 45.98 | 36.56 | 28.02 |
| Mortality rate, under–5, female (per 1,000 live births) | India | 239.08 | 224.48 | 208.1 | 183.68 | 158.32 | 138.14 | 120.66 | 104.02 | 85.66 | 68.02 | 51.24 | 37.34 |
| | China | – | 112.9 | 93.18 | 68.12 | 54.26 | 51.68 | 48.32 | 39.16 | 27.2 | 17.4 | 11.74 | 8.04 |
| | Disparity Index | – | 111.58 | 114.92 | 115.56 | 104.06 | 86.46 | 72.34 | 64.86 | 58.46 | 50.62 | 39.5 | 29.3 |
| Mortality rate, under–5, male (per 1,000 live births) | India | 227.22 | 214.06 | 197.86 | 174.5 | 150 | 129.86 | 111.56 | 93.9 | 76.88 | 61.38 | 47.18 | 35.84 |
| | China | – | 117.75 | 98.1 | 72.72 | 58.58 | 56.02 | 52.8 | 43.26 | 30.62 | 19.84 | 13.38 | 9.08 |
| | Disparity Index | – | 96.31 | 99.76 | 101.78 | 91.42 | 73.84 | 58.76 | 50.64 | 46.26 | 41.54 | 33.8 | 26.76 |

*Source:* World Development Indicators, World Bank Data.

In addition to key health status indicators, there are other important health indicators which show significant differences between the two countries. India experiences much more deaths than China due to communicable diseases and maternal, prenatal and nutrition conditions. Figure 9.3 shows the death rates in India and China, categorized by cause for the years 2000 and 2019.

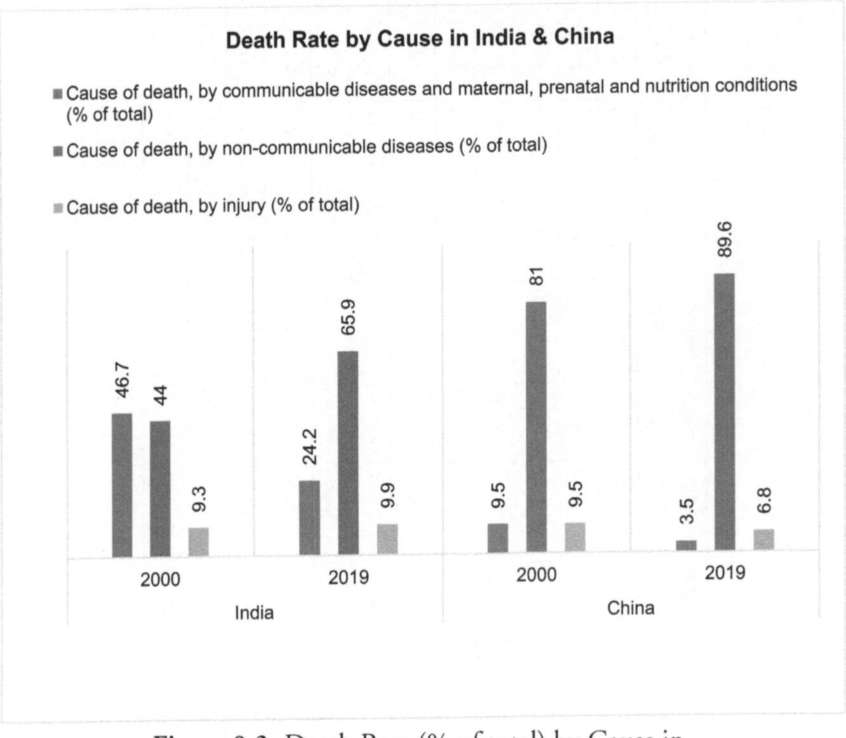


**Figure 9.3:** Death Rate (% of total) by Cause in India & China in the year 2000 & 2019

*Source:* World Bank.

In India, deaths due to communicable diseases and maternal, prenatal and nutrition condition decreased from 46.7 percent in 2000 to 24.2 percent in 2019, whereas that in China was much lower than India in 2000 which further decreased to only 3.5 percent in 2019. In India, deaths due to non-communicable disease increased to 65.9 percent in 2019 which was 44 percent in 2000. China experiences even more deaths due to non-communicable diseases, which increased from 81 percent in 2000 to 89.6 percent in 2019. This shows that there is a need to control communicable diseases in India. Also, women health and supply of nutrition to the population should be focussed to improve the health status in India.

## 9.5 Health Infrastructure in India and China

Policy approaches introduced in India and China for tackling the health problems differed significantly due to the politico-administration system in both the countries. Also, the system of the provision of health in India and China is quite similar but do have some differences. In India a three-tier hierarchical system of providing health care is adopted in case of rural areas. China also adopted a three-tier hierarchical system of providing health care but in case of both rural and urban areas. China has a vast network of rural health clinics for providing primary healthcare services to nearly all the villages, while in case of India, there are much smaller number of rural sub-centres. Also, the existence of variations in health infrastructure is evident from the number of hospitals, hospital beds, physicians; nurses vary in both the countries. However, total numbers of hospitals increased over the time in both India and China. Health care infrastructure includes physical infrastructure such as hospitals, hospital beds, blood banks etc and human infrastructure such as doctors, nurses, midwives etc. Table 9.4 shows the comparison between health infrastructure as well as health expenditure of both the countries India and China.

Hospital Beds per 1000 population in China increased whereas it gradually decreased in India over the years. In the year 1990, India had 0.72 hospital beds per 1000 population which decreased to 0.65 in the year 2000, which further decreased to 0.55 hospital beds per 1000 population in 2019. China, whereas had 1.59 hospital beds per 1000 population in 1990 and it started sharply increasing from 2008 which reached to 4.79 hospital beds per 1000 population in 2019 that is much higher than that in India. Doctors per 1000 population in both India and China increased over the years but the improvement in India was not as rapid as in China. In 2000, India had 0.53 doctors per 1000 population which increased to 0.93 doctors per 1000 population in 2019. China, whereas had 1.24 doctors per 1000 population in the

**Table 9.4:** Health Infrastructure of India and China; 2000–2019

| Year | *Current Health Expenditure (% of GDP)* | | | *Hospital Beds (Per 1000 population)* | | | *Doctors (Per 1000 population)* | | | *Nurses (Per 1000 population)* | | |
|---|---|---|---|---|---|---|---|---|---|---|---|---|
| | *India* | *China* | *Disparity Index* | *India* | *China* | *Disparity Index* | *India* | *China* | *Disparity Index* | *India* | *China* | *Disparity Index* |
| 2000 | 4.03 | 4.47 | –0.44 | 0.65 | 1.68 | –1.03 | 0.53 | 1.24 | –0.71 | 0.71 | 0.97 | –0.26 |
| 2001 | 4.26 | 4.22 | 0.04 | 0.64 | 1.66 | –1.02 | 0.54 | 1.26 | –0.72 | 0.73 | 0.98 | –0.25 |
| 2002 | 4.24 | 4.35 | –0.11 | 0.63 | 1.7 | –1.07 | 0.56 | 1.12 | –0.56 | 0.75 | 0.99 | –0.24 |
| 2003 | 4.01 | 4.38 | –0.37 | 0.61 | 1.73 | –1.12 | 0.56 | 1.17 | –0.61 | 0.74 | 0.95 | –0.21 |
| 2004 | 3.96 | 4.26 | –0.3 | 0.49 | 1.79 | –1.3 | 0.57 | 1.2 | –0.63 | 0.76 | 0.96 | –0.2 |
| 2005 | 3.79 | 4.14 | –0.35 | 0.41 | 1.84 | –1.43 | 0.59 | 1.22 | –0.63 | 0.77 | 0.99 | –0.22 |
| 2006 | 3.63 | 3.92 | –0.29 | 0.42 | 1.91 | –1.49 | 0.6 | 1.25 | –0.65 | 0.77 | 1.01 | –0.24 |
| 2007 | 3.52 | 3.66 | –0.14 | 0.41 | 1.99 | –1.58 | 0.62 | 1.27 | –0.65 | 0.78 | 1.07 | –0.29 |
| 2008 | 3.51 | 3.88 | –0.37 | 0.41 | 2.13 | –1.72 | 0.63 | 1.32 | –0.69 | 0.79 | 1.16 | –0.37 |
| 2009 | 3.49 | 4.32 | –0.83 | 0.44 | 2.29 | –1.85 | 0.65 | 1.4 | –0.75 | 0.81 | 1.24 | –0.43 |
| 2010 | 3.27 | 4.21 | –0.94 | 0.47 | 2.47 | –2 | 0.69 | 1.44 | –0.75 | 0.86 | 1.36 | –0.5 |
| 2011 | 3.25 | 4.33 | –1.08 | 0.63 | 2.69 | –2.06 | 0.74 | 1.47 | –0.73 | 0.87 | 1.5 | –0.63 |
| 2012 | 3.33 | 4.55 | –1.22 | 0.49 | 3.01 | –2.52 | 0.7 | 1.55 | –0.85 | 0.99 | 1.63 | –0.64 |
| 2013 | 3.75 | 4.71 | –0.96 | 0.49 | 3.29 | –2.8 | 0.72 | 1.64 | –0.92 | 1.11 | 1.8 | –0.69 |
| 2014 | 3.62 | 4.77 | –1.15 | 0.52 | 3.55 | –3.03 | 0.72 | 1.7 | –0.98 | 1.22 | 2 | –0.78 |
| 2015 | 3.6 | 4.89 | –1.29 | 0.58 | 3.79 | –3.21 | 0.73 | 1.78 | –1.05 | 1.37 | 2.15 | –0.78 |
| 2016 | 3.51 | 4.98 | –1.47 | 0.48 | 4.02 | –3.54 | 0.76 | 1.88 | –1.12 | 1.45 | 2.3 | –0.85 |
| 2017 | 3.54 | 5.15 | –1.61 | 0.53 | 4.31 | –3.78 | 0.78 | 1.99 | –1.21 | 1.5 | 2.48 | –0.98 |
| 2018 | 3.54 | 5.35 | –1.81 | 0.54 | 4.57 | –4.03 | 0.85 | 2.11 | –1.26 | 1.53 | 2.68 | –1.15 |
| 2019 | 3 | 5.41 | –2.41 | 0.55 | 4.79 | –4.24 | 0.93 | 2.24 | –1.31 | 1.73 | 2.87 | –1.14 |

*Source:* World Development Indicators, World Bank Database.

year 2000 and which reached to 2.24 doctors per 1000 population in 2019 that is also higher than that in India. Also, nurses per 1000 population in both India and China increased over the years 2000 to 2019. In 2000, India had 0.71 practicing nurses per 1000 population which increased to 1.73 nurses per 1000 population in 2019. China, whereas had 0.97 nurses per 1000 population in 1990 and it reached to 2.87 nurses per 1000 population in 2019 which is much higher than that in India. It can also be seen those variations of major indicators of health infrastructure i.e., hospital beds, doctors and nurses per 1000 population between India and China increased over the years.

Also, from Table 9.4, it can be seen that there is a sharp decline in health expenditure (% of GDP) from the year 2000 till 2011, which again started rising from 2012 but again started declining from the year 2014. It further decreased to 3 percent in 2019. On the other hand, in China health expenditure (% of GDP) which was 4.47 percent in the year 2000 increased to 5.41 percent in 2019. The gap of health expenditure between India and China increased over the years.

## 9.6 Dynamics of Educational Performance in India and China

The first and second largest education systems in the world are respectively hosted by India and China. Both the countries together hold about 45 percent of the world's primary school-age children. India and China are the two countries whose organizational and political structures are completely different but the challenges and considerations they faced were similar as they underwent rapid industrialization and social transformations. The transformations in both the countries started in late 1940s underneath comparable conditions. Also, in late 1940s, both the countries India and China started their national education systems. The deviation in educational performance between them which took place was due to different policies, strategies, and historical circumstances (Shah, 2013). China is much ahead of India in terms of educational enrolment at various levels. In case of primary and secondary education, China has outperformed India in terms of the access, quality, and equity. Whereas, India's higher education have a competitive edge over China (Goldman *et al.*, 2008). However, at the beginning of the 21st century, it can be said that the performance of China is much better than India along a broad spectrum of education indicators.

### 9.6.1 *Overview of Education System in India and China*

India's educational system is relatively steady whereas education system in China was in quite unstable condition. Since the time of independence, it was centrally planned in India to give attention in reconstructing the education system in the country which was required for meeting its scientific, technical and manpower needs. A university commission was appointed under the chairmanship of S. Radhakrishnan in 1948 and in 1952, under A.L. Mudaliar, a secondary education commission was appointed. India had inherited a higher education system from its colonial time and since the time of independence focused on its secondary and higher education, rather than primary education. High-quality institutions were built at different parts of India such as Indian Institutes of Technology (IITs), Indian Institutes of Management (IIMs), etc. However, these are not equally distributed in all over India. Also due to absence of the physical and technical infrastructure, system failed to reach its target. A huge chunk of graduates from such institutions either emigrated or were underemployed and another problem which arised in India was mass illiteracy and it was continued to be neglected. For checking on this unbalanced educational development, Kothari Commission (1964–1985) recommended that government should provide free and compulsory education for all the children up to the age 14 and also give priority to research and scientific education. It also recommended the use of Indian regional languages. But most of the recommendations stayed in papers and were not implemented due to lack of necessary resources. In 1986, the National Education Policy (NEP) was announced, according to which more organizational and financial support should be provided for improving educational system so that several disadvantaged groups such as women, SCs, STs, etc have educational access and the overall educational standard improves. However, though the NEP 1986 laid emphasis on secularism but it also laid continuous emphasis to promote privatization.

China, on the other hand, have an educational system which experienced several bold moves, shifts during the last five decades from the foundation of People's Republic of China in1949. In the earliest fifteen years after independence, the government of China tried to make access the basic education to its masses and also made a strong base of higher education. China adopted the Soviet Model for achieving economic success and as well as for planning its education system. The newly formed communist government in China in 1950s focused on strengthening the education system and the result was the restructuring of comprehensive universities segregating into various specialized colleges and polytechnics. Both the higher institutes and the college going students experienced rapid growth at their level. China in its initial period could successfully and quickly expand primary education but due to the economic crisis resulted from Great Leap Forward, since 1958, the strong base which was built for primary education started to decline continuously. China shifted from Soviet Model to two-tiered model keeping a balance between traditional Confucian style and modern i.e., western style education. Also, it was the period of 1966 to 1976 when there was the Great Cultural Revolution in China which was launched for reviving the spirit of revolution among youths of China. Due to this proletarian revolution, the goal of national education which was primarily preparing skilled labour shifted to provision of ideological knowledge. The way in this period, there was disruption of the earlier achievements in secondary and higher education, on the other hand, there was unintentional expansion in access to primary education in China. However, the elitism which was present in the education system of China got reversed. This shift and the outlook of the communist government started addressing the problem of mass illiteracy. Education policies were reverted to the policies initiated during the early 1960s, by reintroducing academic standards and emphasizing on access and quality rather than quantity. In the late 1970s, half of the population in China was educated at primary level or higher, when it embarked on the land reforms and economic reforms. A compulsory nine-year education policy was introduced in 1985. But the closing and merging of schools in the time of Cultural Revolution, left some of the rural areas were without primary schools resulting decline in enrolments. However, in most of the states, enrolments in elementary schools were higher. Since the early 1990s, students in China opted for general secondary education, increasing the possibility of growth of higher education.

## 9.7 Status of Education in India and China

To examine the status of education in India and China, the flow and stock of education in both the countries can be reviewed. Flow of education can be measured by indicators like enrolment and intake rates in different levels and the stock of education measured by indicators like literacy rate, years of educational attainment, and percentage of adult educated population etc.

Table 9.5 shows the status of education in both the countries—India and China and the indicators taken to compare the two countries are Adult Literacy Rate, Pupil- Teacher Ratio (Primary, Secondary and Tertiary), School Enrolment (Primary, Secondary and Tertiary). The overall performance of China is much better than that in India.

Adult literacy rate means the percentage of people with age of 15 and above who is able to both read and write, also understand short and simple statements of everyday life. From Table 9.5 it can be seen that though the adult literacy rate in India increased from 34.45 percent in 1970 to 74.37 percent in 2018, but that in China was much higher over the years. Adult literacy rate in China increased from 65.51 percent in 1981 to 96.84 percent in 2018. There was considerable gap of adult literacy rate between both the countries, but it slightly decreased from the year 1991 to 2018.

Pupil-teacher ratio means the number of students for a teacher. Lower the pupil-teacher ratio, better is the condition. The pupil-teacher ratio (primary) in both the countries are showing a positive trend and indicates that educational systems of both the countries is recognizing the importance of reducing the ratio as much as possible. In India the ratio was 41.45 in 1970 which reduced to 32.74 in 2018 which was much higher than that in China. In China, the ratio was 28.87 in 1970 which reduced to 16.43 in 2018. In case of secondary education, the pupil-teacher ratio in India which was 21.92 in 1970 increased hugely in the year 1991, decreased to 25.92 in 2011 and further increased to 28.52 in 2018. In China pupil-teacher ratio (secondary) decreased from 20.60 in 1970 to 13.26 in 2018. The pupil-teacher ratio (tertiary) in both the countries has an increasing trend which is not a good sign. However, from Table 9.5, a sizable gap of pupil-teacher ratio between India and China can be seen.

Table 9.5: Status of Education in India and China, 1970–2018

| *Years* | *Country* | *1970* | *1981* | *1991* | *2001* | *2011* | *2018* |
|---|---|---|---|---|---|---|---|
| Adult Literacy Rate | India | 34.45 | 40.76 | 48.22 | 61.01 | 69.3 | 74.37 |
| | China | – | 65.51 | 77.79 | 90.92 | 95.12 | 96.84 |
| | Disparity Index | – | –24.75 | –29.57 | –29.91 | –25.82 | –22.47 |
| Pupil-teacher ratio, primary | India | 41.45 | 38 | 43 | 40.15 | 35.15 | 32.74 |
| | China | 28.87 | 27.25 | 21.93 | 22.21 | 16.79 | 16.43 |
| | Disparity Index | 12.58 | 10.75 | 21.07 | 17.94 | 18.36 | 16.31 |
| Pupil-teacher ratio, secondary | India | 21.92 | 38 | 42 | 33.44 | 25.92 | 28.52 |
| | China | 20.6 | 18.88 | 14.43 | 18.92 | 15.15 | 13.26 |
| | Disparity Index | 1.32 | 19.12 | 27.57 | 14.52 | 10.77 | 15.26 |
| Pupil-teacher ratio, tertiary | India | 12.96 * | 11.82 | – | 23.8 | – | 24.73 |
| | China | 0.79 | 4.41 | – | 15.97 | 19.49 | – |
| | Disparity Index | – | 7.41 | – | 7.83 | – | – |
| Enrolment Rate (Primary) | India | 78.51 | 82.44 | 91.15 | 94.11 | 108.32 | 112.96 |
| | China | 107.04 | 109.72 | 124.38 | 112.34 | 99.05 | 100.22 |
| | Disparity Index | –28.53 | –27.28 | –33.23 | –18.23 | 9.27 | 12.74 |
| Enrolment Rate (Secondary) | India | 23.84 | 28.86 | – | 45.15 | 66.25 | 74.38 |
| | China | 27.47 | 43.24 | 38.98 | 60.08 | – | – |
| | Disparity Index | –3.63 | –14.38 | – | –14.93 | – | – |
| Enrolment Rate (Tertiary) | India | 4.92 | 4.96 | 6.03 | 9.69 | 22.76 | 28.06 |
| | China | 0.13 | 1.13 | 2.89 | 9.79 | 25.65 | 50.6 |
| | Disparity Index | 4.79 | 3.83 | 3.14 | –0.1 | –2.89 | –22.54 |

*Source:* World Development Indicators, World Bank Database; Indiastat.
*Note:* *indicates the year 1973.

School Enrolment for all primary, secondary and tertiary level also has an increasing trend in both the countries. In case of primary enrolment, the gap between India and China was positive from 2011 i.e., India's primary enrolment was higher than China. It can be due to the double counting problem in the gross enrolment ratio which includes dropout rates. Due to unavailability of data, only gross enrolment rates can be given. Tertiary enrolment rate in India was 4.92 and was higher than 0.13 of China in 1970. From 2011 to 2018 there was a huge increase in the tertiary enrolment rate of 50.60 in China which was much higher that India's 28.06 in 2018. India had a history of giving importance to the tertiary education. In case of tertiary enrolment, the gap between India and China was negative from 2001 i.e., China's tertiary enrolment was much higher than India.

However, since the independence in 1947, in India, the number of universities increased 16-fold and that of colleges increased 20-fold. In 1960s and 1970s the annual growth rate of institutions was about 13 percent which in 1980s decreased to 4.5 percent and the total enrolment was 9.4 million students. During the year 1985, the percentage of adult population attaining post-secondary education was 2.8 in India and that in China was 1.2 percent (UNESCO, 2004). Since 1990s, the post-secondary enrolments in India increased from 5 to 13 million, while that in China increased from 5 to 27 million.

## 9.8 Education Infrastructure in India and China

Both the countries—India and China have entirely dissimilar economic, political and social structures and both the countries, for their economic and social development, depend on education. A study on comparison of educational system of both India and China would help to determine some of the forces that have helped in shaping the inputs and outcomes of education. Due to increase in the enrolment rates, the pressure increases on the existing educational infrastructures which necessitates the development of educational infrastructure. Thus, education infrastructure is one of the measures of the quality of education of a country. If there is the lack of basic amenities of education, it is likely that there will be discouragement among the students from enrolling and completing education. (Goldman, Kumar & Liu, 2008). Also, to increase the educational

**Table 9.6:** Educational Infrastructure in India and China

| Years | *Education Expenditure (% of GDP)* | | | *No. of Teachers, Primary* | | *No. of Teachers, Secondary* | | *No. of Primary School* | |
|---|---|---|---|---|---|---|---|---|---|
| | *India* | *China* | *Disparity Index* | *India* | *China* | *India* | *China* | *India* | *China* |
| 1971 | – | 1.39 | – | 1376176 | 3612000 | 964445 | 1212599 | 408378 | 961131 |
| 1981 | – | 1.95 | – | 1599182 | 5226000 | – | 3171564 | 495007 | 917316 |
| 1991 | – | 1.65 | – | – | 5581810 | – | 3631500 | 566744 | 729158 |
| 2001 | 4.25 | 4.26 | −0.01 | 2835044 | 5860316 | 2164558 | 4572065 | 638738 | – |
| 2011 | 4.34 | 3.25 | 1.09 | 3918312 | 5939088 | 4387444 | 6431127 | 748547 | – |
| 2019 | 5.35 | 3.01 | 2.34 | 4339390 | 6363952 | 6103309 | 6474893 | 826842 | – |

*Source:* World Development Indicators, World Bank Database; Indiastat.

efficiency, technology is one major aspect and it may make it easy to have access to education. The government of India and China appreciated the importance of technology for developing the education. Some scholars in fact argued against the incorporation of technology into the educational system in India as it is too high (Konana & Balasubramanian, 2002).

Table 9.6 is given below showing and comparing the educational infrastructure and also education expenditure in both the countries—India and China.

From Table 9.6, it can be seen that the number of teachers in case of primary and secondary level in both the countries India and China increased over the years but the gap of that between the countries was considerable as China outperformed India over the years. Also, number of colleges in India increased from 2247 in 1971 to 39931 in 2019. Number of colleges in China can not be given due to unavailability of data. Number of universities in India increased from 82 to 993 over the years 1971 to 2019. In 2011 the number of universities in China was 2409, whereas that in India was only 621. In 2019, the number of universities in China decreased to 1270 but was also larger than the number of universities in India (World Development Indicators, World Bank Database; Indiastat).

However, though education expenditure in both the countries increased over the years, but that in India was higher than that in China from 2011.

## 9.9 Conclusion

This comparative study of health and education performance in India and China shows that, though both the countries were in the similar position after independence but over the years China over-performed India. In case of HDI rank India is far behind China. There is a considerable gap of GDP growth rate and gross capital formation between India and China which must be addressed. China's PCI increased at a double than India over the years. Also, the performance in industrial sector is worse in case of India with increasing youth population, which must be given attention to.

Statistics of all the health outcomes taken up in the study i.e., life expectancy at birth, infant and under 5 mortality rate, crude death rate indicates that, though the gap of such indicators between India and China is decreasing over the years but the improvement in health status is much more significant in China. Also, the variations in life health outcomes for India and China are greater for female than male over the years. In India, deaths owing to communicable diseases and maternal, prenatal and nutrition condition is much higher than in China which means India failed to control the prevalence of communicable disease, and have not focussed properly on women health and supply of nutrition to the population. In case of health infrastructure also China is in better position than India. There is significant variation in primary health care provision between India and China. The statistics shows that there are significant variations in health infrastructure in terms of hospital beds, doctors, nurses per 1000 population and the variations in major health infrastructure indicator between India and China increased over the years. Also, current health expenditure (% of GDP) gradually decreased in India whereas it increased in China over the years 2000 to 2019. This may be one of the reasons of higher out-of-pocket payment (% of current health expenditure) in India. India experiences much more out-of-pocket health expenditure driver poverty than China.

Also, the status of overall education in China is in better position than that in India. The gap of adult literacy rate and pupil-teacher ratio (primary, secondary and tertiary) between India and China is increasing over the years. In case of primary enrolment rate India is in better position while in case of tertiary enrolment China is in better position. But due to unavailability of data, gross enrolment rates are taken which also includes dropout rates. In case of educational infrastructure, both human and physical, position of China is better than India. Number of teachers in case of primary and secondary level in both the countries increased but however, China outperformed India over the years. Also, number of colleges and universities in both the countries increased over the years, since independence but India is still behind China. However, though education expenditure in both the countries increased over the years, but that in India was higher than that in China from 2011.

Looking up to China, Indian government can focus on the following: Increasing spending on health, especially public health; reducing out-of-pocket expenditure; focusing on controlling communicable disease, women health etc; and rather than curative care, India must invest in preventive health care services. Also, health infrastructure, access to health care must be improved so that health outcomes reach at a better position. However, health infrastructure is not the sole factor on which health status depends on. Health status also depends on other non-medical, social and economic factors etc on which any country, especially India must look up to. Both countries should also learn from the strengths and weaknesses of each other's education system. China has been successful in ensuring increasing its enrolment rate. One of the major steps strategies that have enabled the country to improve its rate of enrolment is lack of overemphasis on higher education. This has led to even development of education at all levels. On the other hand, India's overemphasis of higher education has been detrimental to the development of education at low levels. This necessitates that the governments of both countries view health and education as major pillars of future economic prosperity.

## References


[1] Akin, J.S., Dow, W.H., Lance, P.M. and Loh, C.-P.A. (2005). Changes in access to health care in China, 1989–1997. *Health Policy and Planning,* Vol. 20(2), pp. 80–89.

[2] Bangdiwala, S.I., Tucker, J.D., Zodpey, S., Griffiths, S.M., Li, L.M., Reddy, K.S. and Tang, J.L. (2011). Public health education in India and China: history, opportunities, and challenges, *Public Health Reviews,* Vol. 33(1), pp. 204–224.

[3] Bhat, R. and Jain, N. (2006). Analysis of Public and Private Healthcare Expenditures, *Economic and Political Weekly,* Vol. 41(1), pp. 57–68.

[4] Dummer, T.J. and Cook, I.G. (2008). Health in China and India: A cross-country comparison in a context of Globalization. *Social Science & Medicine,* Vol. 67, pp. 590–605.

[5] Goldman, C.A., Kumar, K.B. and Liu, Y. (2008). Education and the Asian surge: A comparison of the education systems in India and China.

[6] Ma, S. and Sood, N. (2008). A Comparison of the Health Systems in China and India. Santa Monica, CA: RAND Corporation. Retrieved from https://www.rand.org/pubs/occasional_papers/OP212.html

[7] Palit, K. and Guha, D. (2018). A comparative study on system of general education in China and India, *International Journal for Research in Engineering Application & Management,* Vol. 4(05), pp. 447–450.

[8] Peters, D.H., Rao, K.S. and Fryatt, R. (2003). Lumping and splitting: The health policy agenda in India. *Health Policy and Planning,* Vol. 18(3), pp. 249–260.

[9] Shah, S. (2013). Higher Educational Entitlement and Economic Development: India after Independence, *Development Dynamics,* Vol. I, pp. 95–103.

CHAPTER 10

# Conceptualizing Cities in Terms of Migrants' Vulnerability and Resilience during COVID-19©

Chandra Kanta Saha and Soumyananda Dinda

## 10.1 Introduction

Vulnerabilities of migrants are overrepresented in any economy in both the phases of migration life cycle, both pre and post migration. After the introduction of globalization and structural reforms, the pace of urbanization has accelerated and there has been concomitant growth of rural-urban migration. In Harris-Todaro model, the rural to urban migration was based on expected urban-rural wage differentials. But in developing countries, the motivation behind rural urban migration was mainly to earn subsistence level of living as alternative livelihood opportunities are scarce in rural sector. Pre-migration phase is characterized by distress migration and this push factor will force the rural people to migrate out to the cities in form of seasonal or circular migration. Again, the skilled workers of rural are also migrated to the cities for better job prospects and to fulfill the needs and aspirations of life. This pull factor also has a role to play mainly for permanent migrants to migrate to cities. This temporary and permanent migration in cities has posed a challenge to urban living though it is an important factor to promote urbanization.

COVID-19 has exposed the lacuna in city planning as major cities in the world have crumbled under the onslaught of the virus. Pandemic has exposed existing vulnerabilities as well as it has added

---

© Authors would like to acknowledge the valuable suggestions and inputs from the reviewer and have tried to incorporate it in the entire writing. The usual disclaimer applies.

new dimensions to existing vulnerability and thus heighten community's sensitivity towards the adverse impact of future disaster. In this background, we have to conceptualize cities in terms of health infrastructure, climate resilient factors, deployment of essential services to the vulnerable, mobility of migrants and social, physical and financial infrastructure as they have an important role to play to build resilience in cities. On the one hand, the paper suggests the areas of vulnerability of migrants within a city and on the other hand an effort has been made to develop city resilience index to prevent crises in the future. An inclusive city approach is the need of the hour to integrate migrants into the cities to ensure full and productive employment, decent work, and protection of labour rights with safe and secure working environment. The paper tries to explore the methodology related with the development of city resilience index and vulnerability index which will help urban planners to plan for the disaster management in future. This city resilience approach will incorporate different aspects of labour mobility, which are hitherto be unexplored, and help to develop disaster preparedness and response plan to accommodate the considerations of its vulnerable populations in the cities. In this regard, management and governance of cities has a huge role to play. Stakeholders should make concerted effort to encourage rural to urban migration, which is one of the pillars of urbanization and should develop strategies to strengthen governance of migration. In this context, the perception of 'managing migration' is more important than 'reducing migration' in the cities.

### 10.1.1 *Urbanization and Migration*

Migration has always been one of the forces that drives the growth of urbanization and poses challenges for cities. Rural to urban migration leads to the growth of economy through the growth of urbanization (Tripathi and Kaur, 2017). Urbanization can be termed as the increasing proportion of a country's population living in an urban area and one of the most important sources that increases urban population. Urbanization can be defined as a structural transformation that have taken place in the economy, politics, legal, social, cultural and demography of a particular society which signals a shift from tradition to modernity (Ojo *et al.*, 2017). According to Neo-Marxists, urbanization is an engine behind capitalism, and poor and less privileged are always sidelined in the process which is inherent in the capitalist mode of production (Ojo *et al.*, 2017). However, urbanization through internal migration (intra and interstate) is an engine of economic growth for the developing countries (Latham-Sprinkle *et al.*, 2019). International migration (mostly to developed countries) also helps the countries of origin with remittances and destination countries are also benefited with human resources. But there is much concern about the pace of urbanization and the capacity of national and local governments to cope with it (Tacoli *et al.*, 2015). Indiscriminate urbanization increases the environmental and socio-economic vulnerabilities of urban poor and their social exclusion. Rapid and chaotic urbanization has been linked to the expansion of urban poverty. Again, during any type of disruption in the city, existing insecurities of urban poor have been intensified and these give rise to disaster. In this regard, local governments should play an important role to ensure that urbanization should be inclusive in nature and be properly implemented by including migrants in their urban development planning. This will help to shape cities to ensure future sustainability.

## 10.2 Objective

The present paper aims to develop an indicator-based universal methodological approach to assess vulnerability and adaptive capacity (resilience) of a city and therefore it does not discuss any household specific or city specific assessment of vulnerability and resilience. The indicator-based framework of constructing vulnerability index and city resilience index will help to identify pandemic related vulnerabilities and inherent vulnerabilities of migrants living in a city and contribute to the city's 'immune system' for effective adaptation and better sustainability. Vulnerability assessment has now been accepted as a prerequisite for developing management capability of a city during shocks. This will help to adopt risk mitigation strategies for better preparedness during disaster. Keeping them in consideration, the present paper takes the following two research objectives:

- To develop Vulnerability Index (VI) of a city
- To develop Resilience Index (RI) of a city

This will help to identify the cities which are liveable and more accommodating for migrants. This city-level vulnerability index will help to capture how vulnerable different cities are in their ability to mitigate and respond to the COVID-19 pandemic.

## 10.3 Preparing Cities for Migration

Migration poses some challenges for cities but cities must accept more responsibility for managing migration and its effects. On the one hand, cities have to pursue policies to encourage rural-urban migration and on the other hand, cities need to supplement efforts towards implementing SDGs and related targets to facilitate orderly, safe and responsible migration. In this context, cities have to implement planned and well managed migration policies. Cities would face the challenges of provisioning affordable housing, education and skill development, access to health services, job creation and additional stress on consumption, natural environment and waste, as a result of migration. To change the perception of migration from an "issue of challenge" to an "opportunity", private sector, civil society and International Organizations have to come forward with various local governments. This multi-stakeholder platform with 'whole of government' approach would enable different stakeholders to participate in the design and decision-making processes of migration related policies which will help to manage migration in the cities. In an effort to support the discussion between different levels of governments on migration governance, IOM has adapted the Migration Governance Indicators (MGI) to the local level (Local MGI). This initiative has an important bearing on the decentralization of migration governance. Its adoption has a significant recognition of the role of cities and municipalities in taking stock of the comprehensiveness of migration policies as well as in identifying gaps and areas that could be strengthened. This type of governmental decentralization will help migrants to be mainstreamed into urban planning. Urban planning should incorporate the specific vulnerabilities that migrants face in the cities and should include recovery and reintegration policies for the return migrants (in the case of remigration from the source region) who have once fled from the city during a crisis. MGI profile of any country shows that city-migration governance is an underdeveloped area of migration management system.

### 10.3.1 *Understanding Vulnerability*

Migration helps in the diversification of income sources and may be a strategy for reducing dependency and vulnerability of individuals at the household level but it can also result in increased vulnerability (Ellis, 1998). In the sense of collective vulnerability of a community, migrants in the cities are also vulnerable to climate change, natural disaster, and environmental change and recently pandemic. Central to the concepts of improving resilience to pandemic and improving human rights protection of migrants is vulnerability, which is not the same as poverty. The Hyogo Framework 2005–2015 at World Conference on Disasters, has adopted vulnerability as a 'set of conditions determined by physical, social, economic and environmental factors or processes which increase the susceptibility of a community to the impact of hazards.' The most vulnerable individuals, groups, classes are those most exposed to perturbations, who possess the most limited coping capacity and suffer the most from the impact of a crisis and who are endowed with circumscribed potential for recovery (Bohle *et al.*, 1994). Therefore, vulnerability can be defined in terms of exposure, capacity and potentiality. Vulnerability is concerned with various risks that affect whether individuals or households are in poverty, or are likely to fall into poverty (Holzmann and Jorgenson, 2000). Within the migration context, vulnerability is defined as a limited capability to avoid, resist, cope with or recover from violence, exploitation, and abuse (IOM handbook: On protection and assistance for migrants vulnerable to violence, exploitation and abuse, 2019). This shows that migrants are not only vulnerable to income poverty but also vulnerable to various hazards-like pandemic. Poverty is an important aspect of vulnerability because of its direct association with access to resources. In this regard, income is a relevant proxy for access to resources in its multifaceted form and correlates with other aspects for poverty relevant for vulnerability (Adger, 1999).

According to a report by the United Nations High Commissioner for Human Rights, vulnerabilities of migrants "can include poverty, discrimination, lack of access to fundamental human rights, including education, health, food and water, and decent work, as well as xenophobia, violence, gender inequality, the wide-ranging consequences of natural disaster, climate change and environmental degradation, and separation from family". Therefore, in any city understanding vulnerability implies understanding the risk factors which is the combination of idiosyncratic risks as well as covariate risks that the migrant faces. A significant aspect of migrant's vulnerability is its multi-dimensionality which is rooted within the political economy in terms of existing social relations of exploitation, unequal bargaining and discrimination and deprivation in terms of human rights-based framework. We have to understand both the risk factors that contribute to migrant vulnerability and the protective factors that enhance migrant resilience within a city.

### 10.3.2 *Understanding Pandemic Related Vulnerability*

COVID-19 has reinforced pre-existing vulnerabilities (inherent risks) of migrants with pandemic induced vulnerabilities (systemic risk) and make cities susceptible to hazard. There is an important linkage between pandemic situation and risk of health hazard, livelihood loss, loss of social network and migrants be stranded due to imminent lockdown and border closure. This type of pandemic related hazard has increased the probability of migrants to remain in poverty (chronic poverty) and has caused perturbations within migrants. Due to the paucity of a clean habitat in a crowded environment in the city and little access to health care facilities migrants are the worst victims of pandemic. COVID-19 lockdown measures may have a disproportionate impact on the migrant population as they are working in precarious or informal job sectors and living in poor housing conditions (Molenaar and Praag, 2022). In addition, as migrants are working in a city with undocumented legal status, they failed to receive the benefits of government programme announced during pandemic. Given the diversity in vulnerabilities, it is relevant to explore that migrants are described as being over-represented among the weakest, most vulnerable social groups within urban communities and are worst affected by the pandemic. This will support advocacy on pandemic-resilient development policies in the cities. Diverse aspects of determining vulnerability can be conceptualized as a set of entitlements and it is the structure or architecture of these entitlements which underpins both security and vulnerability of migrants within cities (Bhattacharya & Banerjee, 2021).

### 10.3.3 *Social Vulnerability of Migrants*

Migration has a direct impact on the population size of areas of origin and destination and hence it is indirectly linked to social structure (Goldscheider, 1987). In a narrow sense, theory of social vulnerability is related with individual command over resources and basic necessities. In wider sense it is about totality of individual rights and social entitlement. It includes susceptibility of migrants to potential losses from extreme events and ability to absorb and withstand impacts. Vulnerability is socially constructed because of differences in complex factors such as institutional development, social relations and political power (Cutter, 1996). Social vulnerability at the individual or household level involves political economy associated with access to resources and ultimately to livelihood entitlements (Adger, 1999). Social vulnerability, appropriate to migrants, has been addressed from causal structure of vulnerability developed by Bohle *et al.* Spatially social vulnerability is defined by three distinctive processes- human ecology (quality of the work environment), expanded entitlement (not only ownership of resources but necessary empowerment to capture social entitlements like public distribution system, social protection policies etc.) and political economy and class structure (in cities, labour process common to all societies is subsumed under specific social form through regime of accumulation and appropriation of surplus by the capitalists through exploitation of distress migrants). Class relations and empowerment are related with the capacity part of vulnerability which helps to identify the ability to cope with stress and shocks. Based on class relations, the ability to cope with shocks has been rooted in social relations of production which has changed dramatically due to migration. Finally, unequal access to opportunities is likely to result in competition, conflict and tension between migrants and natives. This has made assimilation, adjustment and integration difficult for migrants in cities. The variables that influence social vulnerability are lack of access to resources, low economic status, lack of social capital (social networks and connection), denial of human rights, limited access to decision making, beliefs and customs etc. Social vulnerability is also driven by precarious livelihoods, the degree of social protection and influence of institutions and rule system in the specific city.

### 10.3.4 *Economic Vulnerability of Migrants*

Economic vulnerability is ascribed to inherent conditions affecting a country's exposure to exogenous shock arising out of pandemic (Briguglio *et al.*, 2008). People migrate for economic reasons as they have very low income in rural. This vulnerability is measured by inequality and economic autonomy of migrants. Gini index and debt repayments as a percentage of GDP are proxies for these two variables. Asset deprivation indicator can also be developed to study this type of vulnerability.

### 10.3.5 *Demographic Vulnerability*

This vulnerability includes demographic characteristics such as age, gender, family structure, occupation and employment as well as access to political power. Among migrants, women and children are more vulnerable than men. Vulnerability is measured by dependency ratio (ratio of the number of dependents to the total working age population in a country or region), urbanization (calculated as proportion of urban households among all households), population density etc.

### 10.3.6 *Housing, Hygiene and Health Vulnerability*

Migrants are more likely to live in substandard housing and suffer from malnourishment. They are less likely to have any health insurance scheme. People per room, non-availability of safe drinking water, inadequate sanitation facilities, chronic diseases, without easy access to public health facility, availability of public hospitals are proxies for hygiene and health vulnerability.

### 10.3.7 *Financial, Mental and Physical Vulnerabilities: The Struggle to Cope with*

COVID-19 pandemic had inflicted several vulnerabilities for migrant workers. Vulnerability in the present context is a dynamic concept in the sense that migrants might not be vulnerable at the beginning of the pandemic, but could subsequently become vulnerable depending on the government response to cope with the crisis (Acharya and Porwal, 2020). In general, physical vulnerability takes into account the probability of exposure to risk associated with natural disaster and it is a sudden process in contrast to social vulnerability which is a continuous process (Sajjad and Jain, 2014). In the case of pandemic, physical vulnerability arises due to travel-bans imposed by the government. Migrants in transit may be particularly vulnerable to rights violations and abuses, particularly when their status is irregular (Latham-Sprinkle *et al.*, 2019). Migrant workers were put in a major financial predicament as they were without jobs and ending of their daily income on which they survived. Most of the migrant workers were running out of food and some of them went without any meal the whole day. Migrants had to suffer mental hardship with no jobs, no money and being isolated from their families due to sudden lockdown with a decrease in their social connectedness (Jesline *et al.*, 2021). The indicators for measuring mental vulnerabilities are psychiatric issues like anxiety disorders, domestic violence, alcoholism etc. It was found that some non-poor migrants had become poor and already impoverished migrants had been entangled in deep poverty (under debt trap) due to these multiple facets of adversities that they went through during pandemic.

## 10.4 Methodology to Measure City Vulnerability

*"We aim to measure vulnerability yet we cannot define it precisely".*
***– (Birkmann & Pelling, 2006)***

The objective is to rank the cities on the basis of Composite Vulnerability Index (CVI) derived from vulnerability indices of different domains of vulnerabilities among urban migrants in the city. The cities which have higher CVI are more susceptible to external shocks than the cities which have lower vulnerability. This methodology will help to map overall vulnerability of a city as well as individual domain vulnerability. Vulnerability at the level of a city can influence poverty and poverty itself may be a source of vulnerability in the city. Vulnerability, addressed on city level (vulnerability of places) based on the vulnerability of urban migrants, will help policy makers to adopt risk mitigation strategies for better preparedness to COVID-19 pandemic and this in turn will reduce poverty for the country as a whole.

Here, an attempt has been made to construct indicators to operationalize city level vulnerability. It is true that indicators are not based on so called one-size-fit-all strategies and any investigation into vulnerability would incorporate other vulnerability indicators relevant to the need of local communities. This paper adopts the vulnerability of places approach (Rygel *et al.*, 2006). Here vulnerability indices are developed to spatially identify vulnerable cities related with the vulnerabilities of urban migrants. First, we have to define principal variables for the above mentioned four domains of vulnerabilities inherent in the city system related with migration. Then we have to define its proxy variables by which we can measure the principal variables. Indicators from different domains of vulnerability can be computed from respective data sources of the country.

For evaluation of CVI, here we followed relative approach used by UNDP for developing Human Development Index (Sajjad and Jain, 2014). Cities should be selected purposely where there is a high concentration of urban migrants and migrant households should be selected randomly from different cities. The questionnaire for this purpose should be open ended so that we can collect qualitative information also.

VI (Vulnerability Index) has to be developed for the $i^{th}$ variable and $j^{th}$ component (domain of vulnerability) and for the $k^{th}$ city for which the vulnerability indices have to be measured. For example, if we want to construct Vulnerability Index for a city for urban migrants then we can proceed as follows:

$$VI_{ijk} = (X_{ijk} - \min X_{ijk})/(\max X_{ijk} - \min X_{ijk}) \quad \ldots (1)$$

$$VI_{ijk} = (\max X_{ijk} - X_{ijk})/(\max X_{ijk} - \min X_{ijk}) \quad \ldots (2)$$

Equation (1) represent normalization of indicators which have direct or positive functional relationship with vulnerability or resilience and equation (2) represent normalization of indicators which have inverse functional relation with vulnerability or resilience (for example, access to remittances, access to relief etc.). Here, $VI_{ijk}$ represent vulnerability index for $i^{th}$ variable in $j^{th}$ component for $k^{th}$ city. Here minimum and maximum is considered on variable i for different cities, for some specific domain on vulnerability.

$$VI_{jk} = \left(\sum_{i=1}^{I} VI_{ijk}\right) / \text{No. of variables in that specific domain.}$$

Where $VI_{jk}$ represent vulnerability index of $j^{th}$ component (domain) and $k^{th}$ city, derived by summing over vulnerability indices for all the variables 'i' related to that domain for that particular city and divided by number of variables or indicators used to express that domain. Here, j is the vulnerability domains (for example, social vulnerability) also known as components and (j = 1, 2, 3, ..., J), i is the variables related to that specific vulnerability j where (i = 1, 2, 3, ..., I) and k is the cities where (k = 1, 2, 3, ..., *K*) for which we have to find composite vulnerability index.Variables denoted by 'i' are basically the proxy variables of the indicators. Numerator measures the extent by which $j^{th}$ component (vulnerability) has performed better in $i^{th}$ variable as compared to the city showing the worst performance in that component and denominator indicates the range. Here range is defined as the difference between maximum and minimum values of that $i^{th}$ variable for $j^{th}$ component (vulnerability). For each variable in that domain, we can determine VI for that particular city and finally by taking average of that we can determine VI for the city in question on that specific domain. In similar vein, we can calculate other VIs for different domains of vulnerability of migrants in that particular city. Therefore, we derive four component vulnerability indices-Economic Vulnerability, Social Vulnerability, Demographic Vulnerability and Health and Hygiene Vulnerability. The overall (composite) vulnerability index of a city is calculated by giving equal weights to each domain to each domain. This is the simplest way to combine component scores into a single measure by using simple average. In most cases, however, vulnerability is insufficiently understood and assigning weights to vulnerability indicators is unwise in the face of disaster as causes of vulnerability change quickly over time and space, rendering many indicators useless (Rygel *et al.*, 2006). But the fact is that all the domains are not equally important for any particular city and in some cities domain specific vulnerability has more practical importance than overall vulnerability. A relationship between overall (composite) vulnerability index and its four components can be developed by using Karl Pearson's two tailed correlation. This will help to detect whether each of the components of vulnerability index has positive or negative correlation with the overall composite index and whether this correlation is statistically significant or not. In this way we can calculate vulnerability score of a city in the context of urban migrants with higher index values indicating higher vulnerability. This city level ranking of vulnerability will provide policy makers the incentive to prioritize reconstruction strategies for affected migrants. This could help the government to identify cities that might have severe consequences of pandemic.

One of the more vexing problems in developing composite vulnerability indices is the method of aggregation (Rygel *et al.*, 2006). In our methodology, in calculating domain vulnerability, equal weights are assigned to each indicator and equal weights are also assigned to each domain at the time of calculating overall vulnerability index (Acharya and Porwal, 2020), without attaching specific weights to each proxy. Simple averages shows that all the components contribute equally to vulnerability but if we decide that certain component contribute more to overall vulnerability then we have to create a weighting scheme. In this context, principal component analysis can be used to weigh the components of overall vulnerability. The standard procedure in using Principal Component Analysis (PCA) as a weight elicitation technique is to use the factor loadings of the first component to serve as weights for the indicators (Greco *et al.*, 2019) and weights are assigned endogenously. However, sometimes the first component alone is not adequate to explain a large portion of the variance of the indicators; thus, more components are needed (Greco *et al.*, 2019). One can also use Data Envelopment Analysis (DEA) to determine endogenously a set of weights which is known as efficiency score. However, these two methods are somewhat criticized relating to their use as a weighting scheme.

### 10.4.1 *Strategies to Foster More Resilient Cities*

Urban resilience is simply defined as "the capacity of a city to rebound from destruction" (Campanella, 2006). Any prescriptive response to vulnerability is to reduce exposure, enhance coping capacity, strengthen recover potentiality and give support to damage control via public and private means (Bohle *et al.*, 1994). Resilience is often used to denote a system's response to hazard/coping mechanism (Briguglio, 2001; Dwyer *et al.*, 2004; van Niekerk, 2007) and is defined as the ability to recover from losses quickly and even capacity transformation when conditions require it. Not all cities or migrants who have integrated in the cities are equally vulnerable when they are exposed to a hazard. This differential vulnerability depends on the coping ability of the migrants or the cities where they live where coping ability has been defined as a combination of resistance and resilience. The scores on resilience index would reflect the appropriateness of policy measures undertaken by policymakers and private economic agents to enable a country to protect or recover from adverse shocks. Resilience is a multi-faceted approach, instead of traditional 'predict and prevent' approach of risk management, that manages change and uncertainty in a more integrated way related with individuals, communities, institutions, businesses and systems of a city.

In India, national lockdown was imposed under the Disaster Management Act, 2005 and severity of COVID-19 epidemic has been equated similar to that of national disaster. Risk is the probability of a loss related with any disaster and is often described as a three-dimensional pyramid with its constituent elements-hazard, vulnerability and exposure. The contribution to capacity to resist, cope with and recover from impact of hazard has been included in the definition of vulnerability.

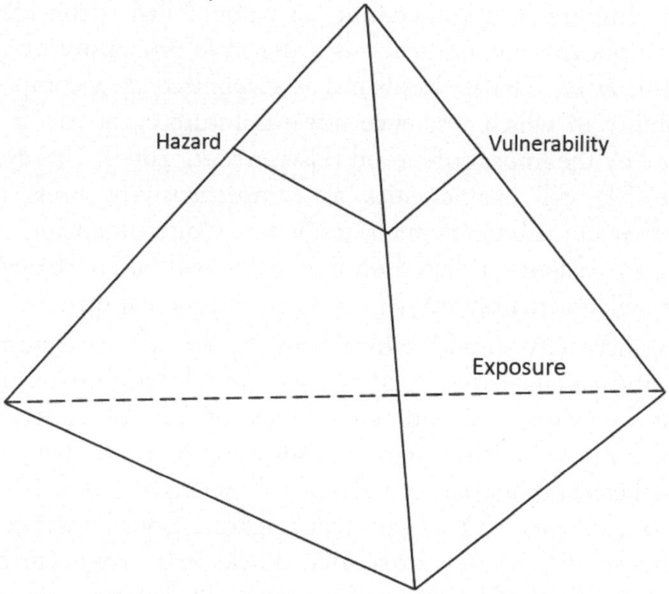


**Figure 10.1:** Risk Pyramid Shows Three Independent Factors that Contribute to Risk: Hazard, Exposure to Vulnerability (developed by Crichton, Dwyer *et al.*, 2004)

Mathematically, in the disaster risk management risk is often expressed as:

| **Risk**<br>of a city being adversely affected by pandemic | = H [ | **Vulnerability**<br>Exposure of a city to external shocks arising from intrinsic features of the city and already present in the city | – | **Resilience**<br>Coping ability which enables the city to withstand or recover from negative shock | ] |
|---|---|---|---|---|---|

Here, H denotes hazard. Hazard in themselves do not constitute disaster but they can exploit human vulnerability and the systems on which it depends (Dewald, 2006). Interaction between hazard and vulnerability translate into disaster risk. In this context hazard is defined as disease pandemic. This itself do not constitute disaster risk. When vulnerability increases disaster risk also increases. Again, disaster risk decreases when coping capacity increases. This shows that when vulnerability of a city increases, resilience also has to be increased to mitigate disaster risk. In this approach resilience is viewed as an integral component of vulnerability or vulnerability is considered as a static component and resilience as a dynamic propensity of a system (Galderisi, *et al.*, 2010). Resilience is recognized as a component of vulnerability in which resilience towards future event can in fact be enhanced by the impact of hazard (Dwyer *et al.*, 2004). City Resilience Index (CRI) will enable cities to comprehensively assess multiple factors that contribute to their resilience. Conceptualizing cities on the basis of resilience is based on how a city will fare in the event of a disaster which is mainly influenced by governmental management.

A resilient city should deliver basic needs; safeguard human life; protect and enhance asset; facilitate human relationship and identity; promote knowledge; defend rule of law, justice and equity; support livelihood and stimulate economic prosperity (City Resilience Index - The Rockefeller Foundation | Arup). These eight city functions are critical to resilience and will protect migrants from idiosyncratic risk and systemic risk of stress or sudden shocks that may occur in cities. City's ability to perform these functions will depend upon efficient leadership in the form of a committed city government and of whole-of-government approach. Any resilient city should be characterized by seven qualities like reflectiveness, robustness, redundancy, flexibility, resourcefulness, inclusiveness and integration. Among these, inclusiveness and integration are the two prominent qualities to build resilience. Inclusiveness imply the need for inclusion of vulnerable groups like migrants in the agenda of city resilience.

Earlier approaches of urban resilience have focussed on either assets or systems. We have to understand the interdependency between systems because interventions to build resilience in one system may have feedback implications in other systems. Development of City resilience index should incorporate multiple city assets, systems and actors simultaneously by considering interdependencies between systems. This is known as performance-based approach of building city resilience. Here, City Resilience Index (CRI) is used which is developed by Arup International Development. This indicator has been developed on the basis of performance-based approach and is based on extensive, evidence-based research and is globally applicable. It recognises the cross-cutting nature of assets and systems and is based on four dimensions, twelve goals and fifty-two indicators. These indicators are assessed through 156 questions and the measurement is based on both qualitative and quantitative information. Indicators related with different goals and dimensions are somewhat overlapped with each other. Therefore, in measuring CRI we have used less indicators relative to the original model but those indicators have been considered which are relevant to particular goals and dimensions related with resilience:

- **Health and well-being:** This dimension considers the extent to which city enables everyone including migrants to meet the basic needs basically in times of crisis.
- **Economy and society:** This dimension relates to the organization of cities with the interaction of economy and society.
- **Infrastructure and environment:** It considers robustness of infrastructure and ecosystem to protect and cope with multiple hazards.
- **Leadership and strategy:** This dimension is characterized by inclusive governance involving government, business and civil society with a whole-of-government approach. Effective leadership and urban management with appropriate government decision making are the key to build resilience.

**Table 10.1**

| *Dimensions* | *Goals* | *Indicators* |
|---|---|---|
| Health and well-being | • Minimal human vulnerability<br>• Diverse livelihoods and employment<br>• Effective safeguard to human health and life | Safe and affordable housing, safe drinking water, effective sanitation, affordable food supply, inclusive labour policies, diverse protection of livelihoods following a shock, adequate access to quality healthcare, robust monitoring and mitigation of public health risk. |
| Economy and society | • Active community engagement and strong social network<br>• Enforcement of law and justice<br>• Sustainable economy | Local community support, participation of actively engaged citizens, proactive corruption prevention, diverse economic base, strong integration between the city's economy and wider economic systems, well-managed public finances. |
| Infrastructure and environment | • Reduced exposure and fragility<br>• Effective provision of critical services<br>• Reliable mobility and communications | Mapping city's exposure and vulnerability to hazard, robust protective infrastructure, proactive management of ecosystems, maintenance and renewal of essential utility infrastructure, reliable communication technology, secure technology network. |
| Leadership and strategy | • Effective leadership and management<br>• Empowered stakeholders<br>• Integrated development planning | Appropriate government decision making, effective coordination with other government bodies, proactive multi-stakeholder collaboration, widespread community awareness and preparedness, effective mechanisms for communities to engage with government, comprehensive city monitoring and data management, consultative planning process. |

*Source:* Developed by author by using City Resilience Index framed by Arup International Development with support from Rockefeller Foundation.

*Note:* The indicators that we have discussed to build city resilience are universal, although their relative importance may vary.

This will be helpful to construct a resilience index just to complement the vulnerability index and also help to assess the degree to which a vulnerable city is moving ahead in coping with or withstanding vulnerability of migrants. As resilience is a multidimensional concept, we have to consider all relevant aspects related with urbanization. Responses from city stakeholders will help to calculate scores for constituent indicators and these scores are obtained between 1 and 5 provided against a worst case-best case scenario (Likert scale). A Qualitative Resilience Profile can be generated by aggregating the responses for each goal. We can transform a qualitative assessment into a quantitative assessment by using an ordinal scale.

## 10.4 Conclusions

In this paper an attempt has been made to develop an overall vulnerability index for cities based on the vulnerabilities of the in-migrants who are likely to live in those cities. The assessment of vulnerability has been addressed mainly to increase the capacity of the city. Vulnerability index as a policy tool will help to identify not only the cities requiring immediate attention but also the specific domains in which efforts could be made to reduce vulnerability for that particular city. The research also aims to shed light on city resilience index as an integral part of measuring vulnerability. In this paper vulnerability and resilience is analyzed in an integrated framework of disaster risk management. But the vulnerability index that we have developed in this study, especially social vulnerability, is very difficult to assess. Assessment of social vulnerability is a continuous process and it would be useful to reassess the relative rankings even after the effect of disaster subsides. Apart from this, City Resilience Index (CRI) that we have developed in this study does not deliver any single score for comparing performance between cities. CRI is basically an indicator-based framework without aggregation and therefore it could not be considered as an index. As resilience is a complex, multi-faceted topic and demands greater transparency, aggregation up to indicator level will provide greater transparency in building resilience for the cities. It will provide a comprehensive basis of measurement including benchmarking performance and is somewhat different from conventional sustainability indicators. The main policy recommendation programme to cope with the vulnerabilities of migrants in the city is the introduction of wage employment programme with a guarantee of work, in-kind transfer, cash transfer and effective use of public distribution system to provide immediate assistance to the marginalized group of people. Paper also recommends the need of national and sub-national micro level data framework for effective management of disaster in future. In this context, the dimension of leadership and strategy has an important role to play.

## Scope of Further Improvements

More research is needed on weighting of indicators and quality of data and validating such data in the context of vulnerability analysis. Study fails to assess the qualities of a resilient city on the basis of a score and their comparison in an evidence-based framework. Further research is required to understand the factors that contribute to the resilience of vulnerable groups like urban poor, especially migrants. It is a dynamic process and priority should be given for improving the factors that makes a city resilient. It is important to note that future research should follow the methodology of constructing an effective index of vulnerability without using the problematic practice of weighting the individual vulnerability indicators.

## References

[1] Acharya, R. and Porwal, A. (2020). A vulnerability index for the management of and response to the COVID-19 epidemic in India: An ecological study. *The Lancet Global Health*, Vol. 8(9), pp. e1142–e1151.

[2] Adger, W.N. (1999). Social vulnerability to climate change and extremes in coastal Vietnam. *World Development,* Vol. 27(2), pp. 249–269.

[3] Adger, W.N. and Kelly, P.M. (1999). Social vulnerability to climate change and the architecture of entitlements. *Mitigation and Adaptation Strategies for Global Change*, Vol. 4(3), pp. 253–266.

[4] Bhattacharya, M. and Banerjee, P. (2021). COVID-19: Indices of economic and health vulnerability for the Indian states. *Social Sciences & Humanities Open,* Vol. 4(1), pp. 100–157.

[5] Birkmann, J. (Ed.) (2006). Measuring Vulnerability to Natural Hazards: Towards Disaster Resilient Societies (Tokyo: UNU Press), pp. 9–54.

[6] Bohle, H.G., Downing, T.E. and Watts, M.J. (1994). Climate change and social vulnerability: Toward a sociology and geography of food insecurity. *Global Environmental Change*, Vol. 4(1), pp. 37–48.

[7] Briguglio, L. (2001) The Vulnerability Index, paper presented at the AOSIS Workshop on Trade, Sustainable Development and SIDS, Montego Bay, Jamaica, 12–15 December.

[8] Chambers, R. (1989). Editorial introduction-Vulnerability: How the poor cope. *IDS Bulletin*, Vol. 20(2), pp. 1–7.

[9] Cutter, S.L. (1996). Vulnerability to environmental hazards. *Progress in Human Geography*, Vol. 20(4), pp. 529–539.

[10] Dwyer, A., Zoppou, C., Nielsen, O., Day, S. and Roberts, S. (2004). Quantifying social vulnerability: A methodology for identifying those at risk to natural hazards, *Geoscience Australia Record*, Vol.14, pp. 1–101.

[11] Ellis, F. (1998). Household strategies and rural livelihood diversification. *The Journal of Development Studies*, Vol. 35(1), pp. 1–38.

[12] Galderisi, A., Ceudech, A., Ferrara, F. and Profice, A. (2010). Integration of different vulnerabilities vs. Natural and na-tech hazards. *ENSURE Project, Deliverable*, Vol. 2, pp. 29–74.

[13] Goldscheider, C. (1987). Migration and social structure: Analytic issues and comparative perspectives in developing nations, Vol. 2(4), pp. 674–696.

[14] Greco, S., Ishizaka, A., Tasiou, M. and Torrisi, G. (2019). On the methodological framework of composite indices: A review of the issues of weighting, aggregation, and robustness. *Social Indicators Research*, Vol. 141(1), pp. 61–94.

[15] Holzmann, R. and Jørgensen, S. (2001). Social risk management: A new conceptual framework for social protection, and beyond. *International Tax and Public Finance*, *8*(4), pp. 529–556.

[16] Jesline, J., Romate, J., Rajkumar, E. and George, A.J. (2021). The plight of migrants during COVID-19 and the impact of circular migration in India: A systematic review. *Humanities and Social Sciences Communications,* Vol. 8(1), pp. 1–12.

[17] Latham-Sprinkle, J., David, F., Bryant, K. and Larsen, J. (2019). Migrants and their vulnerability to human trafficking, modern slavery and forced labour, *International Organization for Migration, Geneva*, pp. 1–112.

[18] Molenaar, J. and Van Praag, L. (2022). Migrants as 'vulnerable groups' in the COVID-19 pandemic: A critical discourse analysis of a taken-for-granted label in academic literature. *SSM-Qualitative Research in Health*, Vol. 2, pp. 1–10.

[19] Ojo, S.S., Tpl, D.B. and Pojwan, M.A. (2017). Urbanization and urban growth: Challenges and prospects for national development. *Journal of Humanities and Social Policy,* Vol. 3(1), pp. 65–71.

[20] Rygel, L., O'sullivan, D. and Yarnal, B. (2006). A method for constructing a social vulnerability index: An application to hurricane storm surges in a developed country. *Mitigation and Adaptation Strategies for Global Change,* Vol. 11(3), pp. 741–764.

[21] Sajjad, H. and Jain, P. (2014). Assessment of socio-economic vulnerabilities among urban migrants in South-East Delhi, India. *Journal of Studies in Social Sciences*, Vol. 7(1), pp. 65–81.

[22] Tacoli, C., McGranahan, G. and Satterthwaite, D. (2015). Urbanisation, rural-urban migration and urban poverty. *IIED Working Paper. IIED, London.* pp. 1–36.

[23] Tripathi, S. and Kaur, H. (2017). Determinants of rural to urban migration in large agglomerations in India: An empirical analysis, MPRA Paper no. 76484, pp. 1–19. Online at https://mpra.ub.uni-muenchen.de/76484.

[24] Van Niekerk, D. (2007). Disaster risk reduction, disaster risk management and disaster management: Academic rhetoric or practical reality? *Disaster Management: South Africa,* Vol. 4(1), pp. 6–9.

SECTION – IV

# Sustainable Development & Environmental Issues

CHAPTER 11

# Technological Progress and Productivity Measurement: Some Conceptual Issues

**Madhusudan Datta**

## 11.1 Introduction

Revolution in information and communications technology has coalesced the world into what has been called the 'global village'. But this coalescence has not reduced disparity or removed misery. However, we are now more aware of the sufferings and needs of people in different countries and regions. This is the context of heightened focus on development cooperation. Urge for development is human passion and cooperation is a humane, rational, and civilized way of living. Development cooperation refers to assistance, not from a sheer profit motive, flowing from the countries or organizations with resources, including knowledge, to countries or regions in need of them. Assistance can be financial or material – that is important in a world of enormous disparity – or in the form of knowledge or technology transfer. Unless the assistance is aimed at overcoming some exigency, one would expect it to be ultimately reflected in an improvement of productivity that is supposed to be concomitant to development. And improvement of productivity is a measure of success of cooperation. But the link is often not so obvious, as we will explain below.

The phenomenon of global warming and possible ways to tackle it is at the centre of all learned discussions regarding economic progress and development cooperation. The exploitation of fossil fuels is being viewed with increasing concern and restraints are being considered and exercised, but that seems to be yielding only limited benefit in fighting global warming. Ultimately, in this divided and competitive world, it seems, we will have to depend on technological progress to meet the challenge. Indeed, technological progress has been happening in all sorts of directions.

In the context of global warming, consider the case of solar electricity. The unit cost of solar electricity has been steadily falling, which means total resource-use (in value terms) per unit of the product has been falling, or, its inverse – productivity – in this line of production has been rising. To keep the motivation of research strong, governments have been giving subsidies to solar batteries. But does the advancement of technology in this field lead to measured productivity enhancement in the broader field of electricity generation? Probably not yet, as the cost of this green electricity is still not less than that obtained by burning fossil fuel, which means that solar electricity technology is still using more resources per unit of electricity generated than that under alternative fossil fuel technologies[1]. The same point can be made about electric cars. One can ask why then are green technologies being encouraged? We know; they have some benefits that are not given due consideration for productivity measurement and therein lies a bug.

In the case of solar electricity, the output of the process is not only the quantity of electricity generated but also the saving of carbon footprint that would be generated by alternative processes of electricity generation. Contrary-wise, output measurement in the case of fossil fuel burning processes does not consider the carbon footprint that is released into the atmosphere without a cost to the producer.[2] If the negative (undesired) by-product could be built into the cost structure, the measured comparative productivity could give a very different result. Economic measurements of output and hence, productivity are thus market-oriented. But even as we ignore, however unreasonably, the non-market externalities that escape accounting but are not inconsequential by any means, the measurement of productivity has other pitfalls that researchers are often oblivious of. Most often we consider several lines of production together like in the case of the manufacturing sector where the output of one line of production

[1] Strictly, this is true under competitive conditions.

[2] Many advanced countries have already introduced carbon tax and other measures as effective cost to the emitters of greenhouse gases.

becomes the input in another line within the sector. For example, steel in used in car manufacturing. Correctly accounting for output, in this case, becomes very important for productivity measurement. The present paper takes up an analysis of some pitfalls in the measurement of productivity. In the following sections, the depth of interrelations between technological progress, prices and measured productivity growth is discussed. In Section 11.2, a short discussion of the measurement complications of output is undertaken. Section 11.3 shows that a non-flat trend of relative prices can lead to divergence in trends of output and GVA and the next section investigates how differential sectoral technological progress may generate systematic movement in relative prices. This relative price movement may cause adjustment of value-added; erosion from the progressive sector and build-up elsewhere undermining the link between technological progress and productivity growth. The import of this discussion is that value-added productivity growth is often not a true indicator of the extent of sectoral technological progress.

## 11.2 What is Output?

Output is apparently an elementary concept of economics, but contrary to common perception the concept is involved enough to bear careful consideration. The ultimate purpose of production is to make goods and services available for use outside the production process. Thus, for a production unit, the purpose of production is to make the (gross) output available for use (or sale) outside the unit. The gross output of the electricity generating sector is what flows out of the sectoral production process for use outside the sector; this amount must exclude the generated electricity used up by the sector itself for running the machinery and lighting up the plants concerned. In this simple example with only one product, the gross output may be viewed in the physical unit as there is no need to add up heterogeneous quantities. But, for broad sectors producing more than one product we need to resort to measures in value terms. Clearly, the gross output of a sector, say manufacturing, viewed as a group of subsectors (like leather goods, metals, transport equipment, chemicals, etc.), is not just the sum total of those of the sub-sectors in value terms, as the (gross) output of the broad sector must exclude intra-sectoral intermediate uses of products of subsectors (but not intermediate inputs taken from outside the sector). "It is not difficult to see that the inclusion of intra-industry flows of intermediate products adds identically to both the input and output side of an industry production function... . This is a form of double-counting and in principle, output and intermediate inputs can be made larger and larger by basing industry aggregates on increasingly smaller statistical units ....." (OECD 2001, p. 31).

The import of the above discussion is that the manufacturing sector's gross output is goods made available by the sector for final use (like consumption, investment or export) and also for intermediate use outside the sector. This is what the sectoral production process generates for use outside the sector. By implication, the gross output (we will refer to it simply as output below) of a sector cannot be obtained by adding up those of its subsectors. For this purpose, the input-output transactions table must be used[3]. To avoid the complexity researchers often take recourse to the concept of net output or its equivalent gross value added (GVA).

GVA (includes depreciation of fixed capital) is the gross output less intermediate inputs taken from outside the sector (like mining, service or other inputs for manufacturing)[4]. At the sectoral level, it is often a maintained assumption, particularly when we do not look beyond a few years, that the intermediate input of a process is proportional to its output, i.e., the intermediate input coefficients are stable. A subtle assumption here is that relative prices are stable too. On this basis, GVA has been used as a proxy for output in productivity studies[5]. This line of thought suggests that GVA and output should follow the same trend; more specifically, the trend of GVA in the manufacturing sector should reflect the trend of the output of the sector. But things often do not turn up so conveniently; GVA and output may diverge in trend; and, indeed, they did so for the Indian economy since the turn of the 1970s (Datta, 2020). In that case, the

---

[3] Annual Survey of Industries does not follow the norm.

[4] At the level of the whole economy net output is the GDP or the sum of final uses (expenditures) like consumption, investment and exports out of domestic production less imported intermediate inputs. All domestically produced intermediate inputs become intra-sectoral (economy-wide) intermediate inputs.

[5] GVA is computationally a very convenient entity. GVA of a sector, unlike gross output, is the sum-total of GVAs of all the sub-sectors.

question arises about which of the two variables would better represent the growth of the sector or its productivity. The choice has the implications for measured productivity growth.

## 11.3 Output, GVA and Relative Price

For simplicity, let us conceive of a simple production setup with only M (manufacturing) and S (services) sectors. The production functions can be specified as:

$$\Omega_M = F_M (\Phi_M, \omega_S) \qquad \dots (1)$$

$$\Omega_S = F_S (\Phi_S, \omega_M) \qquad \dots (2)$$

Here, subscripts are used to denote sectors, $\Omega$ stands for gross output, F represents production function and $\Phi$ stands for the primary factors of production. Each sector takes intermediate input from the other sector; $\omega_S$ is intermediate input of manufacturing originating in the service sector and $\omega_M$ is that originating in the manufacturing sector but employed in service production.

An important point to note here is that a production function is a relationship among real variables. So, we take all the variables in equation (1) and (2) as real quantities. However, value-added is a monetary quantity expressed at current prices[6]. So, writing V for GVA and following the definition:

$$V_M = P_M\Omega_M - P_S\omega_S = (P_M - P_S\,\mu)\,\Omega_M \qquad \dots (3)$$

$$V_S = P_S\Omega_S - P_M\omega_M = (P_S - P_M\,\lambda)\,\Omega_S \qquad \dots (4)$$

where, $\mu$ and $\lambda$ are assumed factors of proportionality between the relevant intermediate input and output.

Clearly, $(V_M/V_S) = [(P_M - P_S\,\mu)/(P_S - P_M\,\lambda)](\Omega_M/\Omega_S)$ ... (5)

Assuming $\mu$ and $\lambda$ to be constant, it is clear from the equation (5) that depending on the trend in relative prices the trend in relative value-added may deviate from that in relative real output. Particularly, if the relative price of manufactures falls consistently, value-added in

[6] Real value added of another period is obtained by using the GDP deflator. The much-touted double deflation method has serious pitfalls leading the Central Statistical Office of India to abandon the method (see Datta, *et al.*, 2015).

manufacturing relative to that in the services sector will go on declining even if outputs of the two sectors remain unchanged. Clearly, it is a real possibility that systematic price movements would whittle away value-added from the output of a sector (and build it up in another sector) making relative sectoral GVA an improper proxy for the relative size (level of activity) of the sector in real terms[7]. It is here noted that the relative value added is the same whether it is considered in real or nominal terms since the value-added deflator is the same for both the sectors. Equation (5) shows the relative price as the essential issue involved in obtaining a transformation factor from relative real output to relative value-added and thus it shows the limitations of conclusions regarding relative sectoral growth based on GVA calculus. We will discuss below that systematic movement of relative prices may be generated by differential sectoral technological progress.

## 11.4 Uneven Technological Progress and Relative Prices

Traditionally technical progress has not been uniform across different sectors of economic activities. Traditionally manufacturing has been the most fertile ground for the adoption of new technologies while the flip side of the picture, perhaps, is to be found in certain services (like performing arts, teaching, medical care and public administration) that are by nature akin to the labour of the service provider. Doubtless, productivity gains happen in this latter category of services also. Nevertheless, in such cases, labour seems to be more organically related to the service. While the reality is not a static bundle of rules and revolutionary changes in technology in several fields have changed the nature of many activities, several studies have attested to the validity of the basic notion of differential productivity changes favouring the manufacturing sector the most (Nordhaus, 2006; Steindel and Stiroh, 2001; Fagerberg, 2000). William Baumol (1967) presented a very simple construct using the assumption that economic activities can be classified into basically two types: one is

---

[7] It may be noted here that obtaining real GVA is not a solution in practical situations. A one percent change in price may change GVA by several percentages depending on the importance of intermediate inputs and their price changes. Further, as the CSO has warned, double deflation procedure may result in negative value added for a vibrant industry. For a detailed discussion see the section.

technologically progressive in that it experiences sustained productivity increases while the other type is technologically stagnant in the sense that productivity increases are relatively small and sporadic. A simple input-output (I-O) model is constructed in the following in order to understand how uneven labour-saving technological progress may lead to divergent trends in relative prices and sectoral shares in GDP.

### 11.4.1 *Uneven Technological Progress and Prices*

Consider a production system, as in the previous section, with two sectors – M and S. Manufacturing is the progressive sector denoted by M; and services, denoted by S, constitute the sector of comparatively stagnant activities. Here we use the following notations: $\omega_{ij}$ = intermediate use of the i[th] commodity in the j[th] sector, and $\Omega_i$= output of the i[th] sector ($i, j$ = 1 and 2 respectively for M and S). Also, we denote $l_i$ = labour used in, and $f_i$ = final demand for the product of, the i[th] sector. The I-O structure is given below:

| | M | S | Final Demand | Output |
|---|---|---|---|---|
| M | $\omega_{11}$ | $\omega_{12}$ | $f_1$ | $\Omega_1$ |
| S | $\omega_{21}$ | $\omega_{22}$ | $f_2$ | $\Omega_2$ |
| Labour | $l_1$ | $l_2$ | | |

I-O flows are real flows per production cycle defining the underlying technology. In practice, the observations are conveniently recorded as money values. At any point of time, we may take advantage of defining units of measurement to do away with the distinction between physical quantities and money values. So, we choose units suitably to set prices of both the commodities to unity; so, the observed values as real quantities[8] initially. The assumption here is that the technology is characterized by fixed coefficients: $a_{ij}$ = $\omega_{ij}/\Omega_j$. We take the norm of using brackets for matrices, braces for

[8] In fact, as argued below, for any vector of final demand (F) and the input-coefficient (A) matrix, the system solves for the output (X) vector; and production structure determines relative prices. Taking any one price as unity the other price is determined. Now the logic is straight forward – if a price is, say, 2 per unit quantity then redefining the unit as half the previous measure, price is reset to unity. This redefinition of unit changes the relevant input coefficients appropriately.

vectors and superscript '*T*' for transpose: $\omega = [\omega_{ij}]; A = [a_{ij}]; \Omega^T = \{\Omega_1, \Omega_2\}; F^T = \{f_1, f_2\}; L^T = \{l_1, l_2\}$. Thus, for given A, $\Omega = (I-A)^{-1}F$, $(I-A)^{-1}$ being the Leontief-inverse matrix with a typical element, $\alpha_{ij}$, representing the total (direct and indirect) requirement of the i$^{th}$ commodity for producing to satisfy one unit of final demand of the j$^{th}$ commodity.

All the elements in the vectors and matrices must be non-negative in order to be economically meaningful. While *A, F* and *L* are given, conditions for obtaining $\Omega \geq 0$ are the well-known Hawkins-Simon conditions:

$$(1-a_{ii}) > 0,\ i= 1, 2;\ \text{and}\ \det(I-A) > 0. \quad \ldots (1)$$

Looking at the uses of products, we have the following relations among inputs, outputs and final demands:

$$\Omega_1 - \omega_{11} - \omega_{12} = f_1,\ \text{and}\ \Omega_2 - \omega_{21} - \omega_{22} = f_2 \quad \ldots (2)$$

We assume initially that there is a single (primary) factor of production, labour, and no fixed cost; so, in a competitive set-up, price equals average (and marginal) variable cost. An assumption[9] of the model is that *the wage rate is equal across sectors*[10]. Then the price equations are:

$$(p_1)\omega_{11} + (p_2)\omega_{21} + wl_1 = (p_1)\Omega_1,\ \text{and}\ (p_1)\omega_{12} + (p_2)\omega_{22} + wl_2 = (p_2)\Omega_2 \quad \ldots (3a)$$

We put the prices in parentheses to highlight the relations among quantities, which are also values in the beginning, as prices are set to unity. In this economy, since labour is the only factor of production, $l_1, l_2 > 0$, it follows from (2) and (3a), putting $p_1 = p_2 = 1$, that aggregate wage payment equals aggregate final uses $(f_1 + f_2)$, which is equal to the GDP of the economy. Thus, the real wage rate can be found from the accounting identity:

$$\text{GDP} = f_1 + f_2 \equiv w\,(l_1 + l_2) \quad \ldots (4)$$

$$\text{More generally, } (p_1)\,f_1 + (p_2)f_2 \equiv w\,(l_1 + l_2) \quad \ldots (4a)$$

[9] This assumption is not strictly necessary; it simplifies the model.

[10] The implication is that the skill levels are of the same order in the two sectors, only skill takes different forms in different sectors.

Using vector-matrix notations we can write (3a) as:

$P^T\omega + wL^T = P^TZ$ ... (3b)

where, $P^T = \{p_1, p_2\}$ and $Z$ is diagonalized $2x2$ matrix form of $\Omega$. Further, let us write the labour coefficients as $\lambda_i = l_i/\Omega_i$, so that, $L^T = \lambda^T Z$, for $\lambda^T = \{\lambda_1, \lambda_2\}$.

Clearly, (3b) gives[11]: $P^T = wL^T(Z-\omega)^{-1} = w\lambda^T(I-A)^{-1}$ ... (5)

Writing in full form: $p_1/p_2 = (\lambda_1(1-a_{22}) + \lambda_2 a_{21})/(\lambda_1 a_{12} + \lambda_2(1-a_{11}))$ ... (6)

Now, so long as $\lambda_i$'s are independent of $a_{ij}$'s, we have:

$\delta(p_1/p_2)/\delta\lambda_1 = \lambda_2\,[(1-a_{11})\,(1-a_{22}) - a_{12}a_{21})]/[(\lambda_1 a_{12} + \lambda_2(1-a_{11}))]^2$... (7)

Similarly, $\delta(p_1/p_2)/\delta\lambda_2 = \lambda_1[a_{12}a_{21} - (1-a_{11})\,(1-a_{22})]/[(\lambda_1 a_{12} + \lambda_2(1-a_{11}))]^2$ ... (8)

Using the two Hawkins-Simon conditions on (7) and (8), we have $\delta(p_1/p_2)/\delta\lambda_1 > 0$; and $\delta(p_1/p_2)/\delta\lambda_2 < 0$. So, if labour-saving technical progress takes place in the technologically progressive M-sector without affecting $a_{ij}$'s, so that the labour coefficient in the M-sector($\lambda_1$)is now reduced, leaving that for the S-sector unchanged, the relative price of the M-commodity will decline and vice versa.

Clearly, from equation (3a), labour-saving technical progress reduces the cost of production in the M-sector by reducing $l_1$ for unchanged *F*. Under competitive conditions, the benefit of cost reduction is fully passed on to the users through lower prices[12]. Intuitively it is clear that, so long as the same final demand vector is being produced, the real GDP remains unchanged, now being produced using less labour due to productivity increase in the M-sector. By assumption, real wage rises uniformly (equation 3) in the two sectors. The result is the *adjustment of value-added through a change in relative price in favour of the stagnant sector*[13] *and the*

---

[11] The expression gives a nice interpretation: price equals the value of total direct and indirect labour used in production of the relevant commodity.

[12] Nordhaus (2006) finds firm support to this hypothesis for the US economy.

[13] One very comprehensive study on the American economy, spanning more than half a century from 1948, by Nordhaus (2006) finds strong negative relationship between productivity growth and price growth, so much so that it concludes that

*corresponding change in value-added per unit of output, again in favour of the stagnant sector. This leads to a decline in the progressive sector's relative share in GDP even without any change in the real output of the two sectors* as, in this model, sectoral GDP is proportional to sectoral employment.

In fact, no assumption of an unchanged final demand vector is necessary to show the direction of change in relative price which is independent of final demands (equation-6). In reality, how the structure of final demand changes depends on several factors affecting the price and income elasticities. The basic point is economising on the use of resources through productivity improvement and distribution of the gain across sectors through uniform wages causing adjustment in relative price and sectoral value-added. So long as the progressive-stagnant classification remains effective and technical progress goes on reducing the opportunity cost of production of the progressive sector, a decline in the relative price of the progressive sector, and a corresponding rise in that of the stagnant sector, will go on cumulatively without respite. This message of the model forms the basic notion that has come to be known as the Baumol disease.

The objective here is not to build a comprehensive model of the economy, but to develop a macroeconomic insight even at the cost of some microeconomic precision. Working out the equilibrium would inevitably require consideration of the demand side (Echevarria, 1997; Kongshamut *et al.* 1997). Our model is admittedly simplistic, but it goes a step further than the original Baumol (1967) model; we have introduced intermediate inputs and thus used the input-output framework simply to show that cost in the progressive sector reduces even though the cost of its intermediate inputs from the stagnant sector rises. Regarding this progressive-stagnant classification of the entire economy, Baumol *et al.* (1985) clarifies: "Outputs, firms and industries do not fall into black and white categories of stagnation and progressivity – they are all shades of grey. Even the most stagnant sectors of the economy have undergone some technological change, varying from one period to another." p.807. We deliberately ignore agriculture and other informal sectors, which are shades of grey. Skill

consumers capture virtually all the gains from technological change (Also, see Fagerburg, 2000).

requirement in these sectors is generally of a lower order, so the tendency to wage equalization does not work. With this clarification, our model may be viewed as an instrument to highlight the intuition that so far as wage hikes tend to get diffused more or less uniformly across the sectors and one sector experiences labour-saving technological progress more consistently and intensively than the other, and so long as prices remain tied to cost, the relative price of the progressive sector will fall. The literature on the subject focuses on differential cost and price changes and growth rates while the present discussion focuses on value-added adjustment.

It is possible to introduce greater generality to the model, without complicating matters much, by introducing cost-plus pricing and still maintain the insight (Datta, 2019). The above narrative of potential cumulative decline in relative price in the progressive sector seems to fit well with observations on the Indian economy. This observation raises a serious question regarding the reliability of productivity estimates (Goldar, 2015) for Indian manufacturing based on the value-added as a measure of output.

## 11.5 Conclusion—Pitfalls along the Road

Growth accounting is a very popular topic for research but productivity estimation needs a lot of caution that is not often evident in the relevant studies. It must be recognized that technological progress and measured productivity growth are not bound by a one-to-one relationship. Though technological progress is supposedly the most important source of measured productivity growth, the growth does not necessarily happen mostly in the sector where technological progress happens. Even when gross output at constant prices is considered, proper accounting for intra-sectoral intermediate inputs must be made and this requires input-output transactions tables and proper price deflation.

The present paper goes through the above issues in some detail. It has been observed that technological progress may sometimes simply mean getting rid of unwanted by-products that, in any case, are not counted as output. In most cases, the by-products are treated as externalities polluting the environment but the implied costs are not internalized giving a partisan measure of output that fail to capture relevant technological progress under the growth accounting approach. Sectoral gross output measure needs a lot of information regarding intra-sectoral intermediate inputs and their prices. To avoid the complexities gross value-added method is often used by researchers only to land into a different problem caused by changes in relative prices. Fruits of technological progress are often passed on to the consumers in a competitive setup leading to a decline in the price of the product where technological progress originates. As a result, relative price and relative value-added of the relatively non-progressive sectors rise, giving a misleading measure of sectoral productivity change. From such considerations, gross output measure is more appropriate for measuring productivity change, but that needs the use of input-output transactions tables which are not available for all the years for the Indian economy. Data provided by the Annual Survey of Industries is not of the right type for the purpose.

## References

[1] Baumol, W.J. (1967). "Macroeconomics of Unbalanced Growth: The Anatomy of Urban Crisis", *The American Economic Review*, 57(3), 409:420.

[2] Baumol, W.J., S.A.B. Blackman and Wolff, E.N. (1985). "Unbalanced Growth Revisited: Asymptotic Stagnancy and New Evidence", *TheAmerican Economic Review*, 75(4), 806–817.

[3] Datta, M. (2020). *Reform and the Structure of the Indian Economy: Output-Value Added Symbiosis*, Cambridge University Press, Cambridge, UK.

[4] Datta, M. (2019). Manufacturing Sector of the Indian Economy: Output-Value Added Symbiosis, *Journal of Asian Economics*, 63, 75–87.

[5] Echevarria, C. (1997). "Changes in Sectoral Composition Associated with Economic Growth", *International Economic Review*, 38, 431:452.

[6] Fagerberg, J. (2000). "Technological Progress, Structural Change and Productivity Growth: A Comparative Study", *Structural Change and Economic Dynamics*, 11, 393:411.

[7] Goldar, B. (2015). "Productivity in Indian Manufacturing in the Post-reform Period: A Review of Studies", in Kathuria, V., Rajesh Raj S.N. and KunalSen (eds.), *Productivity in Indian Manufacturing*, Routledge.

[8] Government of India, Central Statistical Organisation website: www.cso.org, *Input-Output Transactions Table: 1993–94*; *Input-Output Transactions Table: 2003–04, 2007–08.*

[9] Government of India, Central Statistics Office (2012), *National Accounts Statistics: Sources and Methods,* New Delhi.

[10] Kongsamut, P., Rebelo, S. and Xie, D. (1997). Beyond Balanced Growth, *Working Paper 6159,* NBER.

[11] Nordhaus, W.D. (2006). "Baumol's diseases: A Macroeconomic Perspective", *Working Paper 12218, NBER,* Cambridge, USA.

[12] OECD (2001). Productivity Manual: A Guide to the Measurement of Industry-level and Aggregate Productivity Growth, Paris.

[13] Steindel, C. and Stiroh, K.J. (2001). Productivity: What Is It, and Why Do We Care About It? April 12, https://www.newyorkfed.org/medialibrary/media/research/staff_report

CHAPTER 12

# Impact of Spatial Arrangement of Road Topology on Landscape Transformation through Machine Learning Technique: Evidence from Sabroom, India and Ramgarh, Bangladesh

**Pradip Debnath, Stabak Roy and Saptarshi Mitra**

## 12.1 Introduction

Spatial interaction is a term used to define the interdependence between geographical areas. Many geographical studies have assessed spatial interaction and interdependency between geographical areas and significant research topics in regional planning. As stated by Ullaman (1945), three crucial factors directly influence spatial interaction; supply at one place meeting a specific demand at another place, intervening opportunities promoting interaction by intermediate transport links and transferability considering the distance friction measured by real-time and travel cost. Spatial interaction takes place when these three conditions are satisfied. The movement of essential goods, particularly in the backward areas, express the interregional relationship and stimulates the regional economy. The development of transport connectivity depends on topography, climatic condition, habitation pattern and other situations like law and order (Osama and Sayed,2017; Pregnolato *et al.*, 2017; Yin *et al.*, 2016. New road construction and connectivity often affect the spatial structure of landscapes through its continuous expansion (Yaxing *et al.*, 2022; Hadi *et al.*, 2021; Jedlička *et al.*, 2019; Li *et al.*, 2016. It often leads to land cover and land use changes through the process of urbanisation. The review undertaken by Acheampong and Silva (2015) indicates that several conceptual modelshave developed, for example; the agricultural models of Von-Thünen (1826), the Residential Models of Wingo (1961), Alonso (1964) and Mills (1972), and Spatial Exploration Model of Gould (1966), King (1969) and Haynes and Fotheringham (2020) and utilised in several transportation research. The authors highlighted that transportation and land use research was undertaken with the help of different types of models, for example, the gravity-based model developed by Lowry in 1964. In the recent past, several transportations and land use theories were developed (Wegener, 2021; Rui, 2013; Wegener, 2013; Echenique, 2011. All the operational theories and models are determined mainly by economic development in relation to transportation and LU, in addition to other factors (Zheng *et al.*, 2021). Moreover, recent studies have examined transport accessibility and LU change and also investigated the relationship between transport connectivity and LU dynamics *(*Patarasuk 2013*)*. Many types of research were conducted to investigate the interrelationship between transportation, land use, and land cover change (Wang *et al.*, 2019; Litman and Steele, 2017; Chaudhuri and Clarke, 2015. LULC change has been deducted based on time series digital satellite images by using maximum likelihood methods (Regasa and Nones, 2022; Zhang and Zhang, 2022; Paul *et al.*, 2021. Indeed, the construction of a new road must have an impact on land transformation. The new road network construction, realignment, and enlargement of an existing network would impact the firm land and choice of household location and changes settlement density (Arowolo and Deng, 2018; Lembcke and Menon, 2017. The long-term impact of road transport infrastructure in promoting, maintaining, and developing the economic system is important (Funderburg, 2010). Changes in LULC have directly influenced a local and regional economies (Arowolo; Deng, 2018). The road network supports various dependent economic activities and integrates the economic system over space. The impact of a new highway on land accessibility and urban land use changes in developing countries has been undertaken by Yaxing *et al.* (2022); Al-Shaar *et al.* (2021). Meanwhile, land use changes affect travel demand and accessibility (Iacono *et al.*, 2008). Changes in LULC result from the complex interaction of many factors, including policy implementation, urbanisation, road network connectivity, and accessibility (Oruonye, 2014; Rui, 2013; Müller *et al.*, 2010). More specifically, the development of the Indo-Bangal road transport connectivity through the Feni River will improve the connectivity and accessibility of India's entire North East region. A classical concern generally evaluates the socio-economic benefits, partially interlinked with the land use evolution, and justifies the financial investment. Very recently, a study was conducted by Dhar and Mitra (2021), an account of the geopolitical and regional sustainability of Sabroom Town. The authors have identified that geopolitical relationship stimulates regional sustainable development and Sabroom became the geopolitical hotspot due to its geo-strategic location and convergent geopolitical relationship with Bangladesh. So, improving road transport connectivity is regarded as a critical factor in regional development (Chatterji *et al.*, 2014). Tripura is comparatively backward state of India with the largest population living in remote areas. Thus this state is unique and endeavour with many natural resources; it depends upon a variety of commodities from the outside and exports local products to the rest of the country, mainly through roadways. Before the partition of undivided Bengal, its transportation networks were mainly interconnected with Bangladesh. Road transportation was an integrated system that supported an integrated economy at the time. After 1947, the Northeast, particularly Tripura, became a landlocked state due to geopolitical consequences, and its transport connectivity has been affected adversely. These links were severed only after partition (Sen *et al.*, 2013). As a result, this region becomes economically weak. For several decades Tripura and Bangladesh have neither trade nor any kind of formal economic relations till 1992. However, the immense potential for a mutually beneficial economic partnership came into focus when Tripura and Bangladesh signed a border trade agreement in 1995. It came into effect in 1998 when the Indo-Bangle border was officially declared open for Border hat. Therefore, the transport network is considered an important infrastructure for eliminating backwardness and connecting the interstate of the country. Tripura is connected with India through Assam-Agartala Highway (Debanath *et al.*, 2021; Debbarma *et al.*, 2017) and the Indian railway. In Tripura, passenger mobility and the exchange of goods and services rely heavily on road transport, where National Highways play a vital role (Debanath *et al.*, 2021). However, the condition of surface topography does not allow the faster inter-state movement of people and goods. Similarly, most of the hilly routes were narrow and steep in a number of places. Primitive conditions of surface roads make the transportation system vulnerable due to seasonal influences. Heavy downpours also pose problems in the interstate connectivity and mobility system. Rather increase the friction of journey distance and puts the state in adverse positions. The positive geopolitical relationship between the two neighbouring counties will foster road connectivity. Because of the uncertainty in the global economy and international trade, the current geopolitical scenario with Bangladesh is expected to undergo a major transformation dramatically. Over the lasttwo decades, the government of India and Bangladesh has undertaken some initiatives to develop international collaboration and cooperation. The two countries governments have implemented several plans and policies for developing regional trade and commerce by improving transport links between the two neighbouring countries (Roy *et al.*, 2021). In recent decades, India and Bangladesh initiated reconnecting road connectivity at the diplomatic level. One of the important notified road links is the Sabroom-Ramgarh road link through Maitri Setu over the Feni River. A very little comprehensive study has been done to identify the scope and strength of cross-border transport corridors stimulating land use and land cover change. Therefore, this chapter attempted to illustrate how spatial movement can stimulate the complex process of LULC changes and analyse strategic factors for regional development in general and North-East India in particular.

## 12.2 Description of the Study Area

The present study has been conducted around the Maitri Setu and extended about 15 km radius Maitri Setu located over Feni River on the Sabroom (Tripura) and Ramghar (Bangladesh) route. Figure 12.1 illustrates the geographical location of the study area covers an area of about 710.75 km$^2$. The average elevation of the study area is 136 m from above the mean sea level. Two countries partially cover the present study area, Bangladesh to the northeast to southwest (400.75 km$^2$) and the Indian State of Tripura (310.00 km$^2$). The Sabroom-Ramghar Highway is an important trunk road connecting India to Bangladesh by land. It is one of the key cooperative projects on

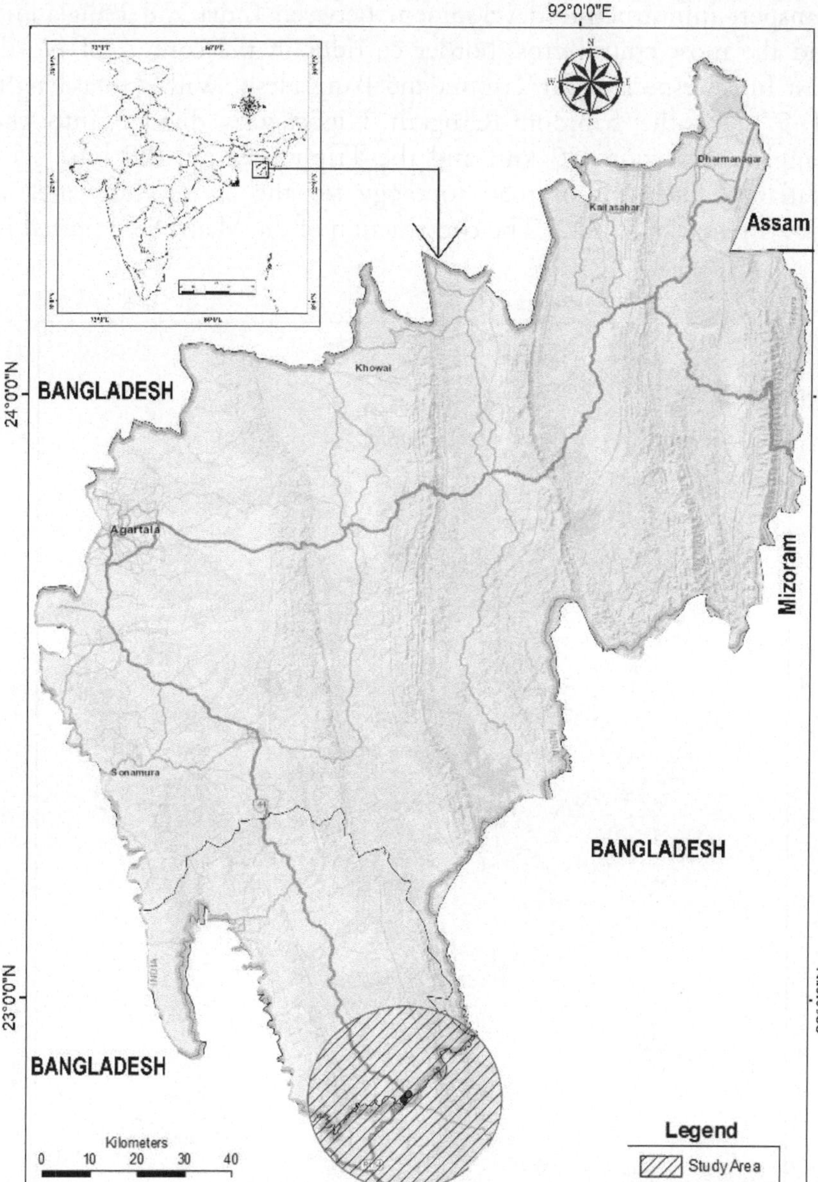


**Figure 12.1:** Geographical Location (maps of the 15 km buffer area of the Sabroom-Ramgarh route and major artery roads) of the Study Area

(*Source:* prepared by the authors using google earth pro data, 2022)

transport infrastructure development between India and Bangladesh and the most crucial cross-border corridor in the context of North East India, especially for Tripura and Bangladesh. With a total length of 57 km, the Sabroom-Ramgarh Highway is divided into the Bangladesh section (38 km) and the Tripura section (29 km). The spatial arrangement of road topology for the entire study area is showing in Figure 12.2. The construction of the Maitri Setu started in

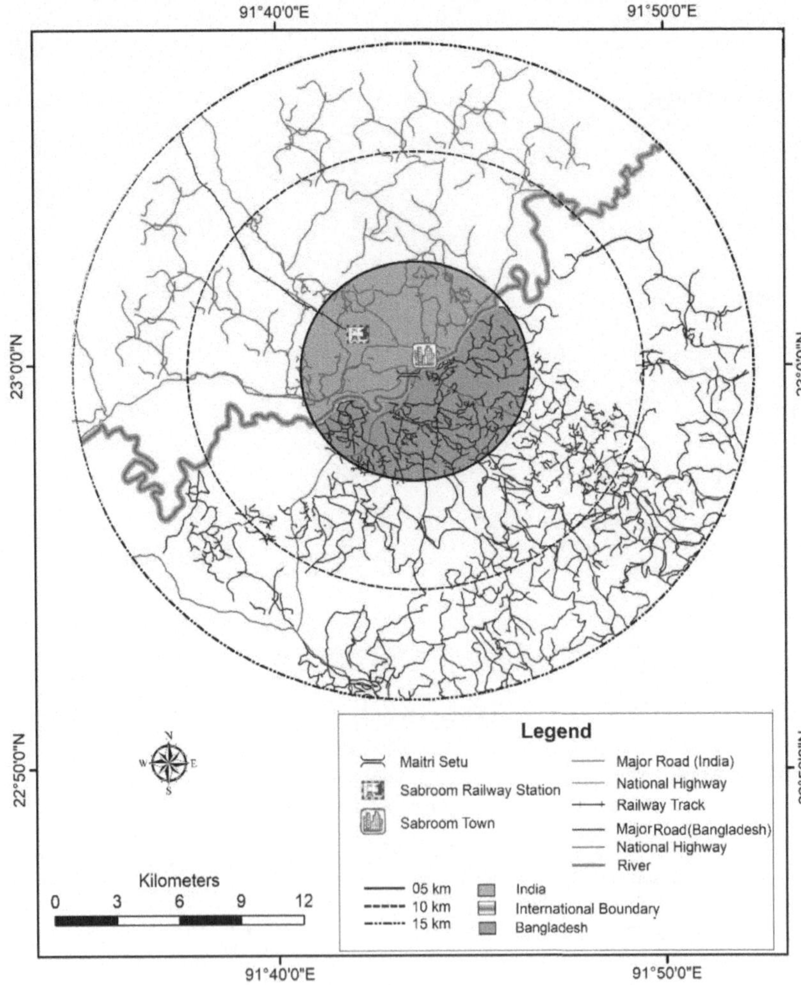


**Figure 12.2:** Road Network of the Study Area (trio concentric zone-5, 10, and 15 km buffer from the centre of Maitri Setu)

2014 near Sabroom Town of Tripura to connect the entire North East India with South East Asian countries. More than 45% of its land is covered as fallow land, while agricultural land covers 32%. In these circumstances, road transportation has become the prime mode of transportation. The high man-land ratio creates huge pressure on agricultural lands.

As a result, the study area became a food deficit area obliged to import food and other necessary materials from elsewhere. Transport cost by road is comparatively higher than railways and waterways transportation (Arnold *et al.*, 2004). Roadways are always a more dependable mode of transportation, especially in a hilly area, wherein during the monsoon, road connectivity is interrupted due to landslides. Indian Highway has played a significant role in freight transport of Tripura.

## 12.3 Database and Methodology

In this study, the satellite images retrieved from Landsat 8 (2007, 2014, and 2021) of 30 m resolution. Remote sensing data were acquired to analyse the spatio-temporal dynamics of land use/cover from 2007 to 2021, and the CA-Markov model has been utilised for the determination of LULC change prediction for the next 14 years i.e., from 2021 to 2035. Five distinct LULC types have been identified based on their characteristics and functions as agricultural land, built-up area, fallow land, vegetation cover and water bodies (Table 12.2). A detailed description of the digital satellite images is listed in Table 131. Software such as, global mapper, google earth engine, and ArcGIS10.8 has been used to process and analyse satellite data. Annual land use and land cover data (2007–2021) were procured from the United States Geological Survey (USGS). Figure 12.3 depicts the flow diagram of the research design adopted for the study. The raster products of agricultural land, build-up area for land uses, vegetations, and water bodies for land cover were classified to examine the dynamic LULC changes along the Sabroom-Ramghar Highway by identifying changes in pixel values with the help of Arc GIS. Maximum likelihood estimation (MLE) has been adopted to understand the impact of spatial interaction on LULC transformation. Supervised classification techniques are widely acceptable in machine learning, panel data, and remote sensing, digital image analysis (Richards, 1999). Maximum likelihood classification determines the probability that a given pixel belongs to a particular class, given that the statistics for each class in each band are normally distributed. In this study, the maximum likelihood estimation has been adopted for processing and analysis of the LULC maps *(Mitra et al., 2021; Richards, 1999)*. The maximum likelihood function is described as follows:

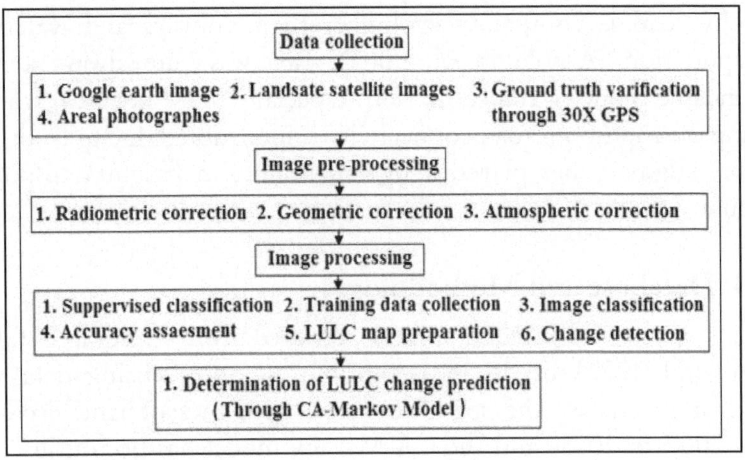


**Figure 12.3:** Flowchart Depicts the Research Methodology for Processing and Predicting LULC Changes in the Study Area

**Table 12.1:** Comprehensive Information about the Data Set and Satellites Imagery Utilized for this Study

| *Satellite* | *Sensor* | *Acquisition Date* | *Projection* | *Spatial Resolution* | *No. of Bands* | *WRS Path/Raw* |
|---|---|---|---|---|---|---|
| Landsat 7 | Enhanced Thematic Mapper Plus (ETM+) sensor | 2007/06/23 | WGS84 UTM Zone 46 N | 30 m | 8 | 136/44 |
| Landsat 8 | Operational Land Imager (OLI) sensor | 2014/07/03 | WGS84 UTM Zone 46 N | 30 m | 11 | 136/44 |
| Landsat 8 | Operational Land Imager (OLI) sensor | 2021/07/03 | WGS84 UTM Zone 46 N | 30 m | 11 | 136/44 |

*Source:* United States Geological Survey (USGS), 2022.

$$g_i(x) = 1np(w_i) - \frac{1}{2}1n|\Sigma i| - \frac{1}{2}(x - m_i)^T \Sigma_i^{-1} (x - m_i) \quad \dots (1)$$

Where:

i = class

x = n-dimensional data, and it represents the number of bands

p $(\omega_i)$ = the probability that class $\omega_i$ appears in the image and is taken to be the same for all classes.

$|\Sigma_i|$ = determinant of the covariance matrix of the data in class $\omega_i$

$\Sigma_i^{-1}$ = inverse matrix of it

$m_i$ = mean vector

For calculating the degree of LULC change over the different time intervals, the annual rate of change and the percentage of change by category have been demonstrated by using Eqs. (2) and (3). Equations 2 and 3 illustrate by the following mathematical notation.

$$pc = \frac{p^2 - p^1}{p^1} \times 100 \quad \dots (2)$$

$$rc(ha/yr) = \frac{p^2 - p^1}{t^i} \quad \dots (3)$$

Where:

pc and rc represents the per cent of change; rate of change; p1 is the initial observed area of LULC category for the time interval 1; p2 represents the final observed area for the time interval 2; ti is the time interval in years between p1 and p2.

**Table 12.2:** Land Use and Land Cover (LULC) Classification Criteria

| *Land Use and Land Cover Classification Criteria* | *Description and Purpose of Land Use* |
|---|---|
| Agricultural Land | Farmland, paddy field, and vegetable land |
| Built up Area | Commercial service, road, urban and other build-up land like residential area |
| Fallow Land | Landfill sites, Exposed soils, and land lying fallow |
| Vegetation Cover | Mixed forest lands, rubber plantations and others vegetation cover |
| Water Bodies | Permanent water bodies, ponds, lakes, and reservoirs |

*Source:* Computed by the authors, 2022.

## 12.4 Radius Analysis (0–5 km, 5–10 km and 10–15 km)

The main purpose of this study is to analyse the comprehensive LULC dynamics driven by spatial interaction as observed before and after the construction of the Maitri Setu and the probable impact on LULC through CA Markhov-based simulation technique. To investigate the simulating LULC changes due to spatial interaction, consider the radial distance between 0–5 km, 5–10 km, and 10–15 km and form a series of circular zones from the the Maitri Setu (Figure 12.2).

## 12.5 Result and Discussion

Maitri Setu has been identified as the centre of the concentric zones signify the LULC dynamics (Figure 12.4). LULC change deduction has been determined employing 30 m resolution satellite data. The applied configuration of the satellite image is discussed in tabular form (Table 12.1). An attempt has been made to investigate the impact of the Maitri Setu on spatial interaction the associated by comparing the pre construction and post-construction scenarios along with LULC change the comprehensive illustration about the study is discussed in different sections.

### 12.5.1 *LULC Transformation (2007–2021)*

The authors investigating the LULC transformation within trio-radial zones at different distances from the centre of the study area. Satellite images have been processed, and five major LULC classes were identified, i.e., water body, vegetation cover, agriculture land, and settlement or built-up area, based on the hybrid classification approach. When the radial zone was 5 km, the LULC transfer for the build-up area was the highest in 2014–2021 (Figure 12.4). The total area of land use transfer to construction land (21.37%), agricultural land (2.24%), and vegetation land (18.44%).

### 12.5.2 *Acceleration on Vegetation Cover*

Change detection shows that vegetation cover was decreased by 21.13%, and built-up area was raised by 23.91% over the study periods. In particular, 7.32% and 4.08% of the land occupied by vegetations was transformed into a build-up area from 2007 to 2014 and 2014 to 2021, respectively. Improvement of road connectivity has distinct and significant impacts (Figure 12.4) on the areal transformation which can play a substantial biodiversity loss at a regional scale.

### 12.5.3 *Historical Changes of the Water Body*

Water body comprises surface water in the form of rivers, ponds, lakes, and reservoirs in the blue texture as regular shape and size. Feni River is the largest river that passes through the middle of the study area and act as a trans Border. Total area under water body was calculated about 5.71% in 2007, 5.14% in 2014, and 3.96% in 2021 from the observation. Table 12.3 illustrates the sequential degradation of the blue infrastructure in the study area.

**Table 12.3:** Spatio-temporal Analysis of LULC Change from 2007 to 2021

| *Purpose of Land Use* | *2021* | | *2014* | | *2007* | |
|---|---|---|---|---|---|---|
| | *Area (sq. km)* | *%* | *Area (sq. km)* | *%* | *Area (sq. km)* | *%* |
| Agricultural Land | 77.08 | 10.84 | 92.95 | 13.08 | 93.91 | 13.21 |
| Built up Area | 234.31 | 32.96 | 82.35 | 11.59 | 64.32 | 9.05 |
| Fallow Land | 18.91 | 2.66 | 15.46 | 2.17 | 9.40 | 1.32 |
| Vegetation Cover | 352.43 | 49.58 | 483.52 | 68.02 | 502.52 | 70.71 |
| Water Bodies | 28.02 | 3.96 | 36.55 | 5.14 | 40.57 | 5.71 |
| **Total** | **710.75** | **100.00** | **710.83** | **100.00** | **710.72** | **100.00** |

*Source:* Computed by the Authors, 2022.

### 12.5.4 *Agricultural Land Use Dynamics*

Figure 12.4 demonstrated that the cultivated land decreased in the area, whereas built-up areas increased over the study period. Agricultural land was about 13.21% (93.91 sq km) of the total area in the year 2007, but it was reduced gradually by 0.13% in 2014 and 2.24% in 2021. Most of the study area is characteristics by low-lying land, and it has been converted into a built-up area agricultural land is decreasing in percentage because it is being converted to other types of land use. Figure 12.4 illustrates that agrarian land use occupied almost 1.74% (93.91 sq km) of the total area in 2007, although it decreased to 2.37% in 2021 with an annual declination rate of 1 sq km/year. A large amount of cultivated land is mostly found on both sides of the Feni River and has been transformed into settlement land and vegetation plantation along the river circle 1 witnessed a rapid decrease in cultivated land between 2014 and 2021. However, the transformation of agricultural land use in circles 2 and 3 has slightly decreased by 2014. Maximum reduction of cultivated land took place within the 5 km radius from the Maitri Setu, which is the prime wideness of the impact of spatial interaction in the study area. Table 12.3 illustrates the conversion of agricultural land into a build-up area on both sides of the Feni river. People in the study area have filled the low-lying depression area to construct houses.

### 12.5.5 *Built-up Land Use Dynamics*

The built-up LU change between the years 2007 and the year 2021 has been determined from the LULC mapping. Figure 12.4 illustrates the chronological modification of landscapes into of the areas to built-up area (2007 to 2021). The year 2014 refers to the terminal point as initially construction of Maitri Setu was started. The increasing regional connectivity and various economic processes stimulate population explosion. This study shows that the expansion of build-up area and road density developed at an exponential rate. This study also focused on examining land use dynamics from non-residential to residential land and demonstrated that road infrastructure investment creates new opportunities. Table 12.3 depicts the build-up land use dynamics in the study area. The built-up area shares about 234.31 sq km of the total study area in 2007 and significantly increased from 64.32 sq km in 2007, 82.35 sq km in 2014 and 234.31 sq km in 2021, with growth rate of 24.28 and 12.14 per cent, respectively. Study illustrates that the increase in built-up land use area between the years 2007 to 2021 is occurring along both sides of the road, and simultaneously, agricultural land use areas decrease significantly for the same period. Maximum build-up growth took place within the 5 km radius from the Maitri Setu through the transformation of vegetative cover, encroachment of agricultural land,

and conversion of water bodies. The circle 1 witnessed built-up land use acceleration in the years 2007 and 2021. However, the transformation of built-up land use in circle 2 and 3 have been slightly accelerated by 2014.

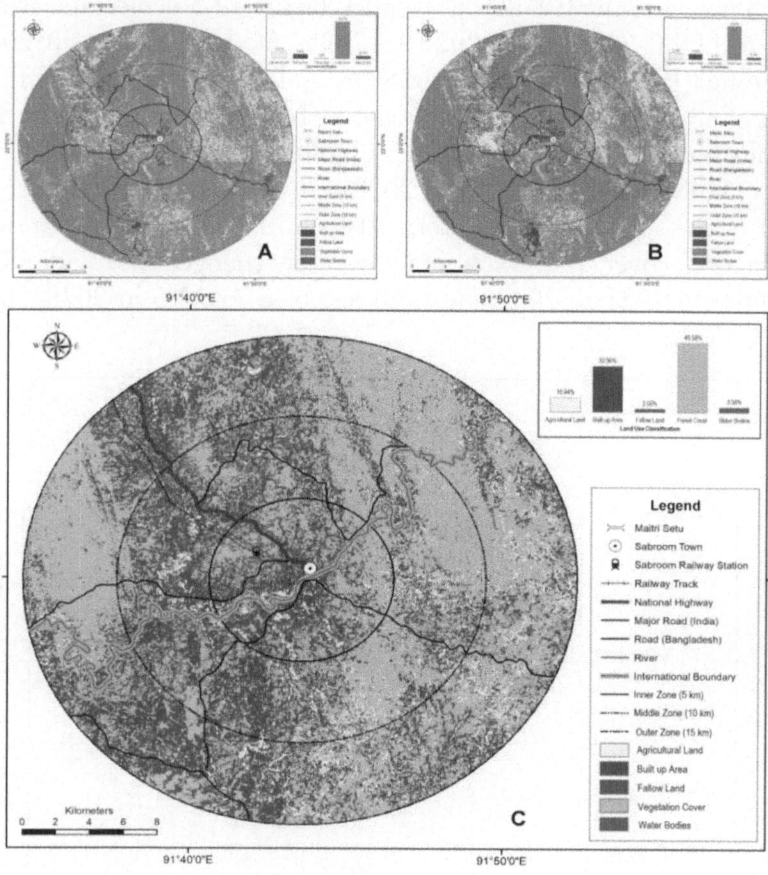


**Figure 12.4:** Spatial Dynamics of LULC Around Maitri Setu (a) 2007, (b) 2014, and (c) 2021

### 12.5.6 *Prediction of LULC of the Study Area*

Assessment of the historical transformation in various types of LULC is a crucial factor for fore-casting and prediction. After monitoring mapping LULC, predicted for the years 2028 and 2035. It was undertaken with the application of the cellular automata–Markov

(CA–Markov) model, which helps in predicting long-time series data. The simulated areal change (%) from 2028–2035 have been illustrated in Table 12.4 and Figure 12.5. The purpose of this chapter is to prepare a comprehensive land use land cover change model and predict what the landscape might look like over the time span of 2028 and 2035 owing to the CA-Markov model. Figure 12.5 depicts the area of future LULC types from 2028 to 2035. As can be seen, in 2028, cultivated land with an area of 8.83%, and constructed land with an area of 53.68% will be the lowest and highest extent, respectively. The results show a significant increase in build-up area from 32.96, 42.48 and 53.68% for the years 2021, 2028 and 2035, and a decrease in the area of the agricultural area from 10.84 to 8.83%, while the areas of vegetation cover and water body will be changed from 49.58 to 41.06% in 2021 to 2028 and from 41.06 to 31.12% in 2028–2035, respectively.

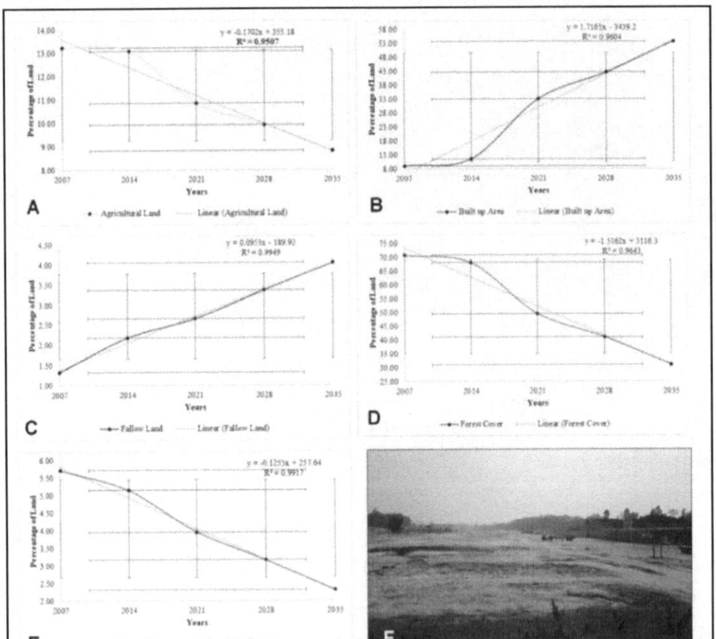

**Figure 12.5:** Predicted Model of LULC Dynamic from 2028–2035 (A) Agricultural Land (B), Built-up Area, (C) Fallow Land, (D) Vegetation Cover, (E) Water Bodies and (F) Transformation of Fallow Land into Build-up Land.

**Table 12.4:** Prediction Model for Spatio-temporal Dynamics of LULC

| *Year* | *Agricultural Land* | *Built up Area* | *Fallow Land* | *Vegetation Cover* | *Water Bodies* |
|---|---|---|---|---|---|
| 2007 | 13.21 | 9.05 | 1.32 | 70.71 | 5.71 |
| 2014 | 13.08 | 11.59 | 2.17 | 68.02 | 5.14 |
| 2021 | 10.84 | 32.96 | 2.66 | 49.58 | 3.96 |
| 2028* | 9.93 | 42.48 | 3.38 | 41.06 | 3.16 |
| 2035* | 8.83 | 53.68 | 4.06 | 31.12 | 2.31 |

*Source:* Computed by the Authors, 2022.

"The study by Mintra and Santra (2020) focused on Agartala city in Tripura, indicates that a significant portion of agricultural land has been converted into built-up areas. This transformation is indicative of urban expansion and development pressures, reflecting broader trends in land use change where agricultural lands are increasingly being urbanized to accommodate growing populations and infrastructural implementation."

*Note:* *Predictive years.

### 12.5.7 *Cost-benefit Analysis for Optimum Utilisation*

Tripura is considered as a landlocked state as because it has no direct seaport connectivity and its freight transportation totally depends on land transportation. Therefore, movement of freight transportation cost is comparatively higher. Due to the proximity to Chittagong port in Bangladesh (92 km from the study area), if connected in near future, it will minimise the transportation cost and Sabroom and Ramghar route will play a significant role and act as a corridor for the entire Northeast region. So there is a huge potentiality to become the gateway of North East India in near future. The cost-benefit analysis of the Sabroom-Ramghar route has been adopted and compared with the Assam-Agartala road. For measuring the cost benefit analysis of road connectivity, basic parameters like the physiographical characteristics of the region, distance, travel cost and duration of the journey have taken into account.

## 12.6 Comparison of Relief and Topographic Configuration

This paper studies the possibilities and potentialities of road connectivity between Sabroom (India) and Chittagong (Bangladesh) for developing regional trade and commerce and its impacts on the neighbouring area of Sabroom (India) and Ramgarh (Bangladesh). Figure 12.6 illustrates the relief configuration of the two different routes like, Agartala Chittagong route and Agartala-Assam-Kolkata route in the study area. Comparing the physiographic configuration of these routes; the Agartala Chittagong route has the minimum altitude rather than the Agartala-Kolkata route via Assam. The Agartala-Chittagong route has a maximum altitude of 253 m, whereas the Agartala-Assam route has about 700 m. It means the journey by the Agartala-Chittagong route becomes much comfortable and smooth than the Agartala-Assam route.

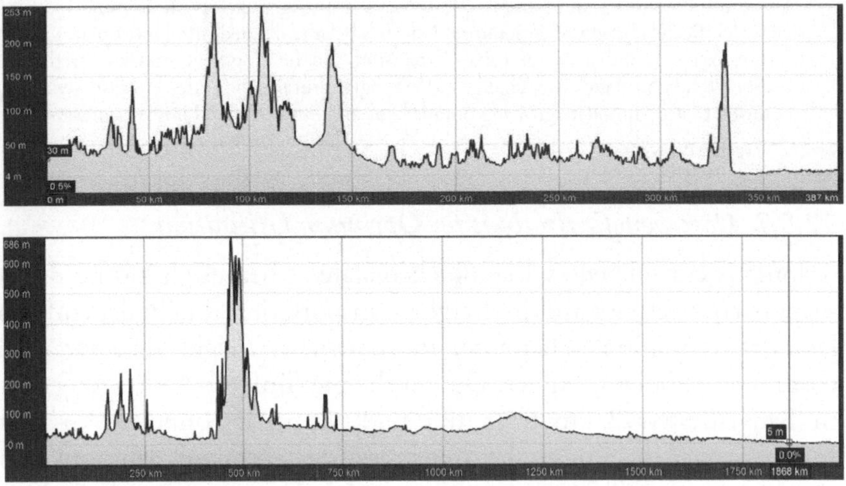


**Figure 12.6:** Relief and Topographic Condition of the Two Important Highways

(*Source:* prepared by the authors using google earth pro image)

### 12.6.1 *Journey Distance*

The present study has been undertaken by considering the existing route distance, journey time, and travel cost as independent factors. Tripura's optimal and alternative freight route connectivity has been developed by examining cost-benefit analysis. Optimum freight route mapping is a crucial and powerful technique for solving real-time transportation problems by saving journey time and reducing travelled distance. The total mileage of the Agartala-Chittagong route is only 423 km, whereas the Agartala-Assam-Kolkata route has about 1753 km, so it is definite lya cost-effective route in terms of travel distance. Duration of journey time is another important factor in transport planning, as the authors earlier mentioned that the Agartala-Assam route has a maximum travel distance rather than the Agartala-Chittagong route. So entrepreneurs always prepared the Agartala-Chittagong route for profit maximization.

### 12.6.2 *Travel Cost*

Identification and selection of the shortest route will help road users and drivers to optimise the transportation cost through minimum uses of fuel, reduce travel time and avoid traffic congestion by diverting the excess traffic flow through less travelled shorter routes. The transport cost model emerged from the pioneering work of Cambridge (2003) and has illustrated that models which determine price changes as a result of transport policy changes are necessary for economic viability. This is the line graph comparing the journey cost between the two routes. In that case, the travel cost is less compared to the Agartala-Kolkata routes. From that point of view, this route has huge international trade and commerce potential.

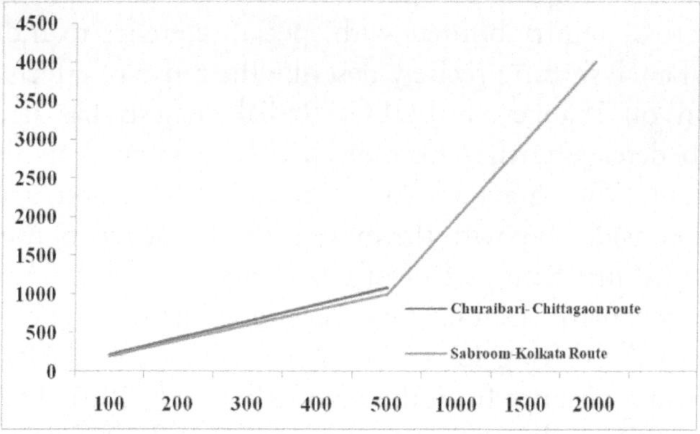


**Figure 12.7:** Cost-benefit Analysis in Terms of Journey Time with Travel Cost

## 12.7 Discussion

The driving forces for changes in land use and land cover are complex. Maitri bridge construction is a major contributor to changing land use changes and land cover. Spatial interaction is considerable attention, and it has an adverse effect on the landscapes. The impacts of spatial interaction on changes in regional land use have crucial concerns. The relationships between spatial interaction and LULC are well understood. Assessment of LULC has rarely been considered across cross borders. Cross-border road projects constitute strategic corridors for the growth of commerce among neighbouring countries and have changed the infrastructure across the land (Bourguignon and Pleskovic, 2008). The impact of spatial interaction on land use and land cover changes has been analysed from two different perspectives; impact on biodiversity and ecological environment, which can be examined in terms of vegetation land and water body conversion; adverse pressure of human disturbance mainly manifested in the construction and expansion of build-up area and encroachment agricultural land. Jimenez *et al.* (2021) argued that the transformation of vegetation cover to other types of land has adverse effects on the succession of the ecosystem. The conversion of vegetation cover to residential areas and planting land represents human activities' negative effect on the natural environment. Most of the relevant research has focused on changes in land use types in urban areas. However, this study investigates the impact of spatial interaction on changing LULC between cross-country borders with special reference to Indo-Bangla. The radial analysis can precisely describe the range of effects of spatial interaction on changes in LULC. Radial analysis has been widely utilised to determine the effect of spatial interaction on the natural environment. The gravitational forces of spatial interaction have decreased considerably with the increasing distance from the centre of the radius (Maitri Setu). Most of the earlier research has investigated the comprehensive LULC dynamics and demonstrates that the influence of the driving forces for LULC changes gradually decreases with the rising distance from the road (Zhu *et al.*, 2001; Long and Li, 2001). In this study, the concentric zone of LULC indicated the dynamic degree of comprehensive changes in LULC. The quantity of changes decreases with the increase of the distance from the centre circle. A similar kind of result has been identified by Zheng *et al.* (2021), Zhu *et al.* (2006). However, the influence of the transport corridor on the buffer zone is not equal and the same. For example, Yan *et al.* (2003) investigated that the Qinghai-Tibet Railway substantially impacts land use changes in a range of 7 km. Other studies have examined the range of considerable effects of the road from Tangela to Glomus Mountain, about 1–3 km (Zhang *et al.*, 2002). A similar kind of study was undertaken by Zhu *et al.* (2006), who analyzed the threshold of impact as 1–5 km around the road because of the geotectonic setting of the area. A very limited research concern is about the comparative study of periods before and after a new highway was constructed. As a result, the authors investigated and measured the degree of dynamic changes in different types of LULC within a 15 km peripheral area of the Maitri Setu.

## 12.8 Concluding Remarks

The results showed that once the Maitri Setu was functioning for spatial interaction, the LULC changes were comparatively higher before it was constructed. Before the opening, the area of significant impact was within 5 km of the buffer zone.The gap between actual and estimated LULC for the period between 2028 and 2035 shows that the impact of the Maitri Bridge led to an increase in built-up areas with an annual growth rate of 3.9%, more than the rate of the precedent trend. The hypothesis proposed in the study is partially validated. The impacts of spatial interaction on LULC change help in the process of urbanisation in adjacent areas, asserting the first part of the hypothesis. Moreover, the result shows that the spatio-temporal interaction among both countries inconsistently influences various types of LULC. The study also attempts to investigate the optimal freight route of Tripura through a cost-benefit analysis. Freight transportation via the Sabroom-Ramghar route is relatively shorter; the journey distance reduces by about 800 km compared to the Assam-Agartala route. This route has adequate potential for providing services and will become the alternative route of the Assam-Agartala Highway. Finally, conclude that the Agartala Chittagong route is the most cost-effective route for Tripura and the entire North-east India and is much more economically viable for sustainable freight transportation.

### 12.8.1 Limitations of the Study

There are several limitations of the study. The authors mainly considered the spatial interaction of a single route on LULC changes and did not consider the effect of other roads on the study area. Analysing the impact of socio-political factors on the study area does not account for which has the spatial impact and can also lead to transforming the various types of LULC. In the future, it is important to examine the strength of other factors' influence on the Highway's condition. Researchers should also use refined information like volume of traffic, commodity flows, and freight traffic for a comprehensive and systematic study on the impact of spatial interaction on LULC change.

## Acknowledgement

The authors highly acknowledged Dr. Samrat Hore, Assistant Professor, Department of Statistics, Tripura University, for his thoughtful and constructive comments and careful review of the manuscript.

## References

[1] Acheampong, R.A. and Silva, E.A. (2015). Land use transport interaction modelling: A review of the literature and future research directions, *Journal of Transport and Land use,* Vol. 8(3), pp. 11–38.

[2] Alonso, W. (1964). Location and land use. Harvard University Press, Cambridge, MA.

[3] Al-Shaar, W., Nehme, N., Bonin, O. and Adjizian Gérard, J. (2021). Impacts of a new highway on urban development and land accessibility in developing countries: Case of Beirut southern entrance in Lebanon. Arabian Journal for Science and Engineering, 46(6), pp. 5783–5800.

[4] Arnold, P., Peeters, D. and Thomas, I. (2004). Modelling a rail/road intermodal transportation system. *Transportation Research Part E: Logistics and Transportation Review,* Vol. 40(3), pp. 255–270.

[5] Arowolo, A. O. and Deng, X. (2018). Land use/land cover change and statistical modelling of cultivated land change drivers in Nigeria. *Regional environmental change,* 18(1), pp. 247–259.

[6] Bourguignon, F. and Pleskovic, B. (2008.) Rethinking infrastructure for development. *In Annual World Bank Conference on Development Economics-2007;* World Bank: Washington, DC, USA.

[7] Chatterji, R., Ray Chaudhury, A., Basu, P. and Sarkar, G. (2014). India Bangladesh Connectivity: Possibilities and Challenges. *Observer Research Foundation.* Kolkata: Observer Research Foundation. Retrieved November 11, 2020.

[8] Chaudhuri, G. and Clarke, K.C. (2015). On the spatiotemporal dynamics of the coupling between land use and road networks: Does political history matter? *Environment and Planning. B, Planning and Design*, Vol. 42(1), pp. 133–156.

[9] Debbarma, D., Mitra, S. and Debnath, P. (2017). A Comparative Assessment on the Working and Living Conditions of the Auto Rickshaw Service Providers of Dharmanagar and Udaipur Town of Tripura, *Global Journal of Advance Research*, Vol. 9(4), pp. 281–289.

[10] Dhar, S. and Mitra. S. (2021). Geopolitical scenario of Tripura: An analytical study on state, people and development policies. Department of Geography and Disaster Management, Tripura University, Unpublished Ph.D. Thesis

[11] Echenique, M. (2011). Land use/transport models and economic assessment, *Research in Transportation Economics*, Vol. 31(1), pp. 45–54.

[12] Gould, P.R. (1966). Space searching procedures in geography and the social sciences (No. 1). *Social Science Research Institute*, University of Hawaii.

[13] Hadi, P.L., Wasanta, T. and Santosa, W. (2021). Land use change due to road construction. *In IOP Conference Series: Earth and Environmental Science*, Vol. 920(1), pp. 1–8.

[14] Haynes, K.E. and Fotheringham, A.S. (2020). Gravity and spatial interaction models.

[15] Hodonín region (Czech Republic). Quaestiones Geographicae, Vol. 38(1), pp. 145–159.

[16] Iacono, M., Levinson, D. and El-Geneidy, A. (2008). Models of transportation and land use change: A guide to the territory, *Journal of Planning Literature*, Vol. 22(4), pp. 323–340.

[17] Jedlička, J., Havlíček, M., Dostál, I., Huzlík, J. and Skokanová, H. (2019). Assessing relationships between land use changes and the development of a road network in the Hodonín region (Czech Republic). *Quaestiones Geographicae*, 38(1), pp. 145–159.

[18] Jimenez, Y.G., Aráoz, E., Grau, H.R. and Paolini, L. (2021). Linking forest transition, plant invasion and forest succession theories: Socioeconomic drivers and composition of new subtropical Andean forests, *Landscape Ecology*, Vol. 36(4), pp. 1161–1176.

[19] Karan, S.K. and Samadder, S.R. (2016). Accuracy of land use change detection using support vector machine and maximum likelihood techniques for open-cast coal mining areas, *Environmental monitoring and assessment*, Vol. 188(8), pp. 1–13.

[20] King, L.J. (1969). The analysis of spatial form and its relation to geographic theory, *Annals of the Association of American Geographers*, Vol. 59(3), pp. 573–595.

[21] Lembcke, A.C. and Menon, C. (2017). The impact of road infrastructure investment on incumbent firms in Korea.

[22] Li, T., Wu, J., Sun, H. and Gao, Z. (2016). Integrated co-evolution model of land use and traffic network design. *Networks and Spatial Economics*, Vol. 16(2), pp. 579–603.

[23] Litman, T. and Steele, R. (2017). Land use impacts on transport. *Victoria, Canada: Victoria Transport Policy Institute*, pp. 1–90.

[24] Long, H.L. and Li, X.B. (2001). Land use pattern in transect of Yangtse River and its influential factors. *Acta Geographica Sinica*, Vol. 56(4), pp. 425–434.

[25] Lowry, I.S. (1964). A Model of a Metropolis, RM–4035-RC. The Rand Corporation, Santa Monica, CA.

[26] Mills, E.S. (1972). Urban Economics. Scott Foresman, Glenview, IL. Putman, S.H., 1982. Integrated Urban Models: Policy Analysis of Transport.

[27] Mitra, S. and Santra, A. (2020). Monitoring urban expansion and land use/land cover changes of Agartala City, Tripura, India. *Indian Journal of Regional Science*, Vol. 52(1), pp. 123–136.

[28] Mitra, S., Roy, S. and Dhar, S. (2021). A Geopolitical and Regional Sustainability of Sabroom Town, Tripura: A Road Map for Future. *In T. Banerjee, Geoinformatics in Research and Development* (pp. 128–151). Kolkata: South Asian Institute for Advanced Research & Development.

[29] Mitra, S., Roy, S. and Hore, S. (2022). Assessment and forecasting of the urban dynamics through lulc based mixed model: evidence from Agartala, India. *GeoJournal*, Vol. 87(4), pp. 1–24.

[30] Müller, K., Steinmeier, C. and Küchler, M. (2010). Urban growth along motorways in Switzerland, *Landscape and Urban Planning*, Vol. 98(1), pp. 3–12.

[31] Osama, A. and Sayed, T. (2017). Evaluating the impact of connectivity, continuity, and topography of sidewalk network on pedestrian safety, *Accident Analysis & Prevention*, Vol. 107, pp. 117–125.

[32] Patarasuk, R. (2013). Road network connectivity and land-cover dynamics in Lop Buri province, Thailand, *Journal of Transport Geography*, Vol. 28, pp. 111–123.

[33] Paul, S., Saxena, K.G, Nagendra, H. and Lele, N. (2021). Tracing land use and land cover change in peri-urban Delhi, India, over 1973–

2017 period, *Environmental Monitoring and Assessment*, Vol. 193(2), pp. 1–12.

[34] Pregnolato, M., Ford, A., Wilkinson, S.M. and Dawson, R.J. (2017). The impact of flooding on road transport: A depth-disruption function. *Transportation research part D: transport and environment*, Vol. 55, pp. 67–81.

[35] Richards, J. (1999). Remote sensing Digital image analysis, Berlin: Springer-Verlag, 240.

[36] Roy, S., Barman, T. and Mitra, S. (2019). Passengers' Perception and Persuasion on Railway Transport System of Tripura, *Indian Journal of Landscape Systems and Ecological Studies*, Vol. 42(1), pp. 115–129.

[37] Rui, Y. (2013). Urban growth modeling based on land-use changes and road network expansion (Doctoral dissertation, KTH Royal Institute of Technology).

[38] Sen, S.K., Gupta, S. and Mukhopadhyay, I. (2013). Economic viability of an alternative internal road network in Tripura: an application of shortest path algorithm. Sen, SK, Gupta, S. and Mukhopadhyay, I. (2013). Economic Viability of an Alternative Internal Road Network in Tripura: An Application of Shortest Path algorithm, Hill Geographer, Vol. 29(1), pp. 25–39.

[39] Ullman, E.L. (1945). Geography as spatial interaction, in transportation geography: ed. by M.E Eliot Hurst, McGraw Hill, New York, pp. 29–44.

[40] Von Thunen, J.H. (1910). Der isolierte Staat in Beziehung auf Land wirtschaft und Nationalokonomie, Perthes, Hamburg.

[41] Wang, Z., Han, Q. and de Vries, B. (2019). Land use/land cover and accessibility: implications of the correlations for land use and transport planning. *Applied Spatial Analysis and Policy*, Vol. 12(4), pp. 923–940.

[42] Wegener, M. (2013). Land-Use Transport Interaction Models. *Handbook of Regional Science*, 741–758. doi:10.1007/978–3–642–23430-9_41.

[43] Wegener, M. (2021). Land-use transport interaction models. Handbook of regional science, pp. 229–246.

[44] Wingo Jr., L. (1961). Transportation and Urban Land Use. Johns Hopkins University Press, Baltimore, MD.

[45] Yaxing, L., Bojie, Y. and Jingjie, Y. (2022). Correlation between Road Network Accessibility and Urban Land Use: A Case Study of Fuzhou City, *Polish Journal of Environmental Studies*, Vol. 31(3), pp. 2915–2922.

[46] Yin, J., Yu, D., Yin, Z., Liu, M. and He, Q. (2016). Evaluating the impact and risk of pluvial flash flood on intra-urban road network: A case study in the city centre of Shanghai, China. *Journal of Hydrology*, Vol. 537, pp. 138–145.

[47] Zhang, B., Li, W. and Zhang, C. (2022). Analysing land use and land cover change patterns and population dynamics of fast-growing US cities: Evidence from Collin County, Texas. *Remote Sensing Applications: Society and Environment*, 27, 100804.

[48] Zheng, F., Huang, J., Feng, Z. and Xiao, C. (2021). Impact of the Kunming–Bangkok Highway on Land Use Changes along the Route between Laos and Thailand. Land, Vol. 10, pp. 991. https://doi.org/10.3390/land10090991

[49] Zhu, H., Li, X. and He, S. (2001). Spatio-temporal change of land use in Bohai Rim, *Acta Geographica Sinica*, Vol. 56(3), pp. 253–260.

[50] Zhu, J.J., Cui, B.S., Yao, H.R. and Dong, S.K. (2006). Land use change and expansion effects caused by road construction in longitudinal range-gorge region, *Journal of Natural Resource*, Vol. 21, pp. 508–515.

CHAPTER 13

# Reimagining Act East Policy

E. Bijoykumar Singh

## 13.1 Introduction

Currently some words have become prominent in development discourse. Inclusive, resurgence, reimagining and mainstreaming are some such words with immense policy implications. Since the eleventh Five Year Plan inclusive development has become fashionable. For quite sometimes, mainstreaming is the word used when one seriously thinks about the lagging northeast catch-up with the rest of the country. Resurgence has also become fashionable after the right wing came to power in India. It is in this context that reimagining has become popular. Inclusive development seeks to ensure that every section of the society can avail of the benefits of development- more of sabkasath, sabkavikas. When we think about mainstreaming, lots of catching up is implied given the fact that the northeast is no longer the vibrant entity at the time of independence. A mainstreamed northeast may acquire the paraphernalia of development at the cost of its identity. The region may no longer be itself. Resurgence extols the virtues of a past and its reappearance will help in solving the current problems. However, the new India and old India are different. Periodization of the past arbitrarily may not give adequate space to every stakeholder in India as in the case of akhand Bharat. Our constitution spells out clearly what we should be and superimposing a part of the past will compromise the vision of leaders like Ambedkar. On the other hand, re-imagination seeks to start afresh. We had a vision in our imagination and our policies are tuned to realize that vision. When we have reason to believe that the vision is getting blurred because of implementation deficit, we can reimagining and come up with a feasible vision. The story of the region is largely a story of missed opportunities as suggested by the coexistence of underdevelopment on the one hand and rich natural resources, local institutions and high quality human resources. The Vision statement of Northeastern Region Vision 2020 states,

1. At Independence, the North Eastern Region was among the most prosperous regions of India. Sixty years on, the Region as a whole, and the States that comprise it, are lagging far behind the rest of the country in most important parameters of growth.
2. The purpose of this Vision document is to return the North Eastern Region to the position of national economic eminence it held till a few decades ago; to so fashion the development process that growth springs from and spreads out to the grassroots; and to ensure that the Region plays the arrow-head role it must play in the vanguard of the country's Look East Policy.

The initiation of Look East policy in the early 1990s and its graduation to Act East Policy in 2015 as a powerful tool for leveraging growth in this region provided an opportunity for introspection and critiquing the extant policies whose outcomes had been of dubious quality. Question arises as to the extent of nation building in the last seventy five years. The issue of identity in the region has been transient – every generation being tagged to a new identity. Sri Aurobindo said that India could serve humanity most by becoming India itself, not anything else. Similarly can the northeast contribute the most to the ongoing nation building process by being itself, not being like Punjab or Maharastra? In that case there are so many questions to answer and it is hoped that the missing development paradigm for the region will emerge out of the narrative. It is in this context that a plea is made to reimagine Act East policy. The Vision document also makes a strong plea for "an imaginative leap in foreign policy, defence policy and internal security policy, as much as in investment, infrastructure and commercial policy, is required to end the Region's geo-political isolation and put it on the path to accelerated and inclusive growth."

The growing prominence of the sustainable development goals, the replacement of the Planning commission by the NITI Aayog and the dislocation caused by the pandemic – all have prompted us to reimagine AEP for the sake of NER in particular and India in general. Becoming a part of India, albeit in different time periods, was the region's first act of reimagining itself. Seventy five years down the line, frustrated by the gap between what we wanted and what we achieved a stage has come for doing another act of reimagining itself. It is based on accumulated knowledge of the seven decades inside and outside the region.

## 13.2 The Dominant View

The reimagining exercise first critiques the policy narrative as propounded by the NER vision 2020 document: after spelling out the development lag the document argues that "The priority sector must be agriculture for with the Region's very high dependence on agriculture and allied activities, comprising over 80 per cent of the Region's gross domestic product, it is only through a Green Revolution that the back of the Region's poverty can be broken and the people as a whole placed on the parabola of progress."

The biggest constraint according to the document is poor infrastructure affecting:

- road connectivity
- rail connectivity
- air connectivity
- cyber and telecom connectivity
- inland waterways
- power

Enhanced resource inflow is also sought "to significantly narrow, let alone eliminate within the next decade or so, the growing gap between growth rates in the country as a whole and much of the North Eastern Region calls for a massive increase in the flow of financial resources to the Region, exponentially much larger than the current or presently envisaged flow."

It then talks about the dubious absorptive capacity of the region. Without it chances of in optimal utilisation of the financial resources available for infrastructure are very high. In addition to the usual leakages to corrupt bureaucracy and technocrats, numerous underground organisations manage to have their shares as well leaving only a fraction of original fund for the actual work. Though the concern for better infrastructure and higher 'gap reducing' growth rates may be justified, the leakages are not. These leakages nourish the vested interest who takes advantage of such investment.

*According to Rao (2009:18)*

"From the early 1990s, there has been an emphasis on forging closer commercial and economic links with markets in the Southeast Asian countries and beyond through the Look East policy. Given the geographical contiguity, cultural ties, and proximity to the countries in Southeast Asia, the policy should have helped to break the economic isolation of the NER states. However, even though the Look East policy has been in existence for more than a decade and a half and even as it has benefited other parts of India, its benefits to the NER have been negligible. For the region, the policy has remained a slogan and has never evolved into a harmonious and productive economic relationship with Southeast Asia.

*Sarma & Choudhury (2018) elaborate it further*

"Given the large unexplored domain of demography and economy of the region, it is no surprise that even after a decade of envisioning Northeast India in the Look East Policy frame, the region continues to be isolated, bounded and land locked. The region has been wrapped in political economy of care. It is caught in the uncertainty of economic gains vis-a-vis the security of the region, that casts doubt on the readiness of the economy of the region to engage with the market-driven economy of South East Asia."

They argue that mainstreaming Northeast India's development issues within the Policy will provide a development framework for the region, and it is important to recognize that the region's locational advantage and rich resource endowment, including manpower, provides an ideal setting for making Northeast India a central part of the Look (Act) East Policy instead of being a mere gateway.

They further argue that "It could be expected that in the course of time the local conditions of the states would be aligned to the requirements arising from the development perspective within the framework of the Look (Act) East Policy."

According to Rao (2009) a major precondition for economic progress is promotion of trade and investment, which calls for immediate effort to end the economic isolation of the region. Development experiences around the world have underlined the importance of trade in both development and promoting social interaction with the outside world. Promotion of trade helps to harness the resources of the region for improving the standard of living and for achieving the technological progress and improving productivity.

*Kathuria and Mathur (2018) argue that*

"NER can capitalize on rising demand for fresh fruits and vegetables, and for fresh, high-quality spices. It can promote bamboo, an environmentally friendly resource. It can push nature-based tourism, as well as trade in medical and education services."

Kathuria and Mathur (2018) suggest a policy framework which focuses on NER's strengths in the context of global trends—growing consumer incomes, purchasing power and awareness in India and abroad and the growing role of services in manufacturing which raise the demand for skilled human resources—arguing that the region's key advantage lies the agriculture and service sectors. They also suggest creating a "Brand North East" focusing on several attributes such as healthy living, environmental sustainability, social responsibility and service orientation which together constitute a unique value proposition. They show that "even with a low base in manufacturing NER can leverage its strengths in agriculture and services to step up its growth". The traditional value chain catering to local or price conscious consumers would be replaced by a new value chain benefitting the women and the poor, motivating at the same time, more private sector players in the field. It seeks to accelerate the transformation of NER into a mainstream participant.

The dominant view is thus that the region should specialise in agro- processing depending on its comparative advantage in agriculture and agro based industries.

### *Why should we reimagine?*

There are two options—make the narrative continuous by stressing on better implementation of extant policies believing in our capability to take care of the constraints or give a break to the narrative by having a fresh look on strengths and weaknesses, in the process, possibly charting a new trajectory.

The environment for policy making when India became independent and when India has turned 75 years needless to say is radically different. Perhaps the earliest attempt to look at the people of this region as they are was Dr Suniti kumar Chatterjee, a famous Indologist in his 'kirattajanakriti' he attempted to understand the people of the Northeastern India as Kirata, the mongoloid group. Commenting on the identity of the people inhabiting this region as early as 1951 Chatterjee (1972:26) asserted that "It is the consensus of opinion among indologists that in Sanskrit the term kirata indicated the wild non Aryan tribes living in the mountains, particularly the Himalayas and in the North-eastern areas of India, who were Mongoloid in origin. These Kiratas were connected with the Cinas or the Chinese, the Bhotas or the Tibetans and other Mongoloid people." (Chatterjee 1972:26)

Unfortunately this perspective seemed to have been missed by social scientists who could have understood the people better coming up with better and more appropriate policy matrix. The potential of the people remains unrealized. He writes

"The Mongoloid peoples in America, as in Mexico, central America and peru produced, quite independently of other peoples civilisations of an original and very advanced type which can compare favourably with the great civilisations of the old world, one of which was the exclusive creation of the mongoloid Chinese people. (Chatterjee, 1972:21)

Rodrik in what is becoming known as Rodrik paradox points out the technological sophistication of Chinese exports has been so high that it cannot be explained simply by the economic fundamentals of a low-income country abundant in unskilled labour. This is attributed to China's industrial policies that help nurture domestic capabilities in machinery and electronics.

The theoretical literature on dynamic comparative advantage gives a key role to investments in knowledge enhancing activities in altering a country's comparative advantage over time. It can be related to specialization in production and trade or relative endowments of factors of production. The new economic geography models assert that high tech production is exposed to increasing returns to scale and is likely to agglomerate in larger countries in the presence of positive trade costs.

Debunking the myth of free trade from the historical perspective demonstrates that there is an urgent need for thoroughly re-thinking some key conventional wisdom in the debate on trade policy, and more broadly on globalization. Chang compares the free trade arguments of countries like the U.K. and U.S.A. with the case of a successful person who kicks away the ladder on which he had climbed the height depriving others the means to rise to the top. The highly competitive industries in these countries grew out of infant industry policy.

Kuznets (1971) talked of six characteristics of modern economic growth.

Rodrik (2004) came up with four stylised facts of development as follows:

1. Economic development requires diversification not specialisation or more specifically that diversification is a key correlate of economic development. Rich countries are rich because of the breadth of their economies and the diversification of goods they produce. We need to learn new things, instead of focusing on what one already does well.
2. Countries with large manufacturing sectors grow and develop faster than those without reinforcing the view that the manufacturing sector is the key driver of development and growth. Growth accelerations within a specific country can be attributed to the performance of the manufacturing sector. Resources moving in and out of manufacturing accounts for stop/start growth in developing nations.
3. Countries that promote exports of more sophisticated goods grow faster than countries promoting exports of less sophisticated goods.
4. Specialisation patterns are not pinned down by factor endowments. Successful countries have pushed the limits of their static comparative advantage and quickly diversified into new activities that are the domain of countries considered more developed than themselves. The sophistication of a country's

exports is in part determined by the country's overall productive capacity and its human and capital constraints yet a policy of setting its sights on sophisticated high productivity sector growth also is important.

In order to grow, a less developed country needs to get onto a track of diversification. Attention should be focussed on the manufacturing sector and within this sector diversification and production of new products should be sought. The more sophisticated manufacturing exports are, the higher the levels of ensuing growth.

According to Chang short term allocative efficiency is different from medium term adjustment and long term development. Comparative advantage is a base line and a country needs to defy its comparative advantage in order to upgrade its industry. Chang argues that

"Given the nature of the process of factor accumulation and technological capability-building, it is simply not possible for a backward economy to accumulate capabilities in new industries without defying comparative advantage and actually entering the industry before it has the 'right' factor endowments."

A country may benefit more from exporting sophisticated products than from exporting unsophisticated and low domestic value-added products, even if its comparative advantage in the current time is in the production of the latter type of goods.

According to Brunner (2010:8) "The NER can only catch up with the rest of India in terms of growth rates and income levels, if the region correctly identifies actual and potential comparative advantages. Comparative advantage is realised only with skilful exploitation of the existing resource base and with the identification of gaps in resources-resources which then need to be acquired in order to successfully fill the gaps which at present isolate the NER from the global markets and demand".

The factor-endowments model is reasonably good at predicting the broad structure of comparative advantage for developing countries. The choice of investment is not simple Hausmann & Rodrik (2002) argue that: "Neither economic theory nor management science is of much help in helping entrepreneurs (or the state) choose appropriate investments among the full range of modern-sector activities, of which there could be tens of thousands, once one moves beyond broad categories such as "labor-intensive products" or "natural-resource based products." They focus on learning on what one is good at.

India is a country that one would have hardly expected to have a comparative advantage in a technology-intensive sector yet IT exports have been growing.

Bangladesh's comparative advantage lies in labor-intensive manufactures. "Hats and other headgear, knitted or from textile material not in strips" constitute Bangladesh's third most important export item to the U.S. after men's cotton shirts and trousers. Pakistan with similar factor endowment specializes at producing bed sheets not hats. Pakistan's major exports are curtains and soccer balls. Honduras and the Dominican Republic concentrate on garment exports, while Taiwan and South Korea focus on computer products. But at the level of individual products, there are again striking differences. In 2000, the Dominican Republic exported $119 million worth of footwear uppers to the U.S. while Honduras is a major exporter of ignition wiring sets. Taiwan exported $279 million worth of bicycles to the U.S. while Korea exports a lot of air conditioning machines. They argue that patterns of specialization are the consequence of historical accidents and serendipitous choices by entrepreneurs.

*Hausmann & Rodrik (2002:26) conclude that:*

"First, for all economies except possibly the most sophisticated, industrial success entails concentration in a relatively narrow range of high-productivity activities. Second, the specific product lines that eventually prove to be hits are typically highly uncertain and unpredictable."

## 13.3 Conclusion

Should our growth continue to be constrained by locally available resources where we seem to have comparative advantage taking gradualist steps? In the last few years the mindset of entrepreneurs has changed significantly and it is reflected in their products and markets. Global and local have become interchangeable. The fermented fish industry is one of the most profitable industries in Manipur. it has grown with dry fish entirely from outside Manipur.

The deepening ASEAN-Indian connectivity will change the economic geography. Examples of changing geography are the commissioning of the Suez Canal joining the Mediterranean and the Indian Ocean and laying of the first transcontinental railways across North America. With India's LEP and AEP, successive governments have sought to revive and strengthen age-old ties with the far east, across the sea and overland across Myanmar. Just as global economic power is shifting from the west to the east, the geography of Asia is changing. Commenting on the implication for such a change in geography Thant Myint (2011) writes:

> "When geography changes, old patterns of contact may disappear and new ones take hold, turning strangers into neighbours, and transforming backwaters into zones of strategic significance. Entire peoples face decline or vanish, others rise in importance."

## References

[1] Brunner, Hans-Peter (2010). ed. "North East India Local Economic Development and Global markets", Sage Studies on India's North east, Sage Publications Pvt. Ltd.

[2] Chang, Ha-Joon (2007). "Bad Samaritans" The myth of Free Trade and the Secret History of Capitalism" bloomsburry press.

[3] Chang, Ha-Joon (2012). "Industrial Policy: Can Africa Do It?" IEA/World Bank Roundtable on Industrial policy in Africa, *Pretoria*, 3–4 July.

[4] Chatterjee, S.K. (1972). "KIRATA-JANA-KRTI the Indo-Mongoloids Their contribution to the History and Culture of India" The Asiatic Society.

[5] Ghose, A.K. (2016). "India Employment report 2016" Institute for Human Development.

[6] Hausmann, R. and Rodrik, D. (2002). Economic Development as self-Discovery. Working paper 8952, NBER.

[7] Kathuria, S. and Mathur, P. Ed. (2020). Playing to strengths: A policy Framework for Mainstreaming Northeast India. Washington D.C., The World bank.

[8] Kathuria, S. and Mathur, P. (2020). A Policy framework to Build on Northeast India's Strengths. In Kathuria, S. and Mathur, P. Ed. (2020) Playing to strengths: A policy Framework for Mainstreaming Northeast India. Washington D.C., The World bank.

[9] Lin, Justin and Ha-Joon Chang (2009). "Should Industrial Policy in Developing Countries Conform to Comparative Advantage or Defy it? A Debate between Justin Lin and Ha-Joon Chang" *Development Policy Review,* 2009, Vol. 27(5), pp. 483–502.

[10] NEC (2008). "North Eastern Region Vision 2020", DONER.

[11] Poon, D. (2009). "China's Evolving Industrial policy Strategies & Instruments: Lessons for development" TIPS Working paper series 2009– 02.

[12] Rao, M. Govinda (2009). "Promoting Trade and Investment in India's North-eastern Region" ADB Working paper series on Regional Economic Integration, No. 30, May.

[13] Sarma, A. (2006). North East as Gateway to South east Asia: Big Dream and Home Truth Borderline, Vol. 1, No. 4, pp. 56.

[14] Sarma, A. and Choudhury, S. ed. (2018). Mainstreaming the Northeast in India's Look and Act East policy. Palgrave Macmillan.

[15] Sarma, A. and Choudhury, S. (2018). Towards a perspective on the Look (Act) East policy and Northeast India. In Sarma, A. and Choudhury, S. ed. (2018) Mainstreaming the Northeast in India's Look and Act East policy. Palgrave Macmillan.

[16] Thant Myint-U (2011). *Where China meets India: Burma and the new crossroads of Asia* Faber & Faber, pp. 3.

CHAPTER 14

# Understanding India's Neighbourhood Challenges through the Lens of Geo-psychology

**Dipikanta Chakraborty**

## 14.1 Introduction

*"To live with a big neighbour (such as the US) is like sleeping with an elephant,"*

**—Pierre Trudeau**

The swearing in occasion of the Prime Minister of India in 2014 marked a history in the political enigma of South Asia. At his coronation, Prime Minister Mr. Narendra Modi invited the leaders of the SAARC nations with a view to strengthen their SAARC tie up. But India's proactive approach towards its confronting neighbour circle has been a great concern since the independence of the country. Most of the South Asian countries are susceptible to Indian interference in their policy making. What their fear is India intervenes in their domestic and external policies. It led the anti- Indian geo-psychology evolved, emerged and sharpened over the years. Anti-Indian sentiments brewed over time in South Asia. Pakistan, being the twin of India has bearded the latter from every front. Despite all the conciliations of UN and various other good offices both the countries have been engaged in the bellicose antagonism. On the other front, both China and India are at loggerheads in terms of security and regional supremacy. China played the prominent role in the formation of India's geo-psychology in its immediate neighbourhood. Most of the South and South East Asian nations including Myanmar, Sri Lanka and Bangladesh have oscillated between India and China, in times to assuage their interest. The gesture of Bangladesh towards

India since 1975 was abruptly curt, especially after India's historical humanitarian assistance to the latter. Bangladesh perceives India potential threat than a strategic ally. Hence, it is quite clear that neither Nehru's idealism nor Modi's realism could offer India a cordial neighbourhood. Researchers may consider it a structural constraint, abstaining India from getting a cordial neighbourhood but it is actually the geo-psychology of India's neighbours that is hurdling the process of peaceful neighbourhood in South Asia. This paper centrally addresses the issue if india is true hegemon influencing both the domestic and foreign policy issues of the nations in its neighborhood circle. This paper examines the geo-psychology of India and its neighbours—Bangladesh and Nepal. The paper has adopted analytical method to evaluate India's gesture in neighbourhood. It discusses how India will appropriately learn from its hegemonic approach to its strategic partners—as anti-Indian geo-psychology prompted Indian neighbours to come closer to China in strategic and economic terms. The objective of the paper is to understand India's South Asian challenges with an aid of geo-psychology, thereby attempting to predict India's astute and calculated foreign policy approach in neighbourhood.

## 14.2 Geo-psychology: Conceptual Understanding

Geo-psychology as a theory emerged out of the epistemological nihility in the study of International Relations. Realism is undoubtedly the dominant theory of international relation but due to its high pessimistic propensity for war, the theory is not full heartedly accepted by the theorists in post-cold war world order. Especially at the advent of globalisation, actors other than the states have become active participants in the world politics which makes the international relation multidimensional in nature. The Indian thinker BM Jain is credited to coin the theory of Geo-psychology in international relation. Jain defines,

> "Geo-psychology is a set of perceptions, images, and belief systems, formed of shared history, culture, nationalism, religion, and ethnicity, which shapes the mindsets and behavioral patterns of non-state and authoritarian actors and communities inhabiting a specific geographical area"(Jain 2021).

Geo-psychology offers a rational and legitimate platform for the researchers to understand the decision making process of the country. It counters the claim of structural realists who supposedly claimed the inevitable role of the structure as the driving force behind exhibiting the same foreign policy by the nation states. Geo-psychology presumes the importance of the decision making process of the states that has been constructed by culture, traditions, societal norms, geography and most importantly human psyche. Geo-psychology may go similar with the theory of social constructivism to some extent, but the propensity of the former for physical location of the states makes it different from the latter. Moreover, Social Constructivism and English school has diverted from the main course of IR due to their less aid on decision making process. Jain further added the geo-psychology can be featured to comprehend "the 'climatic and geographical effects' as a natural environment, as a social environment, and as a historical cultural environment in a given geographical region". Geo-psychology is determined by the agglomeration of the three factors like—History, Geography and Ethnicity. Each nation has its own political history that deserves to be considered in international relation. For example, the state formation process of India and Pakistan is different but it is seemingly analogous in case of Pakistan and Bangladesh as both the nations got independence from their parent states due to cultural conflicts. The second important factor of geo-psychology constitutes ethnicity. The present controversy over nationalism in various states of Asia brings out the typical ethnic formation as well as its human psyche of the state. It triggers off a crucial understanding the ethnicity of a place. For example, Pakistan could not succeed over Bangladesh in 1971 despite all the efforts of western countries like UK, USA, and France. It was because Pakistan was unable to understand the ethnic tradition of the folks of erstwhile East Pakistan. The third factor geography deserves a special mention in the state's sovereignty due to the fact that the nation states have a territorial demarcation and that creates geography induced perception. The theory of geo-psychology centres on the human psychology that has been created against geographical location of a country but while doing so the Geo-psychology theory does not exclude the non-state actors rather theory of geo-psychology perfectly encompasses the nature and activities of the Non-state actors. In the present complicated political web under globalisation, the non-states actors have become the indispensable agents of global politics.

The region of South Asia is portrayed strategic due to its unique location being surrounded by the busiest maritime borders from three sides. The interpenetration of the nuclear powers—India, China and Pakistan has elevated its importance in global politics. It is further accentuated by the interest of America in curbing the meteoric rise of China as an Asian dragon and its catch up with the four Asian Tigers. Furthermore, the proposed BRI sheath of China, dissolving the boundaries of the South Asian nations, thereby coalescing all the land and maritime borders in the region and beyond raised the essentiality of South Asian region. Most of the South Asian nations are not only geographically but also culturally connected and known for sharing common history. The nations in this conflict ridden region are closely clustered due to identical social structures. The thin barbed line could not separate people and their customs. For instance, the people from India and Pakistan share common cultures and history, yet both the nations were engaged in three war fares. Adding on, The India-Pakistan conflict on Kashmir issue, perhaps, has been the biggest hurdle in the development of South Asia. To understand the daedalian political culture of South Asia a psycho analysis is must.

The spread of India's social, spiritual and political culture had have dominated the entire South and South East Asia. India, being the influential and emerging global power, has given considerable importance to its neighbourhood but it fails to pay due attention to the psychology of its neighbours. In case of China, India adopted an 'anti-China' policy throughout, instead of going for a proffer with it. Eventually an anti- China sentiment evolved amongst the Indians and vice-versa. The decision of India to join the Quadrilateral Security Dialogue (QUAD) along with America, as against of the Chinese Belt and Road Initiatives indicates an imprecise understanding of Chinese geo-psychology by Indian decision making bodies, thereby hampering the collective role of de-colonized states in the rise of global South. The geo-psychology of India- Pakistan has been systematically constructed over time. The media houses in India show Pakistan, an ideogram of terrorism. On the other hand, India has been conceived as a drastic abhorrence by the social media in Pakistan. Despite its overall dependence on India, the geographically landlocked Nepal treated India with suspicion, over the years. Fearing of India's regional dominance Nepal conflated with China. India's bountiful material assistance to its neighbours and succour at the grave days has been taken for granted by the countries in its nearest vicinity. Adding on, In 1971 India fought its ever successful war with Pakistan for the liberation of Bangladesh. Though India was successful in establishing Bangladesh as a separate nation free from autocratic rule but subsequently it came to accept the confrontation from Bangladesh. In the post- Mujib era the government of Bangladesh preferred maintaining distance from India. It is because the Bangladesh government found India a potential threat for its existence. Bangladesh wanted to make its separate identity distinct from India. For that, Zia Ur Rehman, the former President of Bangladesh changed the term 'Bangalee' to 'Bangladeshi'. The geo-psychological approach investigated that it is due to the threat of existential crisis or a sense of insecurity, the countries like Nepal, Bangladesh, Sri Lanka and Afghanistan prefers maintaining distance from India. It assumes that India's appropriate understanding of the geo-psychology of its neighbours and based on the same a systemic application of its foreign policy will manoeuvre a cordial upper hand in neighbourhood.

As a discipline, Political Science is all encompassing in nature that includes subjects like psychology. As an offshoot of these two, Political Psychology emerged that analyses political phenomena from socio-cultural and economic perspective. Psychology also gives cognitive understanding of the world politics and enhances the ability to grasp the uncertainty of International Relations. The state's course of action to accrue highest possible interest is well can well be viewed through the lens of cognitive psychology. Moreover, the idea of national interest which is the central point in the edifice of international relation, habitually changes over time and context. Nevertheless, the inevitable role of geography in international churns out the increasing role geo-psychology in world politics. The explanatory element of geo-psychology helps in understanding the dynamism in the state's actions induced by the anarchic nature of international relation. Its normative aspects enable us to analyse the behavioural changes of the various actors in international relation—both state and non-state and thereby predicting their future course of action to avoid extremism.

## 14.3 India's Challenges in Neighbourhood

Since its independence, India made a heroic appearance in the politics of South Asia. Nehru's policy of non-alignment and detachment from bloc-ism had made the country, a pathfinder, at least during the cold war. India's large territory, prodigious population, ancient civilisation, glorious history, wealth and cultural affluence made it the figurehead in the region. But India's regional ascendancy is at stake despite its most decorated 'neighbourhood first' dictum. Most of the countries in South Asia have been the irredentist part of Indian sub-continent; consequently it made India having undefined borders with its neighbours. Since partition India faced territorial disputed with Bangladesh, Bhutan, China, Nepal, Pakistan and Myanmar and maritime border conflict with Sri-Lanka that flared up tension in the region sporadically. China's overall growth in the region also convulses India. Mostly due to its spatial disagreements and undefined border demarcations, the neighbouring countries in closed spatial circle of India are found tilted towards China. India's historical mistake of not joining ASEAN when invited in 1967 makes it distanced from the giant economies of Asia. Notwithstanding India's earnest efforts the country fails to get the confidence of its neighbours. Consequently India is facing number of challenges from its neighbouring circle in this day and age.

### 14.3.1 *Regional Ascendancy*

India and China are emerging powers of Asia. Both the countries preferred to maintain their relationship not in amity but in antagonistic terms. With all its adversities, the growth of China has undoubtedly shapes the political discourse of South Asia. Nevertheless, Chinese One Belt One Road Initiative, may seen as a potential irritant for India as it competes with the latter in regional ascendancy but the advancement of China surely cuts the path for the regional development and South-South cooperation, reducing the economic dependence of the countries on major powers. India deprecated China's BRI due to its duplicitous nature. On the one hand Xing ping Government is seeking India's support for its BRI. On the other China is closing India's door to its neighbour by largessing alms. India's regional ascendancy is not only challenged by China; countries like Sri Lanka, Nepal and Bangladesh also challenged its supremacy with euphemism. India's generosity in the region is inculpated as interference by many. For example, the anti-Indian sentiments are high in Nepal and Bangladesh—two closest neighbouring states of India. Being a sovereign state Nepal wants equal status; it doesn't want to be treated as India's younger brother. Accusing India for its domineering behaviour, people took to the street in Kathmandu refusing India's affectionate policy (Rae, 2021). The controversy over the birthplace of Lord Buddha sparked inveigh. Modi's speech at United Nations General Assembly- "We are a nation that gave the world Buddha not Yuddha (war)" has further anguished the Nepalese sentiment (PTI, 2019).

After the dethronement of Afghan Republic by the Taliban force, India has discontinued its diplomatic relations with India. The recent visit of Indian team in Afghanistan after the Taliban came in power indicated the restoration of bilateral relationship between these two but like most of the Indian neighbours the Afghanistan government also fretful about India's intervention (Wire, 2022). The Taliban spokesperson Abdul Qahar Balkhi requested India to resume the India-Afghanistan healthy bilateral ties but he raised the issue of India's interference in Afghanistan's domestic affairs.

### 14.3.2 *Border Conflicts*

Following the accession of Kashmir with India in October, 1947, the prolonged territorial dispute between India and Pakistan started. The territorial conflict over Kashmir has been a centrepiece in India-Pakistan relations so far. This border dispute on Kashmir has not been solved yet despite the negotiation of various countries as good office and intervention of the United Nations in regular intervals. It is because the conflict over Kashmir is more a geo-psychological issue than political hostility. Both India and Pakistan failed to analyse the psyche of Kashmir, its ethnic formation and history. The movies made in both India and Pakistan to justify their claim over Kashmir deflected the main issue of development. The people of Jammu and

Kashmir have witnessed carnage, threats, suppression of civil rights, discordance with mainland India etc. The continuous and violent gunfights between Indian armies and insurgent groups killed many innocent lives. The Indian soldiers are often confronted by the folks of Kashmir. The youth, being easily approachable, are often manipulated to join militant groups. Their resentment at being demoted by India adds fuel on this repugnance. The Indian policy makers could not understand the ethnic formation, the history and geographical set up of Kashmir that constitutes the human psyche. The initial policy of isolation given to Kashmir in the form of separate constitution, and inapprehensive policies of Indian government thereafter has shoved Kashmir away. Thence, it would not be an exaggeration to say that the Kashmir issue has been systematically constructed over time to challenge Indian sovereignty. Apart from Kashmir, India and Pakistan also disagree upon Siachen Glacier and Saltoro Ridge in Karakoram region and the riverine border of Sir Creek.

The country shares borders with eight countries and having protracted border disputes with most of these neighbouring states. Aksai Chin, Kaurik, Nelang, Barahoti, Depsang Plains, Nelang, Pulam Sumda, Sang, Jadhang and Lapthal; Trans-Karakoram Tract are the disputed land between India and China (Gilani, 2020). Both the countries are at loggerheads as they got involved in the Galwan Valley border skirmish in recent days after four decades. In the same year India faced another confrontation from its *fidus Achates*, Nepal. India's road construction towards Mansarovar has been halted due to the objection raised by Nepal government. Almost four hundred square kilometer bordering area coming under Indian dominion has been challenged by Nepal. The relationship got strained when the Nepalese Parliament introduced a new map including kalapani region, culminating into the India's stand upon economic blockade in Nepal.

In case of India and Bangladesh, the borders dispute has been apparently solved. Though India and Bangladesh disentangled their long lasting border issues through the Land Boundary Agreement (2015), but the debate over Muhari Char in Tripura (India) is still going on. The land Boundary Agreement (LBA) is a milestone achievement in Indian neighbourhood policy under which India surrendered fifty one enclaves to Bangladesh and got 111 enclaves in return.

### 14.3.3 *Vaccine Diplomacy*

The spread of Covid-19 has brought structural changes in South Asia like any other regions. India's dedicated assistance during the pandemic to the neighbouring countries has championed its 'neighbourhood first policy'. Being the 'pharmacy of the world' its prompt response to the countries in neighbourhood and beyond has escalated its claim of regional super power. In the post-Covid world order, Indian vaccine diplomacy has added a new wing to its foreign policy. India gifted vaccine to 71 countries. Its benevolent vaccine assistance to the world showed not only the resurgence of India's soft power policy but also builds a strong footing in neighbourhood. With all its adversities, the Covid-19 has given India a chance to normalize its neighbourhood distraught. India was the first from the region to respond to the great crisis. But the second wave of the pandemic had a devastating effect on India. New Delhi could not go far with its 'Vaccine Maitri' programme. India's inability to fill the crisis of vaccine in South Asia sweep in China as a largest vaccine provider, competing India. China sent 8,00,000 doses of vaccine to Nepal (IANS, 2021) as grant. As a result, Nepal confirmed to buy 4 million Chinese vaccine. The spread of Covid-19 originated from Beijing; ignoring this fact most of the South Asian countries contrived China as ally and accepted Sinopharm's vaccine when India refused to export.

### 14.3.4 *Rudimentary Domestic Policy*

In 2019 the Government of India took a storming decision to conceptualize the Citizenship Amendment Act, 2019. The act is not only brought significant changes in the core structure of the Constitution by adding religion but also targeted its neighbourhood policy. The recently enacted Citizenship Amendment Act has raised protests from different segments of people across the country. It is widely criticized for making discrimination on religious grounds. The act included religion as a determining factor to get citizenship of the country (Chakraborty, 2021). This act consciously excluded the Muslim from the purview. Section 2 of the act reads:

> Provided that any person belonging to Hindu, Sikh, Buddhist, Jain, Parsi or Christian community from Afghanistan, Bangladesh or Pakistan, who entered into India on or before the 31st day of

> December 2014 and who has been exempted by the Central Government by or under clause (c) of sub-section (2) of section 3 of the Passport (Entry into India) Act, 1920 or from the application of the provisions of the Foreigners Act, 1946 or any rule or order made there under, shall not be treated as an illegal migrant for the purposes of this Act; (The Gazette of India, 2019)

This decision got tremendous reaction from international community but New Delhi did not pay heed to this and stayed back with its decision. Following the same vein India repealed Article 370, thereby bringing Jammu and Kashmir under the direct purview of Indian government. This issue raised the concern over suppressing the rights of the people of Kashmir. This authoritarian turn again befell India to trace the psychology of Kashmir. Moreover, India's decision on the implementation of National Register of Citizen (NRC) in Assam to identify the illegal Bangladeshi migrants raised their concern. Fearing that Bangladesh has to shoulder the load of shoved citizen from Assam, various groups in Bangladesh triggered off their protest against India. The present controversy over the tweet of Nupur Sharma, the former BJP spokesperson on Prophet Muhammad has ignited furors across the country. Two persons were beheaded in public for allegedly supporting Nupur Sharma. This tweet has been demurred by many countries in extended neighbourhood. Afghanistan condemned the provoking statement of Nupur Sharma and demanded her eviction. Modi government's indolence over this remark has divulged India's *Hindu Rasthtra* image. India's external policies have always targeted to be more generous, liberal and secular but its domestic policies made a harsh imprint to its neighbours.

### 14.3.5 *Secessionist Movements*

One of the biggest challenges to India from neighbouring states is secessionist movements incited by the countries in close circle. Entire South Asia is under the span of Indian culture. The close cultural affinity as well as geographical proximity of India with the South and South East neighbours resulted in multitudinous separatist rebellions. For instance, the Chinese support to guerrilla train the militant groups of Northeast India, especially the Naga groups; insurgents groups from Tripura, Mizoram and Assam got shelter in Chittagong hill tract from time to time, turmoil in Tamil Nadu related to the Tamil issue as an offshoot of communal tension in Sri Lanka, the demand of Indian inhabitants of Nepali origin in Darjeeling for separate state possesses serious threat to Indian sovereignty. China's new border law is a concern for India. Under this enactment the villages on the Chinese side of India-China borders are provided with infrastructure and better connectivity. No doubt, the rapid development process in the bordering areas put pressure on India, on the one hand. Concomitantly, this initiative will help in gathering people's support.

## 14.4 Conclusion

An appropriate understanding of the geo-psychology of India's neighbour will enable it to decide its future course of action. India's off beam foreign policies have distanced it from its closest neighbours, eventually keeping China the only reliable option to them. India has to understand the psychology of its neighbours. India has to focus on analysing its own image that has been constructed in the region. China understood it and through aids, loans and vaccines it created its image by wiping off the old slate. Over the time, a rival psychology has been brewed up in South Asia against India. One cannot endure someone of its own kind to maintain its uniqueness. India's cultural similitude with its neighbours along with its spatial and material vastness imposes threat to them. Countries like Bangladesh, Nepal and Sri Lanka want to maintain distance from India so that their unique national identity or nationalism does not get engulfed under India's influence. India's over concern for the Tamil minority in Lanka seems to be an irritant to their idea of nationalism. Being an officially recognised Hindu nation Nepal extricated its relations with India and has been playing its China card in times. In India-Nepal relations the real problem lies at the grass root level as the people of Nepal are opposing Indian establishment and Indian government fails to understand the psychology in this regard. The comments of Indian actors and politicians mocking Nepal fuelled the anti-Indian sentiments. India's bureaucratic as well as big brother syndrome has inflamed the abhorrence. Despite its generous efforts and aids to various countries in immediate and extended neighbourhood the country could not get success in its cordial and compatible neighbourhood policy. It is for the obvious reason that India could not understand the geo-psychology of South Asia. India is not a regional but a global power, if not a hegemony. India's animosity with Pakistan and contention with China, though stuck in mind set, has been a big hurdle in its super power status. At this situation, India has to construct the compatible image in the region.

## References

[1] Chakraborty, D. (2021). "Neoteric Nationalism in India: Secular or Religious?" *International Relations and Diplomacy*, pp. 342–353.

[2] Gilani, I. (2020). "India's border dispute with neighbors", Retrieved 06 2022, from AA: https://www.aa.com.tr/en/asia-pacific/indias-border-dispute-with-neighbors/1859854#

[3] IANS (2021). Nepal to procure 4 mn Covid vaccines from China under non-disclosure deal. Retrieved June 2022, from Business Standard: https://www.business-standard.com/article/current-affairs/nepal-to-procure-4-mn-covid-vaccines-from-china-under-non-disclosure-deal-121061700560_1.html

[4] Jain, B.M. (2021). The Geo-psychology Theory of International Relations in the 21st Century, Lexington Books, London.

[5] Pant, H.V. (2021). *Politics and Geopolitics.* New Delhi: Rupa Publications.

[6] Lama, N. (2022, June 4). Why Nepalis Hate India and How That Can Change. Retrieved 7.11.2020, from My Republica: https://myrepublica.nagariknetwork.com/news/why-nepalis-hate-india-and-how-that-can-change/

[7] Rae, R. (2021, September 12): *In a 'bhai-bhai ka rishta', Nepal refuses to be India's younger brother. It wants equality.* Retrieved July 7, 2022, from The Print: https://theprint.in/pageturner/excerpt/in-a-bhai-bhai-ka-rishta-nepal-refuses-to-be-indias-younger-brother-it-wants-equality/731591/

[8] Shringla, H.V. (2018). India-Bangladesh Relations: An Indian Perspective. *Strategic Analysis*, pp. 524–528.

[9] Wire (2022, June 02). *India Plays Down First Official Visit to Afghanistan; 'Sign of Good Beginning,' Says Taliban.* Retrieved July 5, 2022, from The Wire: https://thewire.in/diplomacy/india-plays-down-first-official-visit-to-afghanistan-sign-of-good-beginning-says-taliban